The English Rebels

When Adam delved and Eve span,
Who was then the gentleman?

THE ENGLISH REBELS

by

Charles Poulsen

Author of

English Episode
Victoria Park
The Word of the King (play)

Journeyman

The Journeyman Press Limited, 97 Ferme Park Road,
Crouch End, London N8 9SA, and 17 Old Mill Road, West
Nyack, NY 10994, USA

First published 1984
1 2 3 4 5 6 7 8 9 printing

Copyright © by Charles Poulsen, 1984

ISBN 0 904526 65 8 *paper*
ISBN 0 904526 66 6 *cased*

Frontispiece: The text of John Ball's sermon illustrated from
an early fourteenth-century manuscript.

Printed in Great Britain by
Redwood Burn Limited, Trowbridge, Wiltshire

Contents

Acknowledgements

The publisher and author would like to thank the following for their kind permission to reproduce copyright illustrations: (4) The British Library; (1, 2, 8, 20) The Trustees of the British Museum; (14) Museum of London; (25) The National Maritime Museum, London; (24) National Portrait Gallery; (13, 17 right, 19) Guildhall Library, City of London; (5, 6) The Dean & Chapter of Westminster; (3) The Parochial Church Council, Parish of St Gregory with St Peter, Suffolk; (16) British Tourist Authority; (15) Mary Evans Picture Library; (18, 21, 22, 23) Mansell Collection; (17 left, 23, 26) BBC Hulton Picture Library; (35, 36) The Illustrated London News Picture Library; (37) reproduced by gracious permission of Her Majesty the Queen.

We would also like to thank B. T. Batsford Ltd for allowing us to reproduce illustrations 9, 10 and 11 from *Life in Tudor England* by Peter Lane; Lawrence & Wishart Ltd for 27 and 28 from *Captain Swing* by Eric Hobsbawm and George Rudé; Andre Deutsch Ltd for 30, 31 and 32 from *The Tolpuddle Martyrs* by Joyce Marlow; Reg Groves for 12 from *The Rebels' Oak*; *Socialist Review* for 38; and Robert Leeson for 29.

Preface

Arising out of the 600th anniversary of 1381, this book is being published to commemorate those popular radical movements that carried its spirit and ideals into later centuries. To many historians the Peasants' Revolt was an unnecessary and unsuccessful rising, the work of illiterate and violent men led by an unworldly idealist and a shrewd organiser; it accomplished nothing but the deaths of many simple men and the murder of some outstanding statesmen. So indeed it is usually taught in our schools, when it is discussed at all, as a kind of unusual aberration in the long series of constitutional, legal reforms that marked England's gradual progress from a feudal, agricultural nation of gentry, priests and peasants to our modern industrial, democratic 'welfare state'.

To those on the left of the labour movement, however, the socialists, communists, trade unionists and others, it is seen as the first great mass movement of the English people, as a heroic and revolutionary episode in which thousands of ordinary people left their families, homes and farms to join a hazardous undertaking which, if successful, would result in the creation of a new and better life for all, based on social justice and personal freedom. And before it was crushed it gave Europe the first socialist analysis of society and the first socialist policy arising out of it; as expounded by Father John Ball when he preached to the rebel serfs at the Mass celebrated at Blackheath on Corpus Christi Day, 1381.

To tell the story of that rebellion against feudalism, to salute its martyrs across the centuries that divide us, and to trace in outline the radical theme in our history, is the purpose of this book.

To
CHARLES HOBDAY
scholar, poet, socialist and friend

CHAPTER I

The Peasants' Revolt of 1381

1. THE MEDIEVAL BACKGROUND

In order to understand the Peasants' Revolt and the risings that followed it, the hopes that activated it and the powers that crushed it, it is necessary for the modern reader to realise that it happened in a society vastly different from our own industrial democracy. It happened in the same England, but much of the landscape would be unrecognisable to twentieth-century eyes. The people involved in it had an idea of themselves, and of their relationship with each other and with the government, very different from that of today. Thus we must first visualise the land and the society in which these events took place.

They occurred when England was still in the Middle Ages, under the feudal system, but when that period was beginning to draw towards its close and the stable, age-old relationships within the social order were beginning to break down.

Let us look at medieval England: an offshore island north-west of Europe, beyond which lay the unending, uncrossed Atlantic. 'Ultima Thule', the Romans had called it, 'the last place'. As the main centres of commerce and civilisation were situated around the Mediterranean, especially at its eastern end, England was a land of the outer perimeter, and developed later and slower than places more favourably placed on the trade routes. (It was the discovery of America and the Cape route to India that reversed this situation.)

Much of the country was covered by dense forest, through which ran the roads built by the Romans a thousand years before, but now much decayed. Later roads were little more than rough tracks. The rivers were unregulated and often overflowed. Bridges were few, and crossing was usually by ford or ferry. The low-lying valleys were damp and marshy. The fens of East Anglia were mostly under water, with the high places standing out like islands. In large clearings in the forests, at suitable places in the valleys, on the dry points in the fens, lay the villages in which most of the people lived and worked. At favourable spots round the coast, at river crossings and road junctions, stood the towns; most of them no bigger than a modern village.

The population of the whole country was probably less than 2,500,000. London, the greatest city, contained some 50,000 inhabitants, and the next largest, York, little over 4,000.

The people of this country were born into a society whose entire structure was based on the ownership and exploitation of the land. It was a nation organised into three distinct classes: the nobility and gentry, the Church and the commons. Squeezed in between the Church and the commons, but part of the latter, were the free citizens of the chartered towns.

The nation was conceived as a kind of broad-based pyramid, with the bottom layer consisting of the commons. The vast majority of them worked and lived on the land. At the topmost peak was the king, the chief of the nobility. He was in theory the ruler of the land, the source of law, the defender of the country. Reserving a large number of estates or 'manors' for his own needs, he let out the remainder in great estates or 'fiefs' to his principal barons. In return, the nobleman had to provide the king with a certain number of soldiers and knights for a stated period, and perform other services. To do this, he kept sections of his fiefs to provide his own income and let off the rest to lesser barons, who in turn had to supply him with armed men and follow him to war. This process was repeated until the lowest section, the knights, held their much smaller fiefs.

Many of these knights sublet further, leasing out parts of their land for a rent in money or in service or in kind to a member of the 'gentry'. He would be a man born free, of good family, allied in status and ideas to the nobility. Later, as we shall see, some wealthier members of the commons also became small landlords, or, as they were called, 'lords of the manors'.

This social system was summed up in the medieval catchword: 'No land without a lord: no man without a master.'

The nobility was an exclusive class; titles were usually inherited. They had their own rigid etiquette and ceremonial and they justified themselves by providing the necessary military caste. Warfare was the base for all their culture, sport and outlook. They viewed with contempt all other social classes. This was the uppermost of the three strata of the population.

Between the nobility and the commons was the second layer, the Church, playing an important part in the life of the nation. It was the literate, educated section, which handled much of the business of running the country. When everybody believed in God, that He had created and administered the world, and that mortal life was merely a preparation for eternal bliss or punishment, and that damnation was the result of neglecting the rites of the Church, that organisation had an enormous influence on mens' lives and thinking. And the Church had grown wealthy and powerful on donations, bequests, tithes, and other forms of contribution, voluntary or otherwise. It provided a large part of what we would call the 'civil service'. It held the monopoly of education. It was the recognised dispenser of charity to the crippled, the sick and the indigent.

It could well afford to do so. When wealth was based on the holding of land the Church was the biggest landlord in England, possessing about one-third of the total; and, as landlord, it had the reputation of being much harsher and more extortive than the secular lords. The most splendid and expensive buildings in the country were its abbeys, monasteries, cathedrals and churches. Its bishops and abbots were accepted as equals by the nobility, and even the king found it difficult to act without its approval. The nobility and the Church, as the two non-productive classes, lived off the labour of the commons.

1.   Breaking up stony ground, c. A.D. 1340, *Loutrell Psalter*.

The third class in medieval society, the broad base on which the whole structure rested, was the commons, most of whom worked directly on the land, for the 'manor' (an estate or part of one). It consisted chiefly of a village, a line or huddle of cottages grouped near its church, and perhaps the manor house of the landlord, which might be a modest country house or a great castle. Close to the village would be the arable land in three large unenclosed fields, totalling several hundred acres. These fields were divided into strips, and, in order that there should be an equitable distribution of the good land and the bad, each of the villagers held a number of scattered strips in each field, and a number were the property of the lord of the manor. There they ploughed, sowed and reaped their main crops. Only two of the fields were planted each year, one staying 'fallow' to regain its productivity. Each cottage would stand in its 'croft', an enclosed piece of land in which the tenant could grow vegetables and use as he wished.

A few of the villagers would be 'cottars', who owned a cottage and croft but no land, and lived by hiring out their labour. In the larger villages there would be a few peasants who were the village craftsmen as well — a smith, a joiner, a thatcher, and so on; but most of them would be serfs or villeins (a distinction which need not trouble us here) who were bound to their land and could not leave it, who paid the rent for their holding in the form of compulsory labour on the lord's land or in farm produce, usually both.

These villeins were not slaves. They could not be sold by their lord, they were not his property like the American slave of the nineteenth century. But neither could they leave their village and go elsewhere, to work or trade. They were 'bondsmen', part of the lord's manor like his sheds, stables, mill and barns; part of the 'means of production'.

2.　Ploughing, c. A.D. 1340, *Loutrell Psalter*.

Around the manor fields would be the 'waste', or common land used by all. Here the peasant would graze his cattle, his horse, his geese and other stock. In the woodlands the village swineherd would drive all the peasants' pigs to let them feed on the acorns and beech-nuts. For all this, the land and its uses, he had to pay rent to his lord. The rent varied from place to place according to that important tradition, 'the custom of the manor'. There was the labour rent, or 'boon-work', usually two to three days of every week when he had to work for his lord and not for himself. And the boon-work took precedence over his own in time of crisis, like a sudden storm at harvest or a fire among the stacks. There were many other obligations enforced on him. Should his lord require labour for mending a road, building or hauling, the villein had to leave his own work and do it without pay. He could not grind his own corn — it had to be done in his lord's mill, and paid for. He was not allowed an oven — he had to bake his bread in his lord's oven — and pay for it; and so on.

There were many other 'dues' or fines that the peasant owed to his lord. When his daughter married, he had to pay a due known as 'merchet'. If she anticipated the ceremony, there was a due for loss of chastity called 'leyrwite'. (Virginity, being an asset of the manor, belonged to the lord and not to the woman concerned.) When the peasant died his heir had to pay his lord 'herriot' as compensation usually his best beast or chattel, and then a tax for inheritance of the rest. There were many other fines and dues that varied locally 'according to the custom of the manor'.

If the villein fell foul of his lord, or transgressed in some way, he would be tried in his lord's own court, where he, or his agent, would be both prosecutor and judge; and the 'custom of the manor' might well be his best defence, which even his judge had to accept.

The manor, as a unit, was self-sufficient, producing almost everything it needed. It sheared its own sheep, wove its own cloth, made its own clothes. Few things were needed from outside — salt, perhaps, and iron. The needs of the villein were small, and he was used to living a little above bare subsistence. Money was not of great importance to the villager. The sums needed for taxes and other purposes were obtained by the sale of surplus crops to the townsfolk or merchants. Only a small proportion of the population relied on wages or commerce for their livelihood. These were mainly the artisans, craftsmen and merchants of the towns, or the personal followers and servants of the wealthier people.

In this feudal economy the towns occupied an important place. Originally settlements of men engaged in trading or in crafts, over a long period of time they were able to buy themselves 'quit' of irksome restrictions by payment or services to their overlord, frequently the king. These freedoms took the form of 'charters', deeds granting specific rights and liberties and exemption from certain dues to the citizens; including considerable measures of self-government. Thus each chartered town became a little centre of freedom in a feudal world; a place where a young man would be apprenticed to a craft, learn it, become a journeyman artisan for a time, then set up as a master-craftsman himself. He owned his own raw materials, worked on them with his own tools, sold the finished product for himself, and acknowledged no master except the mayor of his town and the livery of his trade guild. He owed no dues or labour to any man, and could come and go as he pleased. It was a satisfying and independent way of life, and has left us the romantic tradition of 'Merry England'.

The merchants would bring in goods from outside or from abroad for sale in the town, and take away some of the town's particular products for sale elsewhere. All this required a more convenient means of exchange than service or barter. With the development of civilisation, especially after contact with higher cultures in the East during the Crusades, the use of money, and the demand for it, grew rapidly. The life of the ruling classes became ever more luxurious and expensive. A suit of modern plate armour cost a lot more than an old-fashioned and vulnerable coat of mail. Valuable clothes and fabrics from Europe, costly sugar and spices from the East were needed by the nobility. The Church needed money to pay for its huge fantastic buildings and for its heads to vie with the lifestyle of the courtiers. The king always needed immense sums to pay for his continual wars.

Much of this money came through the merchants in the wool trade, who found an ever-growing demand for good English wool in the weaving towns of north-west Europe. So profitable was this wool trade that some landowners began to lay out their estates as sheep-walks, thus encroaching on the ancient rights of the commons. By the fourteenth century many landlords found it profitable to allow their serfs and villeins to make a money payment for their rent instead of labour, and as 'quittance' for all the old feudal dues. Even the great barons began to pay 'scutage' — shield money — to the king instead of providing military services. This brought a greater measure of freedom to the peasant. He earned the money to buy his freedom, where it could be bought, mostly by selling his surplus products to the landless townsmen. Thus he began to produce for the market, not just for his own needs, and needed all his time and labour for himself.

The king never had enough money for his wars and expenses. The nobles claimed it for their luxurious lifestyle. The peasants, hitherto thought to need little more than the beasts they tended, began to demand freedom and the money to buy it with. Some among them became relatively prosperous and began to hold extra land themselves and even to employ labour at certain times like harvest.

Thus the old and stable feudal system, which its people thought had been ordained since Adam, and was the only possible and God-given way of life, began to exhibit strains and tensions. Life began to change. The Church, which dominated the minds of men, opposed the new ways and refused to 'manumit' the rents and dues from its huge estates for money payments. Heretics appeared in the body of the Church itself, condemning its wealth and calling for a return to the simple virtues of early christianity. Unknown in the long history of feudalism, a time of crisis and change was approaching.

Into this situation there suddenly came an unwelcome visitor from the Far East — the Black Death.

2. THE BLACK DEATH AND ITS AFTERMATH

In August 1348, in the reign of King Edward III, plague appeared in the ports of Weymouth and Southampton. It caused little concern at first. Plague was a frequent problem in the unsanitary conditions of the middle ages. It usually came in the summer and died out in the winter, and was accepted as an unpleasant fact of life; as we accept the 8,000 or so now killed on the roads each year.

This plague was different. It began in China, spread across Asia and was brought into Italy by travelling merchants. It worked its way across Europe until infected seamen brought it into England. The symptoms were violent sneezing, inflammation of the lungs and the spitting of blood. Black spots appeared on the limbs, giving the malady its name. Then large tumours grew in thighs or armpits and death usually followed. The primitive medicine of the time was powerless to find cause or cure. It is now known to have been bubonic plague, caused by a parasite of the black rat, then common.

So severe were the ravages of the Black Death that it seemed to foretell the end of the human race. In the absence of accurate records it is estimated that in Europe its victims numbered 25,000,000 and in England about 1,500,000; that is, between one-half and one-third of the entire population died in those terrible months. When the pestilence ended it left large areas of the country almost unpeopled. The mortality was highest among those who were less well nourished and lived in the worst conditions; so much so that it was dubbed 'poor man's plague'. The harvest rotted in the fields unreaped, cattle and sheep were left to wander and die of hunger, neglect and disease.

Henry Knighton, a churchman of the time, wrote:

> Many villages and hamlets were depopulated, and there were no houses left in them, all who lived in them being dead . . . In the following winter there was such a shortage of servants for all sorts of labour as it was believed had never been before.*

This great shortage of labour was an important social outcome of the plague. The landlords were at their wits' end for workmen. Wages rose drastically as they competed with each other for the available free labour, often having to give more than double the sum formerly paid. 'Thatchers . . . who formerly received 1d per day now earned 2½d. In one village alone the cost of harvesting rose from £3.13.9 to £12.19.10.'†

Prices soared, too, as less was produced. Knighton tells us that 'necessaries became so dear that what had been previously worth 1d was now worth 4d or 5d'. The landlords reacted sharply. Where villeins had commuted their dues for a money payment, they tried to restore the old system of boon-work. In manors where this 'manumission' was in progress the lords stopped it, as the feudal bonds kept their peasants tied to their land. Some bargained and

---

Chronicon Henrici Knighton.
†Quoted in Fagin, *Nine Days that Shook England.*

offered favourable conditions to attract free labour to their manors to replace the dead. And the peasants, too, reacted. All over the country villeins began to run away from their manors to lose themselves in distant parts of the country where they could earn the high wages of free men. In the chaos of the time the chances of detection and punishment were small. If caught, the absconder was liable to branding and imprisonment. But if he could remain unclaimed in a chartered town for a year and a day, he could legally demand his freedom.

King Edward and his counsellors also reacted. He had not abated the luxurious excesses of his court throughout the plague. Nor had he ceased to demand money and men for his endless wars in France. In 1351 he called a Parliament, the first time since the pestilence, (which was of course not representative of the country as a whole) and passed the legislation known as the 'Statute of Labourers'. This was an elaboration and enaction of some previous measures which had had but little effect. It was probably the first attempt on the part of the state to regulate wages,* and it took account of all interests except those of the peasant and wage-earner. It is the earliest application of that universal remedy so beloved of modern governments — the wage-freeze.

The Statute of Labourers was an attempt to restore the past by legislation. Among other things it solemnly decreed that no workman was to demand or accept more pay than he would have earned 'in the twentieth year of the present king's reign', i.e. 1347, before the Black Death, and he was forbidden to refuse work offered at that rate. Employers were also forbidden to offer more, and the workman was banned from leaving his master. Offenders were to be punished by fines and imprisonment. It also outlawed all combinations of workmen, as such 'brotherhoods' tended to keep labour dear. The Statute was to be enforced by a new order of Justices of the Peace, enrolled from the landowning gentry.

The Statute failed to achieve its objects. The level of wages fell, but not to pre-plague levels. Knighton records: 'From that time forth they served their masters worse from day to day than they had done previously.' Many peasants ran from their manors, and the resentment generated against the Justices of the Peace and the state was to find its expression later.

It must be borne in mind that all the reports and records that we possess for this period, and the revolt that followed it, come from the pens of people who were the natural supporters of the state, the crown, and the Church, who regarded their social order as something

---

*This was one of the functions of the trade guilds, which set the wage rate in its own 'mystery'. Agricultural wages were determined largely by 'the custom of the manor'.

sacred and eternal, and the common people as a 'mob' that in the interests of Christian civilisation must be rigorously controlled, whose function within society was to work and live contentedly on what they earned or won, to accept without question the decrees of their betters and leave the direction of affairs to them. Our knowledge of the events of the time come largely from the chronicles of a few 'clerks' and some lay writers, all of them strongly biased against the peasants. The commons themselves, being mostly illiterate, left no written records, nor would it have been safe for them to do so.

There survive some accounts of court proceedings both for breaches of the Statute and for participation in the later rebellion, and from these scanty reports the story must be pieced together. Naturally, historians disagree among themselves as to what actually happened, and why and how. Of the resistance of the commons there can be no doubt, but what form it took is dubious.

Because of the spontaneous nature of the revolt, outbreaks occurring simultaneously in areas far apart, the high level of organisation shown in action, the appearance of an ambitious political policy ready-made for the movement and accepted by all from both north and south of the Thames, some have argued that this implies the existence over many years of a large, illegal, underground organisation which drew up the policy, planned the revolt, and carried it out. It would have been known as the Great Company or the Great Society, or a similar name. Its decisions and communications would have been carried and delivered by couriers who may have been pedlars, merchants, musicians, entertainers, friars, masons, builders or other free craftsmen going from job to job.

There is no surviving evidence of such an organisation, and some historians dismiss it as a romantic invention of later years. But the story of ensuing events seems to make it a strong probability.

In 1377 the senile Edward III died. It was symbolic of his dissolute and corrupt court that immediately the breath was out of his body the rings were pulled off his fingers by his mistress Alice Perrers, on whom he had lavished enormous wealth. The English armies in France suffered defeat after defeat. Now the French were successfully raiding the English coast. The cost of the war, soon to be known as the Hundred Years War, was more than the nation could bear. The rival groups round the throne were bitterly fighting for power. There was mass discontent in the countryside and social conflict in the towns. The government was bankrupt. No further means of raising money presented themselves. In these conditions the new reign, that of King Richard II, began.

It was unfortunate that at this time of crisis the new king was a boy of eleven years of age. He was strongly under the influence of his uncle, John of Gaunt, Duke of Lancaster, who grew to be the most hated man in the kingdom. The actual work of government devolved upon the Royal Council. The king and his new Parliament were desperate for money; even the crown jewels had been pawned. They thought up the novel idea of a poll tax, a personal tax on every individual in the country. This is attributed to John of Gaunt. A levy of one groat (about four old pence) was made on everybody over fourteen years old, male or female, rich or poor. The proceeds were quickly spent on the war or absorbed by corruption, and were followed by a 'graduated' poll tax. And in the year 1380, in a move suggested by Simon Sudbury, Archbishop of Canterbury, a new poll tax of three groats (or one shilling, old style) per head over the age of fifteen was levied. There was a maximum payment of twenty shillings from men whose families and households numbered more than twenty, thus ensuring that the rich payed less than the poor. A shilling was a considerable sum for a working man, almost a week's wages. A family might include old persons past work and other dependents, and the head of the family became liable for one shilling on each of their 'polls'. This was basically a tax on the labouring classes, and the response was a unity of opposition among the commons that overrode all their many divisions.

The tax was to be collected at source by commissioners sent out by the county authorities. In the villages a roll of inhabitants would be compiled and each head of a household would be called upon to come forward and make his payment. Before the commissioners arrived there were often mass desertions from the villages and boroughs. Whole families fled and hid themselves in the woods and wastelands. False returns were made on the rolls and the true numbers suppressed. Out of the £100,000 expected by Archbishop Sudbury, now also Chancellor of England, a mere £22,000 was brought in.

The government, aware of the widespread evasion, decided to send again to the towns and villages, but this time with escorts of armed men under charge of a Justice of the Peace. Full checks were to be made of the population figures, oaths were to be administered, and, once the true figures had been arrived at, the taxes due were to be collected under threat of force and imprisonment.

This was rumoured to be the plan suggested by one John Legge, a sergeant-at-arms of the king. True or false, it was to cost him his life.

3. INSURRECTION

On 30 May 1381, Thomas Bampton, commissioner for the collection of poll tax, rode into the Essex town of Brentwood, accompanied by several clerks and a small armed escort. He called on the people of the villages of Fobbing, Corringham and Stanford-le-Hope to appear before him to pay their due taxes. They appeared, about a hundred strong, refused point-blank to reply or to pay, and stoned the commissioner's party out of the town. What happened next is described in the *Anonimalle Chronicle,* a record of the time:

> Sir Robert Belknap, Chief Justice of the Common Bench, was sent into the country . . . wherefore the Commons rose against him and came before him to tell him . . . he was maliciously proposing to undo them . . . Accordingly they made him swear on the Bible that never again would he hold such sessions nor act as Justice in such inquests . . . And Sir Robert travelled home as quickly as possible.

This seems to have been a predetermined signal. All over Essex and across the Thames in Kent, the commons left their villages and assembled with what weapons they could arm themselves. And not only the peasants: with them came many of the smaller gentry and knights and artisans from the towns. Even some priests left their parish churches to join their flocks. It seemed to be a united action by all the lower sections of society.

In Essex, one Abel Ker of Erith appeared as a leader. Messages were sent to centres in Kent, Suffolk and Norfolk calling for support and aid.

The immediate steps were to settle accounts with the feudal landowners. Monasteries, abbeys, the houses of repressive landlords were attacked, the records and charters of labour and other dues dragged out and burnt. These varied from district to district and once destroyed could not easily be replaced. Along with these old parchments disappeared, it was hoped, the oppressions of serfdom and villeinage. Some buildings were also burnt or pulled down. Little mercy was shown to clerks and lawyers, who were regarded as the main enemies of the commons as it was they who operated the old laws, taxes and dues. They were beheaded wherever they were caught. Few were taken, as most of them had enough warning to escape.

Abel Ker crossed the Thames at Dartford with a hundred men and made contact with Robert Cave, the local leader there. A conference was held, and the first statement of aims and policy was announced. This proclaimed loyalty to King Richard and accused John of Gaunt of wishing to usurp the crown. People living within four miles of the sea were told not to join the rebellion, but to stay at home and guard the coast against French raiders.

Within a day or so thousands of people were assembling in south-east England, and in many other areas risings were beginning. Then, on 6 June, the Kentish rebels marched off to attack their first major objective, Rochester Castle. An absconding serf who had sought refuge in Gravesend had been claimed by his lord, against the will of the citizens, and imprisoned there. The great Norman keep surrendered after a long day's fighting, and all the prisoners in the cells were released. Many of them were there for breaches of the Statute and tax regulations.

There was important business to be done at Maidstone, where a strong rebel body arrived on 7 June, with no resistance from the citizens. And it is here that the great leaders of the movement first appeared. Among the prisoners released was the priest John Ball, sentenced yet again for preaching while under the ban of the Church. John Ball quickly assumed his place as the theoretician of the rising and its spiritual father. Whatever the masses thought of the temporal Church, they all considered themselves to be good Catholics.

Given his due, John Ball would occupy an honoured place in English history. Much of his early life is obscure, and our first knowledge of him derives from accusations made against him in clerical courts. He was at first the priest of St Mary's, York, but quickly roused the opposition of his superiors by the nature of his preaching and was banned from the pulpit and later excommunicated. He seems then to have made Colchester his centre, whence for some twenty years he had wandered the country as a kind of Christian agitator, denouncing the rich and their exploitation of the poor, calling for social justice and freedom and a society based on fraternity and the equality of all people.

Sir John Froissart, a courtly writer of the period, tells us that Ball had been imprisoned three times by succeeding Archbishops of Canterbury for illicit preaching. And he writes:

> This priest used oftentimes on Sundays after mass, when the people were going out of church, to go into the cloister and preach . . . and he would say thus: 'Ah, ye good people, the matters goeth not well to pass in England, nor shall do till everything be common, and that there be no villeins nor gentlemen, but that we may be all united together, and the lords be no greater masters than we be . . . let us go to the king, he is young, and show him what servage we be in, and show him how we would have it otherwise . . .' Wherefore many of the mean people loved him.*

And later:

---

*Froissart, *Chronicles*.

'And when this John Ball was out of prison, he returned
again to his error.'*

Without doubt he was loved and supported by the 'mean people'.
How else could he have lived 'on the run' for twenty years? And he
had foreknowledge of events. According to Walsingham, at his
Maidstone trial he told the court that 'soon twenty thousands of his
friends would come and free him'†, as indeed they did. They, at least,
never thought of him as 'the mad priest of Kent'.

He was in the habit of sending messages to his friends in the form of
little verses, some of them in a kind of code. One found in the pocket
of a rebel about to be hanged was probably an encouragement to the
insurgents. It read:

> John Ball greeteth you all
> And doth to understand he has rung your bell.
> Now with right and might, will and skill,
> God speed every dell.

Another ran:

> John Trueman doth you to understand
> Falsehood and guile hath reigned too long
> And Truth hath been set under a lock,
> And Falseness reigneth in every flock. . . . .

Some combined ethical criticism of society with political instruction:

> Now reigneth pride in price,
> Covetise is holden wise,
> Lechery without shame
> Gluttony without blame.
> Envy reigneth with reason
> And sloth is taken in great season. . . .
> . . . . Know your friend from your foe,
> Take enough and cry Ho!
> And do well and better and flee from sin,
> Seek out peace and dwell therein
> So biddeth John Trueman and all his fellows.

It is in Ball's words that we find the early concept of the equality of
all men, as opposed to the rigid class divisions, privileges and injustice of feudalism; equality as justified by scripture and expressed
as fraternity, that was to continue as a basic ideal of the English
radical tradition.

---

*Ibid.
†Thomas Walsingham, *Historia Anglicana*.

At last his day had come. The commons had risen, their work was bearing fruit, and now for the decisive struggle out of which would emerge the new kingdom of fraternity and peace that was God's plan for mankind.

At Maidstone the leadership of the whole rising was given into the hands of Wat Tyler. He, too, emerges out of an unknown past into the centre of the stage of history. Like Ball, he was to have only a few days left to live, but those days were to be crowded with activity, with victory, and with betrayal. He was from Colchester, probably a tiler by trade. A real working man, with a great pride in himself and his fellows. He was said to have served in the French wars, where no doubt he was quick to learn the lessons of organisation and discipline now to stand him in such good stead. He belonged to the lowest social group in the kingdom, but he was, in the name of the commons, to send for the highest men in the land, and the highest came. And Tyler faced them with natural dignity and confidence as spokesman for the people of England. He showed the same pride in the customs and manners of his own class as the noblest baron would for his. For nine days he was to be the unacknowledged ruler of England. Even his enemies admitted his worth grudgingly. Walsingham called him a 'cunning man, endowed with much sense if he had applied his intelligence to good purposes'. Froissart summed him up as 'an ungracious patron'.

There was a brief conference in Maidstone in which Tyler was elected leader, and a policy was announced in four clauses:

1. Allegiance to King Richard.
2. Opposition to John of Gaunt.
3. No taxation of the commons except for the accepted tax of one-fifteenth.
4. Readiness to act for these objects.

Now the main lines of the programme were clear. The aim of the rebellion was to present their case to young King Richard, to assure him of their loyalty, to separate him from his 'evil councillors', to replace them with 'good men of the commons' and to persuade the king to abolish serfdom and villeinage, thus making all men free. From the towns and villages of Kent and Essex great bodies of armed men began to march towards London.

Tyler, with a large party, made for Canterbury, the shrine of St Thomas à Becket. It was a walled city of some strength, but its gates were open wide and the citizens welcomed them in with cheers and offerings. They entered the cathedral, mother-church of all England, as the monks were ending midday mass. All knelt and crossed themselves and Tyler climbed into the pulpit. There he addressed the startled monks, telling them to find themselves a new archbishop as

Simon Sudbury, also Chancellor of England, had been condemned to death by the commons.

The archbishop's palace was ransacked, all the records and accounts were piled up in the courtyard and burnt. The mayor and the corporation, in full civic splendour, wearing their municipal regalia, backed by the townsmen, took an oath of loyalty to King Richard and the True Commons, and swore to operate and defend the new order. Three men, pointed out as 'traitors' and oppressors, were put to death.

Tyler left to rejoin the main body, taking with him 500 recruits from the city. The road to London, to the king, to freedom, was before them.

4. JOHN BALL AND THE MEETING ON BLACKHEATH

On 12 June the great mass of Kentish rebels, some 60,000 strong, more than the entire population of London, arrived at Blackheath, a high, bare place four miles from the southern end of London Bridge. Across the Thames most of the Essex men settled down at Mile End, a mile east of the city wall.

There was much activity by rebel detachments during the night. From their high position the Blackheath commons could see London clearly across the Thames-side flatlands, and the glow of great fires burning around the city. In the south blazed the two prisons, King's Bench and the Marshalsea, with their prisoners freed. The Bankside brothels, rich source of income to their landlord the Bishop of Winchester, gleamed redly in the river. Further west, Sudbury's Lambeth Palace burned fiercely, and in the north flamed Treasurer Hale's priory at Highbury.

Within the city, too, all eyes were on the flames. Rent by social struggles, with the trade guilds, once the free societies of artisans and traders, fallen into the control of the new class of rich merchants and masters, the burghers heard no call for its militia to turn out and man the walls. The great bell of St Martin-le-Grand failed to sound the tocsin which would call the Londoners to arms to defend their city. The rulers of the city did not trust their people to assemble armed, once the right of free men.

The mayor, William Walworth, a member of the Fishmongers' Company and of the new class of mercantile plutocrats dominating the London government, had a large investment in the Bankside vice area, and its burning filled him with rage and loss. He ordered the city gates to be barred and the drawbridge raised, and sent messengers to Blackheath to warn the commons to come no nearer as they would gain no entrance to London. Among these messengers was an alderman, John Horne, who had private speech with Tyler and told him to ignore the mayor. The bulk of the London folk would welcome the rebels, he said, and see that they entered unopposed; steps were being taken to that end.

The next day, 13 June, was Corpus Christi Day, one of the Church's great festivals. The commons observed it with honour. An altar with snow-white linen was prepared, and over it flew the great red-cross flag of St George, patron saint of England. Another flew before the assembly, drawn up in an open square before the altar. Among the host sixty pennons fluttered in the upland breeze, and away to the north-west the clouds of smoke still drifted around London.

The huge crowd knelt, and John Ball celebrated mass. He then preached a unique sermon to his unique congregation on this unique occasion; and his text was to ring down through succeeding centuries of English thought. He took it not from the scriptures but from a popular saw of the country people.

> When Adam delved and Eve span,
> Who was then the gentleman?

This seems to have been the first known expression in Europe of the equality of all men. There is, of course, no verbatim report of this oration. We know of it only through unreliable extracts from the pens of opponents. Walsingham states: 'He tried to prove . . . that from the beginning all men were created equal by nature and that servitude had been introduced by the unjust and evil oppressions of men against the will of God.'*

John Stowe, about two hundred years later, reports Ball's words as he had received them:

> If it had pleased God to have made bondsmen He would have appointed them from the beginning of the world, who should be slave and who lord. They ought to consider, therefore, that now was a time given them by God, in the which, laying aside their continual bondage, they might, if they would, enjoy their long-wished liberty't

According to Stowe, Ball then outlined the plans of the rebellion — the Archbishop, the king's councillors, the lawyers and justices were to be killed, as one weeds the ground before planting. On this

---

*Walsingham, *Historia Anglicana.*
†John Stowe, *Chronicles.*

basis a society of equals was to be constructed, under the crown, 'with equal liberty all one nobility and like authority and power'.*

The chroniclers reported, naturally, what horrified them most — Ball's claim for the political equality of all men. By thus stressing this concept, he was attacking the fundamental ideas of feudal society, the elaborate class structure with its many social levels and its codes of service and duties. But there is little doubt that he would not let such an opportunity pass without introducing and developing his further point, that things could not go well until 'all was held in common', probably envisaging some simple form of common ownership of the land and its fruits.

The sermon was received with acclamation. Walsingham said that it found high favour with the common people, who cried out that he alone was worthy of the office of archbishop. And Stowe commented drily: 'Many more such mad devices preached he.'

To the modern reader it will seem strange that this mass rising, threatening the very roots of society, which had now been under way for nearly two weeks, had met with no organised opposition except for a few local skirmishes and the defence of Rochester Castle. This was long before there existed a standing army or a police force. A revolt of the commons was considered as unlikely and unnatural as a rising of the horses or the cattle. The leaders of the revolt had chosen their time well. The one army the king possessed then was at sea, bound for Portugal and beyond recall. John of Gaunt was away with his men in Scotland. There was no armed force ready at hand to oppose the rebellion. Sitting in his palace at Westminster the young king, now in his fourteenth year, and his royal council, looked out at the fires, heard the reports, and moved into the safer quarters of the Tower of London.

Although it would dishonour a nobleman to parley and bargain with such a rabble, there was no course open but to appease the mob, to satisfy it for a while, to play for time while an army was raised to disperse it and drive it back to its plough-lands and cowsheds.

To the Tower came riding a knight, Sir John Newton, shamefaced and humbled, bearing a message he had unwillingly sworn to deliver. He was ushered into the anxious presence, apologising profusely for acting as herald to a cause he loathed.

'Say on,' said Richard impatiently, 'We hold you excused.'

The embarrassed knight told the king and council that the rebels assured King Richard of their loyalty, and stated that they had come to save him from his evil councillors, especially Archbishop Sudbury and John of Gaunt, who had misgoverned the realm to the great dishonour of the kingdom and the oppression of the people. And

*Ibid.

they respectfully begged the king to come before them without fear, so that they could state their desires in full and tell his majesty things that he should know.

The court felt some relief at this message. As long as the mob retained their loyalty to the king, there was hope for them all. This could be used to keep them in play without too great harm, until they could be crushed. Once the king lost their trust, they would all be doomed. As the old Earl of Salisbury said, 'It will then be all over with us and our heirs, and England will be a desert.' The wretched dishonoured Sir John Newton, whose sons were held as hostages for his oath, returned to tell Tyler that the king would be graciously pleased to meet his loyal commons down river, on the foreshore at Rotherhithe, on the following morning.

Rotherhithe was a royal manor on the south bank of the Thames, and there by the riverside a great crowd awaited the king. The small number with a few pieces of armour stood in the front row, and over them flew the great banners of St George. At the brink waited the group of leaders, headed by Tyler and Ball. The great historical moment was approaching — the first-ever meeting between king and commons to discuss honestly and boldly the problems of the people. All eyes were turned upstream and eventually the royal barge appeared, glittering with gold and scarlet, a magnificent vessel rowed by many uniformed oarsmen. High at the stern was a throne under a tall canopy, and a staff flying the royal banner in embroidery of gold and silver thread. The barge moved steadily on, escorted by four smaller boats, until it backed water and lay, rocking slightly, twenty yards from shore. With the king were all the royal council and all the courtiers who could find room on board, including those that the commons saw as their bitterest oppressors, Sudbury and Hales among them.

A great noise of shouting and cheering broke from the crowd. Some cheered the king, others shouted at their enemies around him. For a while there was pandemonium, while the leadership waited in respectful silence. Then the long-awaited dialogue began. The king cried over the water in his thin immature voice, 'Sirs, what is your will? See, I have come to talk with you!'

The rebels shouted to him to land and come among them. What they had to say could not be shouted over a distance. On the barge there took place a short anxious discussion. The nobles feared the loss of the security they had in the royal presence if he landed. The king feared for his own safety and the debasing proximity of serfs and peasants. Then the Earl of Salisbury stood up before the king and shouted across.

'Gentlemen,' he said, 'It may not be. See, you are not properly dressed nor in a fit condition for the king to talk with you.'

The oars began to move and the barge turned and made off towards the Tower. The peasants roared in anger and shook their fists. Many cried, 'Treason!' A large number of them carried the famous English long-bow that could kill at 200 yards. But none were bent at the barge, and it drew off in peace.

Thus ended the first meeting between King Richard and his commons. The courtiers, cowering from the expected arrows that never came, knew now that as long as they held the king they were safe in his shadow; and that young Richard was the one weapon with which the commons could be defeated, and their ownership of England retained.

5. THE REBELS IN LONDON

It was now clear to the leaders, and to every thinking peasant, that a critical point had been reached. The king had not talked with them, as promised, and again the 'evil councillors' had prevailed. What now? The great rebel host could not stay idle like a paid army. The food they had brought with them was almost gone, few had any money, and there was no possibility of obtaining supplies in the countryside. Men were thinking of their homes and families and the work to be done on the farms if they were not to starve in winter. The issue had to be decided quickly, or the whole mass would melt away. In London there was everything they needed — food, drink, shelter and the king. But London was invincible, safe behind its great wall and its fortified gates, approachable only by the narrow bridge. Defended, it could never be taken.

From the city galloped Alderman Horne, true friend of the commons. The worried leaders gathered round him, the peasants sat and talked and waited. Then Tyler gave the order. Forward to London! With a cheer the crowd rose to its feet, formed its ranks and set off, a banner depicting St George waving overhead.

Now they stood before London Bridge. In front of them was the high stone fort of the gate-house, its portcullis down, its battlements manned. Beyond, was the raised drawbridge and the iron gleam of the river, then the narrow roadway lined with houses. And across the Thames the great wall girdling the city topped by the crowded roofs covering the little hill, with more than a hundred towers and spires forming a diadem, up to the great cathderal of St Paul that towered over all and the steeple shooting five hundred feet towards the sky. In the eastern corner, the fortress of the Tower, high and impregnable, where the king was. There was no army in the world that could successfully assault this city. Must the whole brave business end here? Had Horne been misinformed, or had he deceived them?

The commons' vanguard was a picked body of archers and spearmen, with Tyler at their head. He stayed them short of the gate, and went forward alone. No bolt or arrow flashed toward him from the battlements. At the gate he spoke urgently through the wicket with its captain, Alderman Sibley, while all watched and waited, Then, suddenly, with a creak and a rattle the drawbridge began to fall and the portcullis to rise, while Sibley came out with a breastplate over his long civic gown and Tyler embraced him. London was theirs!

Over the bridge the rebels came, and into the city. On each side of the narrow overhanging streets the townsfolk stood and cheered them, rolling out tuns of ale, offering food of all kinds. From every window people leaned out to wave and call a welcome. On to the wide space by Paul's Cross, where the Londoners held their meetings, they marched, and then a new roar arose as the Essex men swept in. They had found Aldgate opened for them. They were led by Jack Straw and Thomas Farringdon, a Londoner.

Now was a testing time for discipline. The wealth of the great city was there for the taking. There was loot here in the great houses of the rich merchants and the noblemen to make them all rich for life by peasant standards; the sack of a city was the customary reward for conquering armies. Yet even the antagonistic chroniclers agree that there was no pillage, no looting. Everything not offered freely was fully paid for. A stern warning was made to all that a quick hanging awaited any rebel or Londoner who might sieze the chance for crime. 'We are zealots for Truth and Justice,' it said, 'not thieves or robbers.'

There was no time to wander round and stare at the sights of London. The peasant army, under orders, divided into detachments. One set off to the Temple, the legal centre, to destroy all records and documents; another to Lincolns Inn on a similar mission. There was no need to take measures against the hated 'clerks and lawyers'; they were nowhere to be found. Men were despatched to destroy the Fleet and Newgate prisons and free the inmates. Many of these would be poll-tax and Statute evaders, although there were also thieves and criminals who no doubt would go back to their trade.

A large section went off to surround the Tower of London and keep it under observation. They camped all round it on the green slopes of Tower Hill, lit their little cooking-fires, and settled down. Another set off for St John's Priory in Clerkenwell and fired it. This was the monastery of Robert Hales, the king's treasurer, popularly known as 'Hobbe the Robber' who was known to be with the chancellor, Sudbury, in the Tower with the king.

The largest troop went to settle accounts with John of Gaunt, Duke of Lancaster, their chief enemy, in his absence. Out of the loot of France (and of England) he had built himself one of Europe's grandest palaces, the Savoy. It occupied a large area between the Strand and the river, and it was high on the rebels' list for destruction. This operation had the enthusiastic support of the Londoners. The Savoy was also the headquarters of the Duchy of Lancaster, and there the Duke kept his treasures and his accounts and records. It was full of jewellery, tapestries, armour, rich clothing, fine furniture and even some of those rare oriental luxuries called carpets. It was probably the greatest concentration of wealth in the kingdom.

The few people in the palace were allowed to leave unharmed. A solemn warning was given to all that this destruction was an act of justice, and that any person found keeping anything for himself would be treated as a common thief. Then they entered and destroyed and broke up everything within. Nothing was spared. Everything was smashed into useless fragments. Jewels were pounded into gleaming dust in mortars brought along for that purpose. The remains were thrown into the river or stacked for burning. One man detected hiding some silver under his clothes was hanged summarily. A group of peasants had made their way into the wine cellar and drank themselves helpless. No effort was made to get them out when the palace was finally set alight, and much of the duke's wealth and power vanished in the flames.

These tasks accomplished, the peasants fraternised with the Londoners, and their leaders adjourned to the house of Thomas Farringdon. There they drew up and finalised the list of demands to put before the king, and made the list of those men whose lives were to pay for their past misrule and whose survival would be a threat to the new, free England of 'King Richard and the commons'. These included John of Gaunt, Archbishop Sudbury for his extortions as Chancellor, the Treasurer Hales, the Bishop of London, John Legge the chief poll-tax commissioner, and others. Messengers were sent off to provincial towns to co-ordinate their actions and keep them informed of events in London.

In the Tower the king and his council, which now included Walworth, mayor of London, sat in helpless impotence. The rebels held the capital, the main towns of Kent and Essex, and the roads nearby. In East Anglia, in Hertfordshire, in Cambridgeshire, many towns and manors had already risen, and there were likely to be more. The furious mayor was in favour of action. He could raise a large body of armed men from the households of the rich merchants, and with the Tower garrison of 600 soldiers and the private army of the mercenary Sir Robert Knollys available at his home not far away, he could assemble in a day a force of several thousand troops. With these he could smash the rebels round the Tower, rally into the streets and drive them from the city. Salisbury opposed this: the attack would peter out in a thousand narrow streets, and if the

London artisans and apprentices joined with the peasants, as well they might, all would be lost. They must play for time, which was on the side of the king, while the provincial gentry raised their forces and built them up. These rebels were simple men, unskilled in statecraft, and would readily believe the word of the king. A few charters would satisfy them. First, he would send out an envoy to test their mood and promise anything that might tend to delay, for with delay the host would melt away as men tired and went home. Then would be the time for military suppression.

It was dark now, and from the Tower could be seen the camp-fires of the rebels and the glow of the burning Savoy. Out of the Tower on to the Hill came two elderly knights, long past their fighting days. One carried a roll of parchment from which dangled the royal seal. The peasants pressed round them as they cried for silence. Torches were brought, and in the flickering red light one of the two, mounted on a stool, read out the king's proclamation: 'Let the peasants return now to their homes, and the king would pardon them all their offences. There they should put their grievances down in writing and send them to him . . . and with the aid of his lords and his good council, he would provide such remedy as shall be profitable to himself, and to them and to the kingdom'.*

Simple men the peasants may have been, but not so simple as to accept a proposal like that. The storm of hooting and shouting it aroused was clearly heard in the royal chamber, and the two old gentlemen were glad to reach the Tower again. A little later a new message was on its way to Wat Tyler, and was shouted by the town-criers in the streets: the king commanded his loyal commons to present themselves before him next morning at Mile End, where he would be graciously pleased to hear their grievances in person, and to grant them what relief lay in his power.

6. THE KING GRANTS FREEDOM

At seven o'clock on the morning of Friday 14 June, the great gate of the Tower of London opened, the portcullis rose, the drawbridge came down gently to span the moat. Out through the stone arch rode a glittering throng. On the proud high-stepping horses were riders clad in brilliant velvets, silks and damasks. The king was going out to meet his commons.

In front rode the heralds in their embroidered tabards showing the royal arms. Then the royal sword-bearer, Sir Aubrey de Vere,

Anonimalle Chronicle.

bearing the great sword of state upright before him. Then the king, a small bright figure on a large horse, with a goldem diadem round his temples. Behind him the whole court clustered as close to his royal person as they could, knowing that he was the one defence of themselves and all they held dear. There were three earls with him, his two half-brothers the Duke of Kent and Sir Thomas Holland, Sir Robert Knollys the captain of mercenaries, and all the nobility who feared to be away. Even the ageing queen-mother followed in a crude carriage. Only two famous and sought-for figures were missing — Sudbury and Robert Hales. These had been left behind, abandoned, it seemed, to the rebels.

It was noted that when the splendid procession left the Tower, the gates remained open and the drawbridge down, although within were the two 'evil councillors' most wanted by the peasants.

It could not have been a pleasant ride for Richard, this trip to sign away his friends and way of life. Crowds lined the route, doffing their caps to him as he went by, but angrily shouting and pointing at persons behind him, gesticulating and threatening. Twice the king himself was stopped by petitioners. Crossing the green fields of Whitechapel his two half-brothers yielded to panic, wheeled off the road, clapped in their spurs, and galloped off across country. The rest rode on.

The great open waste at Mile End was crammed with people. Never before had such a crowd gathered in England. The chroniclers could only estimate: The *Anonimalle Chronicle* says there were 100,000 people, Froissart, 60,000. In front, under the flapping banners, stood the small group of leaders. At their backs, drawn up in ordered ranks as for battle, were the armed men of the host in what pieces of armour they had — archers, spearmen, bearers of ancestral swords and bucklers, and the famous 'brown bills'; and behind them the drab lines of peasants in their homespun clothes carrying pitchforks, sickles, cudgels, quarterstaffs and axes. The king approached, and halted. Then, as though a great wave swept across them, the entire crowd fell on its knees and cried out in one voice, 'Long live King Richard and his true commons'. The shout rolled away, and the leaders stepped forward — Wat Tyler, John Ball, Jack Straw and others. They marched boldly up to the king, made obeisance, and Tyler, speaking for them all, requested of his majesty the right and authority to take any man that the commons deemed to be a traitor to the king and his people, and put him to death if necessary.

The king was pale and looked worried. At times of stress a slight nervous stammer crept into his speech; this happened now, but he fought it down. He answered that any man accused would be legally tried in the courts. The rebels began to talk about the nature of the courts, and the courtiers became restive. So the king granted Tyler the right to take any man who could be proved a traitor, and deal with him justly.

Tyler then produced a written document and read out its clauses. These, somewhat condensed, were as follows: 'That all men should be freed from their bondage, and that no man should serve another but of his own free will; That any man should be free to buy, sell and trade in any place in England; That there should be an amnesty for all acts done by any man during the rising, and that no prosecutions should follow'.

No doubt the courtiers were shocked at this programme. They might well be. It meant no less than the end of their epoch, which they had been brought up to think, if they ever indeed questioned it, God-given and eternal. This is not the place to subject these demands to close political analysis; but for the commons they meant a revolutionary change: the end of centuries of injustice and suffering, the opportunity for a new life.

Only the king showed no emotion; he had been well schooled in his role. Gravely he listened and nodded down at them from his saddle. He accepted it and he agreed with it all, and would see that it was put into practice at once. And for that purpose he would have his clerks draw up a charter for each district that would make it the law of the land. He solemnly presented Tyler with a banner bearing the royal arms, thereby granting him authority to act and taking him under his own protection. Flushed with victory, Tyler knelt to receive it. The king then rode slowly along the ranks of the commons, acknowledging their homage, while his heralds proclaimed to them all his acceptance of their requests.

The peasants were jubilant, leaping, cheering, shouting, embracing. Now they were all free men! The young king, good at heart, the anointed and consecrated lord of them all, freed from his evil councillors, was, they considered, the natural head and leader of his commons.

Richard rode back, not to the Tower, but to a strongly fortified building in the city called the Royal Wardrobe, by Carter Lane near St Paul's, where much of his valuable clothing and goods were stored. The Tower of London, left open, seemed to have been abandoned, and it was not long before the peasant guard around it were drinking and fraternising with the soldiers of the garrison; 'stroking their beards', the old chroniclers called it. Had they manned the walls and gates, the rebels could never have gained admittance.

Tyler came there straight from Mile End with a picked following. His royal banner gained him immediate entry, and they began at once the search for Sudbury and Hales, left there for them by the king. In the beautiful little chapel of St John, deep in the heart of the keep, they were found at prayer before the altar. They knew that they were

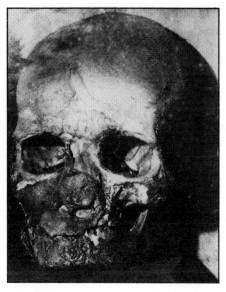

3.   Reputedly Archbishop
Sudbury's head, preserved at
St. Gregory's Church, Sudbury.

doomed men, and they made a brave end. Sudbury had spent the morning at mass where he had shriven and absolved Hales; he had himself been shrived by his chaplain. So both men stood up calmly to face their fate.

'Here I am, my sons, your Archbishop', said Sudbury. 'If you harm me, the Pope will lay all England under interdict and your souls will be lost for ever.' But they were taken out to Tower Hill and stood before a log which was to serve as a block. Sudbury prayed, forgave his executioners and knelt down. The unskilled axeman had to take several strokes before the head rolled off. Hales then shared his fate, with John Appledore, the king's confessor and John Legge, the poll-tax man. In accordance with the custom of the time, the heads were impaled on poles and exhibited on the gate of London Bridge. They were spared the penalty of the king's own punishment for treason — half-hanging, cutting down, disembowelling while still alive, and then chopping the body into four parts, each to be exhibited at a different place. This was the sentence called in law, 'hanging, drawing and quartering'.

Meanwhile, around St Paul's and along Cheapside, trestle tables had been set up at which the king's thirty clerks were busily writing out the charters of freedom for the manors, as promised. When written, the clerk melted sealing-wax over a taper, dropped a blob on the document, pressed it with the royal seal, and it became official. Some of these strips of parchment have survived in local archives. One, for Hertford, reads:

> Richard, by the grace of God, king of England and
> France, and lord of Ireland, to all his bailiffs and
> faithful men to whom these present letters come,
> greetings. Know that by our special grace we have
> manumitted all our liegemen, subjects and others of
> the county of Hertford; and we have freed and quitted
> each of them from bondage by the present letters. We
> also pardon our said liege men and subjects for all
> felonies, acts of treason, transgressions and extortions
> performed by them or any one of them in whatsoever
> way. We also withdraw sentences of outlawry declared
> against them or any of them because of these offences.
> And we hereby grant our complete peace to them and
> each of them. In testimony of which we order these
> letters of ours to be made patent. Witnessed by myself
> at London on 15 June in the fourth year of my reign.*

All the rest of that day, and the day following, the rebels roamed
the London streets brandishing their charters, enjoying their
freedom, demanding that all men take the oath of fealty to 'King
Richard and the true commons'. Where men were pointed out by the
citizens as notorious extortioners and oppressors, they were
questioned and often forced to make good their exactions. Some
were even beheaded, as the king had authorised them to do,
including John Imworth, Warden of the Marshalsea Prison. He was
dragged from sanctuary in Westminster Abbey and executed. Even
the hostile *Anonimalle* chronicler described him as 'a tormentor
without pity'.

The massacre of about 160 Flemings, an unpopular national
minority in London, has long been blamed on the rebel peasants, but
is now considered the work of Londoners. The Flemings had in no
way incurred the enmity of the peasants, most of whom were
unaware of their very existence. Originally from what is now Belgium
and Holland, most of them highly skilled weavers, they were hated as
rivals by the London cloth and weaving guilds who took the
opportunity to settle old scores. These unfortunate people were
dragged from their homes and churches and butchered in the streets.
A quick test was devised to ensure that no Londoner was mistaken
for a Fleming. Everyone was ordered to say 'bread and cheese', a
phrase often pronounced by Flemings as 'brod and case'. If a man
answered thus, he was at once murdered. The homes of many of the
Lombardy bankers and usurers were raided and pulled down, but this

---

*Quoted by Thomas Walsingham, *Historia Anglicana*.

too was the work of the citizens, probably organised by their business competitors and debtors.

Now many of the peasants began to return home. Their mission successful, their freedom won, they longed to return to their families and farms, and the host began slowly to dwindle. For some reason Tyler took no action against the royal council. He set no guard on the Wardrobe, allowed anyone to come and go unchecked and unhindered, nobles, heralds and messengers. And within it the council sat on round the king, and seemed to regard the Mile End meeting and its outcome as a charade. It issued a proclamation as though it was still ruling the land, ignoring the fact that it was now superseded. Power lay in the hands of the commons.

7. THE REVOLT IN THE PROVINCES

While these events were taking place in London, the commons elsewhere were active in their own interests. Despite the slow rate of communications, governed by the speed of a horse travelling along bad roads, or a walking man, provincial centres were well informed of the progress in the south, though there was some lapse of time in news arriving. In Hertfordshire, Suffolk, Norfolk, Cambridgeshire and elsewhere mass movements were developing almost simultaneously with the march on London. These usually took the form of local risings directed against local landowners, and the largest and most conservative of these, and the harshest, were the great abbeys and institutions of the Church. Frequently the local abbey, priory or monastery was the overlord of the town as well as the land, and therefore townsmen played a greater part in these actions and their grievances were mainly urban.

East Anglia was among the wealthiest districts of England, and most of the villeins on secular manors had already been manumitted and paid money rents. The Church opposed any such innovation on its numerous estates, and its people remained serfs. Towns like St Albans and Bury St Edmunds, as implied by their names, were more or less the property of those abbeys, which rigorously enforced every ancient feudal right that they possessed or had assumed. Other towns had purchased themselves charters of freedom from their overlords, and within limits governed themselves and arranged their own conditions of trade and work. The Church steadfastly refused to agree to this, thus greatly restricting the development of manufacture and commerce.

At St Albans the burghers claimed that the Saxon King Offa, in the eighth century, had given them a charter of rights but that the monks had stolen and hidden it. Also, Henry I, three hundred years earlier, had also granted them a charter which the abbey illegally held. The town had risen in arms three times against the abbey and were defeated each time by troops sent by the king. They had challenged the rights of the abbot in the courts of law, but the abbot always prevailed; the feudal courts could give no other verdict. One case concerned the right of the townsfolk to grind corn to make bread in their own mills instead of having to pay heavily to have it ground in the abbey mill. When the abbot won, he siezed all the town's millstones and used them to pave his dining-room. It was not a comfortable floor, but it humiliated the citizens and showed them who was the master. Thus the relationship between town and Church fell somewhat short of the Christian ideal, and the revolts in the provinces were more anti-clerical in their nature than in the south.

An influential leader of the St Albans' citizens was Will Grindcobbe, a man of some standing who had been educated, ex-communicated and imprisoned by the abbey. On hearing the news from Blackheath, he led a small party to London, and fell in with some Essex peasants on their way to burn John Hale's priory at Highbury. They went on to meet Wat Tyler and confer with him on future action. Tyler advised them to return and confront the abbot, and, if needed, he would come to their aid with 20,000 men, 'to shave the monks' beards.'*

Grindcobbe then went to the Mile End meeting, where he knelt before the king and asked for a letter from the royal hand commanding the abbot to yield to the demands of the burghers and produce the ancient charters. In accordance with his policy of appeasement the king complied, and Grindcobbe rode the thirty miles home that same day without rest or pause. The people of St Albans rose at his call and began by breaking down all the gates and fences of the public land that the abbey had enclosed, as they claimed, illegally. They forced the abbey's own private prison and released the prisoners, re-trying them all again as a kind of 'people's court'. They freed all but one, who was beheaded. His offence is not known. The next morning they sent to the abbot himself and commanded him to appear before them, on pain of the firing of the abbey. He at first refused, but was persuaded by his terrified monks, and came out to meet the delegates of the townsmen who awaited him in the great church, now the cathedral. Abbot de la Mare stood up to them boldly and claimed his rights under the law, to be told that the old laws no longer applied, the commons were making new laws. The old charter of King Offa never existed, he said, or was long lost.

---

*Walsingham, *Historia Anglicana*.

That of Henry I was the abbey's property and he had no authority to yield it. The king's letter was then presented. It ran:

> Very dear in God — At the petition of our beloved lieges of the town of St Albans, we will and command that (as law and right demands) you cause to be delivered to the said burgesses and good men of the town certain charters in your custody which were made by our ancestor, King Henry, to the said burgesses and good men concerning common, pasture, fishing rights and several other commodities mentioned in the said charters; so that they may have no reason to complain hereafter to us for this reason. Given under our signet at London, 15 June, in the fourth year of our reign.*

The abbot read it carefully and surrendered. His rulings, records and documents were burned in the market-place, while the citizens revelled. Then they dug up their old millstones from his refectory floor and carried them away. Thus the commons, backed by contingents from the abbey's other manors, won their demands without the loss of a single life, except for the prisoner they executed.

At Bury St Edmunds the abbey had withstood and put down four popular risings against it in the past hundred years or so. Here the leader was a priest himself, John Wrawe of Sudbury. When the Essex rising began, he had been vested with authority by Wat Tyler and marched to his home town where the citizens awaited him. He led them off to Bury St Edmunds, his strength increasing at every village on the way. The abbey was stormed and the monks, under Wrawe's orders, wrote out a charter renouncing all their claims on the town, and handed over to him all the deeds and documents of the abbey's holdings.

For eight days John Wrawe and his supporters ruled Bury St Edmunds and maintained order.

At Cambridge the townsfolk rose, led by the mayor, and renewed their ancient struggle against the university, itself a great wealthy ecclesiastical institution. In Norfolk, Suffolk, Winchester, Lincoln, as far west as Bridgwater and as far north as York and Scarborough there were large-scale actions by the commons apparently co-ordinated with events in London and making similar demands.

The leader of the Norfolk men was a dyer, Geoffrey Lister, who by his power and wide following acquired the unofficial title of 'king of the commons'. He entered Norwich in triumph and set up his headquarters in the castle itself. He acted in alliance with a local

---

*Ibid.

squire, Sir Roger Bacon, who carried the rebellion into Great Yarmouth and the country around.

There was mass action in many other parts of the country, but most of it went unrecorded for lack of a chronicler. Our knowledge of the movements in the provinces can only be pieced together from accusations, indictments and evidence given in the trials of participants that followed their suppression.

The rebellion had now been operative for more than fifteen days, and the rebels had held and occupied London for three of them. Within the Wardrobe Tower king and council deliberated without great hope. Tyler and his men had proved themselves well able to maintain order, organisation and discipline. There was no looting, no pillage to alienate the Londoners, whose bonds with the peasants were growing stronger. Only those officially condemned by the leaders were executed, for which they could cite the powers given them at Mile End. The massacre of the Flemings had not been their work. The news that came in from the counties and the countryside seemed to indicate that the whole kingdom was ripe for revolt and eager to embrace the policies of Tyler and Ball, and that the days of the feudal order were numbered.

Yet in the country round London and on the great baronial estates there were thousands of armed men, mercenaries and retainers and liegemen of the nobility, members of their private armies, with good armour proof against the improvised weapons of most of the villeins, soldiers needing only assembly and leadership. In a pitched battle in open country these well-equipped professionals would make short work of the vast mass of countrymen. And in London itself the rich merchants, the new class of 'princes of commerce' who now dominated the guilds and the city corporation, were growing apprehensive and would gladly offer their large armed households to get the peasants out of their city. Yet the rebels were unassailable in the narrow streets, backed by the populace. They had to be lured out into the fields, satisfied that they had won all they sought, where they would straggle home in careless bands that grew smaller at each crossroad. But how was this to be done?

At last, after long debate, the council decided on a plan. Its authors were probably Mayor Walworth and the Earl of Salisbury. The king himself, their only shield and hope, must himself supplant Tyler as the unquestioned leader of the commons. The great respect in which they held the crown, their reverence for his semi-sacred majesty, had already partially prepared them for this. Was not their main catchword 'King Richard and the commons'? He need only lead them for a very short time, just long enough to get them out of London and into the power of an army brought up to crush them finally.

This could only be achieved by the elimination of Tyler. He had to be killed and his place taken without the knowledge of his followers, in a condition of some confusion so that the king could present himself to them as the natural authority. It was a hazardous policy. If it failed, as Froissart pointed out, it meant the end of the English nobility, its wealth and its power. Everything depended on the courage and self-control of a youth of fifteen years of age. There was no alternative. It would have to be attempted. Out of the Wardrobe, without hindrance, the messengers galloped away to organise and instruct the soldiers and men-at-arms. Although the commons had won, on paper, most that they had set out to gain, Tyler had asked the king for a further meeting to hear proposals for a legal system for the new, free nation. He was too wary to be lured into a meeting of the council where he could be quickly disposed of. As the king was the shield of the nobility, the massed commons was the shield of Wat Tyler. So it was only before the commons that the plan could be carried out.

Soon the town-criers were bawling in the streets that the king commanded his commons to present themselves before him the following day at dusk at Smithfield, just outside the city wall.

8. SMITHFIELD: MURDER AND BETRAYAL

King Richard and his court rose sombrely on the morning of Saturday 15 June 1381; their mood was that of men preparing for a perilous venture. If everything did not proceed exactly as they had planned it, if suspicion or rage provoked the commons, they might well all be dead before nightfall. They dressed themselves like men going into battle, not to a peaceful conference. Armour was never worn at civil meetings, it would arouse suspicions at once. Only the customary sword or dagger, part of everyday wear, was permitted. But the courtiers put on their heaviest breastplates and thigh-pieces, proof against sword-stroke or dagger-thrust. Over their armour they wore long loose robes from neck to ankle, and the armour was completely hidden.

No effort was spared to win divine favour for the proposed murder and deception. They took leave of their womenfolk like men going to their doom, and rode off to the shrine of Edward the Confessor in Westminster Abbey. There the monks came out to meet them in barefoot procession carrying a great jewelled crucifix of silver. All dismounted, the king kissed the cross, and they followed him into the Abbey and made their way to the sanctuary, where they knelt in prayer around the holy tomb of the sainted king. The precious relics were brought out of their chests to be passed round, adored and kissed. It is reported that the noblemen wept with the passion of their supplications till the tears streamed down their cheeks, and beat their breasts in anguish. Then all went to confession like men under sentence of death. There was in the Abbey a hermit of extreme sanctity, an anchorite who had not left his cell for many years and spent his days in fasting and penance. To him the king confessed himself and received absolution and the blessing of the Church. Then, newly shriven, sanctified and fortified, they set out for Smithfield two hundred strong. Close behind the king rode the Mayor of London, William Walworth.

Smithfield was then a large open space west of the city wall where was held the weekly horse and cattle market, and annually the great St Bartholomew's Fair. On the east side was the large Priory of St Bartholomew, and the hospital founded by it two hundred years earlier, still know to today's Londoners as 'Bart's'. Within the hospital was its own little church, St Bartholomew the Less. On the west side it sloped down to the river Fleet, which now flows underground. From end to end it was about three hundred yards; the hour fixed for the meeting was Vespers, when the sun was down below the trees and the mist from the river thickened the fading light.

In the hazy London dusk the commons were drawn up on the east side, by the city wall and before the hospital. The flags of St George flew in the evening breeze, and here and there along their front were the banners given them at Mile End, signifying the king's trust and protection. The royal party arrived at the west side and halted. The two formations, across that darkening space, saw each other as shapeless masses.

A herald cantered across to the commons, blew his trumpet, shouted a summons and rode back. From the commons emerged Wat Tyler, mounted on a little horse, in his everyday attire of a hood with a hanging pipe, loose tunic, hose and boots. His usual short dagger hung from his belt. He was accompanied by one comrade, also mounted, who carried his standard of authority, the very one given him by the king himself.

Of what happened next the chroniclers give conflicting reports. The account that follows is the gist of the matter and the most probable sequence of events.

Tyler and his standard-bearer halted before King Richard. The court was drawn up as a shallow crescent with its points forward and the king in the centre. Tyler dismounted and knelt. The king extended his hand to be kissed, but Tyler shook it as he would have shaken the hand of a friend and equal.

'Brother,' he said. Brother, to the king! No doubt to Tyler this was the highest and noblest form of address. But the courtiers gasped at the incredible insult.

'Brother,' said Tyler happily, 'Be of good cheer and joyful, for soon you will receive the fifteenth pledged by the commons, and we will be good comrades.* (This was a reference to the tax the commons had proposed and agreed. Wat may have noticed that the king was looking nervous and worried, and said this to put him at ease.)

Richard then asked why they still remained in London and under arms, having had all their wishes granted. Tyler replied that they had sworn they would not go until these last demands were accepted; adding, as he looked around him, that it would be the worse for the lords of the realm if they were refused. Then he read them out to king and council.

They were: that no law should prevail in England but the Statute of Winchester; that no man should be made an outlaw by judges and lawyers; that no man should exercise lordship over the commons; that there should be but one bishop over all England ('since we are oppressed by so great a horde of bishops and clerks'); that the property and goods of the Church should be taken and divided according to the needs of the people of each parish, after making provision for the existing monks and clergy; that there should be no more villeins in England, but all men to be free and of one condition.

Despite the simple phrasing, this was probably the most radical programme ever put before an English government. It implied a new legal code based on the Statute of Winchester enacted by Edward I some eighty years before. What the commons chiefly admired about its numerous clauses was that it placed the responsibility for preserving law and order on the people themselves, in arms for that purpose, and their right to administer justice. The terrible punishment of outlawry, used so often against the peasants, meant that legally a man ceased to exist: he could hold no property, had no legal rights whatever and could be robbed, ill-treated or killed by any man. The reform and expropriation of the Church was a revolutionary demand that pulled up the very roots of the feudal system; and with 'all men free and of one condition', added to the results of the Mile End meeting, would usher in a completely different form of society and state.

Yet the king just sat on his horse and nodded his head, as though he had been asked a minor boon. These profound political clauses seemed to mean nothing to him. He probably failed at the time to realise their significance; or he did not care, knowing that his words were hollow deception, and he was instructed to grant anything.

Wat himself was beginning to feel the tensions of this important occasion, standing in the midst of his enemies with only one

---

* *Anonimalle Chronicle.*

companion. He alone was on foot among two hundred horses, breathing the dust stirred up by their hooves. It made him hoarse and dizzy, and he asked for ale and water to clean his clammy mouth and clear his head. After a little while it was brought to him. In the manner of the people, unabashed, he rinsed his mouth with water and spat it out, raised the ale-pot to the king, and drank a long refreshing draught, 'In a very rude and villainous manner,' commented the well-bred *Anonimalle* chronicler. Feeling better, he mounted his horse and turned again to the king.

Now the royal plan began to operate. In the darkening gloom, too far for the assembled commons to see clearly what was happening, the two ends of the line of courtiers began to move slowly inwards, hemming Wat in and concealing him further. From the crowd behind them a page began shouting, in a nervous treble, that this villain Tyler was known throughout Kent as a thief and a liar. (This accusation was obviously contrived and untrue, as Tyler was an Essex man little known in Kent before the rising.) Tyler demanded that the lad be brought before him, he who was now the king's accepted counsellor and spokesman for the commons, to make good his words. The page was unwillingly pushed forward. It seemed then that an argument developed before the king, in which every insult was heaped on Wat in an effort to provoke him into drawing his dagger; and to draw steel in the royal presence meant death, legally and justifiably. Wat kept his hands on his reins. There was some jostling and pushing. Wat and his comrade found themselves cornered, their retreat cut off, unseen by their own people. Suddenly Mayor Walworth thrust himself next to Tyler, laid his hand on his shoulder and cried in a loud voice, 'I arrest you!' Wat brushed it off and his hand dropped instinctively and naturally on to his dagger. Walworth himself then drew his dagger and stabbed Tyler twice, once in the neck and once in the head. Now Wat drew, and thrust at Walworth. The blade pierced his gown and turned harmlessly on the armour beneath. Then Wat knew that he was betrayed, to be murdered under his own royal banner.

Now the others joined in, thrusting their swords into his body. He spurred his horse with his last strength, seeking to break out and get back to his own people. But after a few paces he collapsed and fell from the saddle. In Froissart's words, 'As soon as he had fallen they environed him all about, whereby he was not seen of his company'. We are told nothing of the fate of his standard-bearer, but he was not likely to have escaped.

The first part of the plan had succeeded; Tyler was eliminated.

Overleaf 4. Wat Tyler is murdered by Mayor Walworth, and Richard II presents himself to the commons as their leader, Froissart's *Chronicles*.

Now it was time for the second, most dangerous part. Walworth galloped away through the city to bring up the forces waiting hidden beyond. King Richard crossed himself, muttered a prayer, and rode slowly forward alone to face the commons.

In the ranks of the waiting peasants there was some confusion. None of them knew what was happening across the field, but some of them caught what seemed to be a flash of steel. Then out of the dusk came a single horseman. Everyone expected Tyler, and there was a hush. To their astonishment it was the king himself, and alone, with his hand raised in peace.

It seems that there was no responsible leader among the commons. Ball was not there, but probably on his way to Coventry. Some uncertainty ensued in this unexpected situation. Some knelt to the king, as they had done before, others strung their bows or drew their swords. The king cried out, as he had been told to do, 'Sirs! All your wishes are granted. And now I myself will be your leader.' At this, some cheered and some stared. Others cried out, 'Where's Wat Tyler? What was that flash of steel?' Richard shouted back, 'I have knighted Tyler! It was my sword that flashed in doing so. He is now Sir Wat. Come, follow me, and I will take you to where he is.' He rode on, looking back and beckoning them to follow as one accustomed to command.

The great crowd hesitated, but there were few signs of doubt. Young King Richard, who had made them free, would lead them now himself. In knighting Tyler, he had honoured all the commons, and now they went to hail Sir Wat. The bows were unstrung, the swords sheathed. Then the first ranks moved slowly after the king, and the rest followed. He led them towards St John's Fields, an area of cornfield surrounded by the walls and buildings of the priory, and cried to them to assemble there in that space. He reined in his horse and stood aside and the commons passed before him, he bowing as they cheered and doffed caps and hoods as they went by. Then he turned and rode back across Smithfield, picked up his escort, and hurried back to the Wardrobe Tower. There his mother awaited him, knowing that the plot had succeeded.

> And when she saw the king, her son, she was greatly rejoiced and said, 'Ah, my fair son, what pain and anguish have I suffered for you this day.' Then the king answered and said, 'Certes, madam, I know it well; but now rejoice yourself and thank God, for it is time. I have this day recovered mine heritage and the realm of England, which I had near lost.'*

---

*Froissart, *Chronicles*.

9. *DEFEAT AND SUPPRESSION*

William Walworth, of the Worshipful Company of Fishmongers, city
magnate, erstwhile brothel-keeper, mayor of London, spurred
through his city and sent messengers off in all directions. Out of the
great mansions of the 'merchant princes' came troops of men-at-
arms, and began to make their way to St John's Fields. Another force
of some 5,000-8,000 men, 'harnessed' in proof armour, passed
through the city to face the commons. At their head rode the captain
of mercenaries, Sir Robert Knollys, with his own private band. In the
restricted fields of St John's, crammed and immobile, hemmed in by
walls, the peasants found their exit suddenly blocked by many ranks
of soldiers: 'as sheep are enclosed within a fold until it pleases the
labourer to choose which he wants to send out to pasture and which
he wants to kill.'* In the ranks of the rebels there was confusion.
Nobody knew what was happening. They had their sealed charters
and their banners. But where was Tyler? What were they to do now?
Why were there all these soldiers? They were soon to find out.

The two friendly aldermen of London, Sibley and Horne, had
watched the meeting at Smithfield from the city wall. These men were
more accustomed to the devious ways of court politics than the
simple mass of the peasants. Unsure of what was happening, they
suspected treachery and sounded the alarm, shouting to the citizens
to shut the gates. They were too late. The Londoners had
disappeared when the soldiers took over the streets, and only
Aldersgate swung shut. By then the troops had marched out.

His men on their way, Walworth and his group rode back to
Smithfield to seek the body of Tyler. He came to the spot, but Tyler
was gone. A trail of blood and trampled grass and dust led them to St
Bartholomew's Hospital; and there they found him. A few of his
friends had left the others and come in search of him. He was still
alive and they carried him into the hospital where they put him in the
master's bed. They were soon overpowered, and Tyler was dragged,
still conscious, into Smithfield. There his head was chopped off and
Walworth, in triumph, impaled it on his lance.

Lines of soldiers, foot and horse, kept the commons jammed
into St John's Fields. Knollys and his men were eager to begin the
slaughter there and then, but the old Earl of Salisbury restrained
them. Though in a hopeless position, they were still a powerful body
of armed men and an attack might restore their unity and purpose; if
it failed it would leave the peasants in fighting mood.

---

*Walsingham, *Historia Anglicana*.

It was quite dark now, and in the dim red light of flickering torches there suddenly appeared Walworth, their arch-enemy, with their leader's dripping head upon his spear. At this terrible sight any remaining vestiges of order collapsed. With cries and tears the host sank to its knees among the trampled wheat. Salisbury had an announcement made. The commons had won all they had asked of the king. Now they were to peacefully follow these knights who would lead them away from London, and disperse to their villages and manors. And the rebels allowed themselves to be ushered away between the lines of armoured soldiers, clutching their charters and waving their banners.

Once they were safely on their way, the soldiers began to 'clean up' London. A reign of terror began in the city. The king vested command there in Walworth (already knighted for his services and now Sir William) who called in Knollys to aid him. Anyone who looked like a countryman was in danger. A block was set up in Cheapside, and soon the paving-stones round it were red with blood. All night suspected rebels were dragged to it and beheaded with no semblance of trial or law. Some of the leaders — Jack Straw, John Kerby, Alan Thredor, were taken in the city. (Had they been with the others at Smithfield the outcome might have been different.) They were all executed without trial. In the morning, a little belatedly, the town-criers shouted in the streets that all persons not resident there for at least a year must leave within twelve hours, on pain of death.

London was now reconquered for the king. The royal council sent out to all the lords and landowners of the surrounding counties, who with their retainers had been hiding in woods and wastes. Within a few days a large army was gathered on Blackheath*; and the work of hunting down the dispersed peasants was thoroughly planned.

King Richard himself, at the head of the greater force, rode out to pacify Essex. On 22 June he flew his standard at Waltham, where there awaited him a group of delegates from a formidable rebel body at Billericay. These men, by the rules of war of the time, had the status of heralds or envoys and were not to be harmed or hindered, but were to deliver their message and depart with the answer. They stood up bravely before the king, showed him the charters with his own seals and demanded that they be made good in practice, stating that they were now free men by the king's own word, and the equal of any lord.

The royal council, which accompanied the king everywhere, drew up a reply and it was spoken by the king himself to the delegates. He said to them:

---

*Walsingham estimates it as 40,000 strong — 'larger than any seen in England before'. This was probably an exaggeration.

Oh, you wretched men, detestable by land and sea, you who seek equality with lords are not worthy to live . . . As you have come here as envoys you may keep your lives until you have informed your fellows of our reply . . . You will remain in bondage, not as before, but incomparably harsher. For as long as we live and by God's grace, rule over this realm, we will strive with mind, strength and wealth to suppress you so that the rigour of your servitude will be an example to posterity.*

On receiving this answer, the Essex peasants deliberated their course of action. They could disperse and each man seek his own safety, which he might well find, or keep their new-found freedom and die like free men defending it. They decided to fight, selected a position in the woods, and fortified it as well as they could. Supporters rallied to them from other villages, to stand and die with them. On 28 June the attack came, storming the weak defences with horse and foot. After a long and fierce resistance, fought without the body armour of the king's men, the peasants abandoned their stronghold and retreated, still in good order, into the woods. They left behind five hundred of their comrades, dead round the stockade. The survivors marched on to Sudbury, where they thought to join up with John Wrawe's bands. But Wrawe had already been defeated and his men dispersed or killed. In Sudbury they made a last defiant stand and were cut down, fighting to the end. Those captured alive were beheaded in the market-place.

All over southern England the gallows sprouted and the blocks ran red. Lord Chief Justice Tressilian had so many hanged that there was a shortage of gibbets, and nine or ten men at a time were hanged simultaneously from the same beam. There ensued a time of horror and fear that was to last the entire summer. Here and there peasant formations continued the fight, making what armed resistance they could, always claiming that they acted in the king's name and with his will, as they could prove by their charters. So Richard issued an official proclamation revoking all his charters, declaring them null and void. 'Serfs you ever were,' was his statement, 'and serfs you shall ever remain.' The slaughter continued. Leaders were usually hanged, drawn and quartered, the others hanged or beheaded.

At St Albans, Grindcobbe was captured by trickery. A jury of selected citizens was empanelled for his trial and ordered to name all the ringleaders and active rebels of their town. The jury reported that: 'They could indict none, could charge none. That all were good

---

*Walsingham, *Historia Anglicana*.

and faithful men of the king and they knew none else among them.'

Tressilian came to conduct the trial, and Grindcobbe was offered freedom and life if he would persuade his fellow-citizens to return the charters and documents to the abbey. This he refused to do, and with fifteen others he was hanged, drawn and quartered, the usual punishment for traitors.

Grindcobbe made a noble end. With the noose round his neck he said to the watching crowd:

> Friends, for whom a little liberty has now relieved the long years of oppression, stand firm while you can and not be afraid because of my fate. If I die in the cause of liberty I count myself happy to end my life as a martyr.*

John Ball himself was captured at Coventry, which probably explains his apparent absence from Smithfield. He was taken to St Albans to stand trial before Tressilian. He denied nothing, he freely admitted all the charges without regrets or apologies. He was proud to stand before them and testify to his revolutionary faith and to suffer for it. He was duly sentenced to death, but the Bishop of London granted a two-day stay of execution in the hope that he could persuade John Ball to repent of his treason and so save his soul. His efforts failed, and Ball was hanged, drawn and quartered on 15 July, his sections being hung up 'in the four quarters of England'.

In East Anglia the suppression was actually led by a prince of the Church, Henry Spencer, Bishop of Norwich. He led his men into battle wearing armour under his clerical robes, wielding a great two-handed sword. John Lister and his band made their final defiance at North Walsham, near Norwich, and the bishop personally headed the charge of armoured cavalry that broke them. It was said that they slaughtered the defeated like men in a frenzy, sparing none, and that the bishop foamed at the mouth like a wild boar as he slashed at them with his heavy sword. Lister was taken alive, to be tried and sentenced by the bishop himself in his own court. After the trial he became a priest again, heard Lister's spiritual confession and gave him absolution. Lister's quarters were nailed on the gates of Harwich, Yarmouth and Lynn, and on the house he had used as his headquarters at Norwich.

Never before had there been such a slaughter of the commons of England, nor was to be again. After the atrocities of the initial suppression there was a return to proper legal procedure, and every suspected rebel was tried by jury before being sentenced. Most leading rebels were given the chance to turn king's evidence and save themselves by informing on their comrades. Out of the large number

---

*Ibid.

tried, we know of only one who did so — the priest John Wrawe of Sudbury. It did not profit him greatly; he was hanged a year later. It took many months before the counter-revolution was successful. New revolts and risings took place in many localities and bands of peasants lurked in the woodlands to emerge and attack small bodies of troops, and fought desperately when cornered. It is difficult to arrive at a figure for the commons who died on the roads home, in fighting, on the gallows or at the block. The historian J.R. Green estimates it at 7,000,* This, as has been said, was when the whole population of the country was less than 2,500,000.

Just as the shortage of labour was a factor in causing the rebellion, it was probably an influence in finally limiting its suppression. In November the king called together a Parliament which ended it and declared a general pardon. It excluded, however, 287 known rebels still at large and certain towns that had acted officially in support of the commons.

10. AFTERTHOUGHTS

The Peasants' Revolt was over. England returned to the old order under King Richard II. The survivors went home to their manors to mourn, to labour, to pay the old resented dues and defer to their social superiors. It seemed that little had changed. A few weeks of upheaval, a great dream of what could be, a vision of a land of free men working in fellowship undivided by class, caste or birth, the deaths of many good men, and then — things were as they always had been.

Yet the peasants did win. It was they and not the king and his council who represented the future of England. Stronger forces than those of Richard were at work: the laws of economic development. In the years to come, villeinage, serfdom and feudalism were to wither away speeded by many further riots and risings, to be succeeded eventually by the capitalist system, in which the descendant of the medieval peasant became a propertyless wage-earner. History proceeds at its own speed. As Jack Lindsay points out, it was left to Oliver Cromwell to complete, 260 years later, what Wat Tyler had begun, and to liquidate the final remnants of the feudal state.

The concept of freedom was not killed in the repression. It was nurtured and grew until it became the cornerstone of the national political structure, changing as life and circumstances changed. To the serf struggling for manumission it meant one thing; to the free

---

*J.R. Green, *Short History of the English People*, Macmillan, 1893.

tenant-farmer of the seventeenth century it meant another; to the poor operative of the industrial revolution yet another; and to the thinking worker of our own time it embraces the new concept of economic freedom, which can only be achieved by the joint and common ownership and control of industry and the wealth created out it. And this would mean the winning of basic human rights still unattained, like the right to work.

If the reader of this book walks into Westminster Abbey by the west door he or she will see, hanging from a column on their right, a large life-size portrait in a heavy gilt frame. It is the first known portrait from life of an English king, and it depicts Richard II seated, crowned and in his state robes. The king is still little more than a boy, and his face has still a youthful innocence and sweetness about it, an expression of gentleness and even weakness. There is no cause to doubt the truth of the painting. Walk on into the Sanctuary and there is his tomb, topped by his effigy in bronze. Richard died at the age of thirty-three, and the effigy shows the swollen, puffed, bleary-eyed

5.   Richard II: The first known portrait from life of an English king.

6.   The bronze effigy of Richard II on his tomb in Westminster Abbey.

face of a man prematurely aged. He did not become one of England's great kings, or maintain that self-possession he had shown at Smithfield. Weak-natured, vain, self-indulgent, despotic, constantly at odds with his nobles and his Parliaments, devoting a large part of his revenues to personal extravagance, ruling through favourites, he was finally deposed by his cousin Henry Bolingbroke, son of John of Gaunt, who succeeded him as King Henry IV. He was then imprisoned in Pontefract Castle, where he was either murdered or he committed suicide by starving himself to death. It is these later years of his life that are explored by Shakespeare in his *Tragedy of King Richard II*.

There are in London, many statues commemorating monarchs, soldiers, statesmen and wars. Plaques on walls announce historic events that have taken place by that spot. At the time of writing there is nothing to commemorate the Peasants' Revolt, though it might be considered noteworthy if only because 7,000 Englishmen were killed in it. At Mile End, at Rotherhithe, at Cheapside, these great events are completely ignored. At Fishmongers' Hall the liverymen will show you with some pride the dagger with which Walworth stabbed Tyler. At Smithfield, where at least 227 people later died a slow and terrible death for their religious convictions, there are two memorial tablets. One, placed there by a small Protestant sect, commemorates three of its martyrs that suffered here. The other, from a Scottish society, records the execution of William Wallace. As Tom Paine wrote two hundred years ago, 'If the Barons merited a monument in Runnymede, Wat Tyler merits one at Smithfield.'

SELECT BIBLIOGRAPHY

Caris-Wilson, E. M. (ed.), *Essays in Economic History*, Vol. 2., Edward Arnold, 1962.
Coulton, G. C., *Medieval Panorama*, Collins
Dobson, R. B. (ed.), *The Peasant Revolt of 1381*, Macmillan, 1970.
Fagan, H., *Nine Days that Shook England*, Gollancz, 1938.
Fagan, H. and Hilton R., *The Peasant Revolt of 1381*.
Froissart, Sir John, *Chronicles of England*, ed. G. Brereton, Penguin, 1968.
Green, J. R., *Short History of the English People*, Macmillan, 1893.
Hilton, R., *Bondmen Made Free*, Temple Smith, 1973.
Lindsay, J., *The Nine-Days Hero*, Dennis Dobson, 1964.
Lindsay, J., *England, My England*, Fore Publications.
Mckisach, M., *The Fourteenth Century*, Clarendon Press, 1959.
Rubinstein, D. (ed.), *People for the People*.
Stow, J., *The Survey of London*, Dents (Everyman), 1912.
Stow, J., *Annales*, ed. E. Howes, London, 1631.
Trevelyan, G. M., *A Shortened History of England*, Pelican Books.

CHAPTER II

Wycliffe, the Lollards, and Others

The Peasants' Revolt was not an isolated incident in England's story. It is one of a long, almost continual series of risings, rebellions, revolts, riots and direct actions that have wrung from the nation's rulers the sequence of reforms and changes that have resulted in today's society. Most of these actions were unsuccessful in achieving their aims. Yet they were to succeed in providing the conditions in which it became advisable for the state to institute the reforms demanded.

The first known rebel to appear in our history, upholding the rights of the common people, was himself a gentleman of good family. William FitzOsbert, who lived in the reign of King Richard I, was better known as William Longbeard; people of Saxon descent would often wear beards to symbolise opposition to the cleanshaven Norman conquerors. He had fought in the crusades, and had long been known as a leader in the forgotten social struggles of his time.

'Fired with zeal for justice and equity, he made himself the champion of the poor,' says the chronicler Roger de Hovenden.

In the year 1194 the government found itself faced with the need to raise an enormous sum of money for the ransom of the absentee king, Richard I, who was imprisoned by the Duke of Austria. A levy was imposed on the whole population; and London, the richest city, had to find a vast amount. Longbeard denounced the system of assessment as corrupt, and accused the rich merchants and aldermen who ruled the city of passing their own contributions on to the poorer citizens. He addressed great crowds of Londoners at their folkmoot by St Paul's Churchyard, and became in every way a popular leader.

The Justiciar, or chief officer of the law, who was then none other than the Archbishop of Canterbury, Hubert Walter, ordered his arrest and sent an armed band to bring him in. A scuffle with his supporters then ensued, in which one of the Archbishop's men was killed. Together with nine of his friends Longbeard fled into the church of St Mary-le-Bow, in Cheapside, and claimed the right of sanctuary. It was the Archbishop himself who profaned this privilege and ordered them to be dragged out. They resisted, and finally the Archbishop set fire to the church. Longbeard and his comrades rushed out choking and were seized. Longbeard was badly wounded in the struggle. Tied to a horse's tail and dragged along the stones to the Tower, he was sentenced to death. At once he was dragged again to Smithfield, where he and his men were hanged in chains before a huge crowd. We are told that the citizens carried away the chains and gibbet as holy relics, and even scooped up the earth on which it stood. People came to pray at the spot, and tales were told of miracles happening there.

Thus died, in 1196, some of the first recorded Englishmen who have given their lives for justice and the people. Matthew Paris, a writer of the next century, wrote: 'So perished William Longbeard, for endeavouring to uphold the cause of right and of the poor. If it be the cause that makes the martyr, no man can be more justly described as a martyr than he.'*

Without doubt there were many acts of defiance and protest taking place all over the kingdom constantly, but they went unrecorded and were unknown outside their localities. There has never been a lack of

> Some village Hampden, that with dauntless breast,
> The little tyrant of his fields withstood†

Individual memory perishes; folk memory endures. One of these is enshrined in the numerous ballads, songs and stories of Robin Hood, handed down, embellished and elaborated by generations of illiterate peasants and artisans. He appears as the leader of a group of outlaws living in the depths of Sherwood Forest, who carried on a kind of guerrilla war against Church and State, who 'robbed the rich and gave to the poor and oppressed no righteous man'; taking up and resolving the grievances and injustices of the poor. It may be noted that they are depicted not as solemn dedicated revolutionaries, but as a jolly band of men, full of high spirits and good humour.

Whether 'Robin Hood and his merry men' ever existed is a subject for historical debate; but they certainly typify the spirit of the Middle Ages.

'The criticism of religion', wrote Marx, 'is the beginning of all criticism.' This was especially true of the Middle Ages. The Catholic Church was not only the largest landowner and employer in the country, but a branch of an international organisation that was governed from abroad by the Papacy, and dominated the minds and thoughts of all men. It claimed rights of self-government that

---

*Matthew Paris, *Chronica Major*.

†Thomas Gray, 'Elegy Written in a Country Churchyard', 1750.

frequently brought it into conflict with the secular state, and every year sent large amounts of English money to its headquarters in Rome. As it held that the existing social order was God-given and had divine authority, any plans for secular reform and a greater degree of equity had perforce to begin by attacking the doctrines and teachings of the Church; first by theologians and philosophers, then by radical laymen who adopted their teachings and spread them among the people. Thus much of the progressive thinking of the English people found its expression in religious forms.

7. The earliest known portrait of John Wycliffe. Woodcut, 1548.

An important early critic of the Church was the priest John Wycliffe, who died in 1384. A learned doctor of divinity occupying the important post of Master of Balliol, Oxford, he began to write and to preach against some of the characteristics of the Church at that time. He attacked it as having departed from the simple spirituality to be found in the scriptures, and denied its right to hold temporal wealth or political power. He agreed that authority derived from God, but held that when persons in authority were not in a 'state of grace' — when guilty of sin or worldly failing — that divine authority lapsed. He called for the wealth of the Church to be used for the relief of taxation, and for the clergy to live solely on tithes and offerings. The wealth of the monasteries, he said, would be enough for the maintenance of all the poor and indigent in the country. He claimed that the decrees of the Pope were only valid when in conformity with the scriptures, which every man had the right to read for himself.

(The Bible then was written in Latin and its reading was confined to the upper clergy, who 'interpreted' chosen passages to the public. When it was at length translated into English and made available to all, it quickly became a major ideological weapon of the radicals.)

Wycliffe outlined the idea of predestination, which was later to play such an important role in deciding the rights and powers of the individual in society. This asserted that all people were destined before birth by God either for salvation or eternal damnation. During their own lifetime, no one could know if they were numbered among the damned or the 'elect'. This applied to everyone. If, for example, the Pope was among the majority predestined to be damned, by what divine authority could he claim his powers?

These daring theological speculations led Wycliffe into deep waters as he began to realise their wider secular implications. Thus we find him writing in 1374, in the treatise *De Civili Domini:*

> Firstly, that all good things of God ought to be in common. Every man ought to be in a state of grace . . .
> This will not happen until they hold all things in common: therefore all things ought to be in common.

This passing thought illustrates the ancient lineage of communist thinking in England. Wycliffe was a scholar, writing in Latin for other scholars, and he remained politically conservative all his life. But his teachings were among those that contributed to the liberation of the human mind and its search for the ideal form of state and society.

He was, of course, attacked by the Church, and his works were condemned as heretical. When he denied transubstantiation — the 'real presence' of Christ in the Mass — he was driven out of his beloved Oxford, but his powerful friends in the ruling class saved him from suffering the terrible penalties for heresy. He died peacefully in his bed, but the Church had its belated revenge. In 1428 his grave was desecrated, his bones dug up, burnt and thrown into the River Swift.

To what extent, if at all, the leaders of the Peasants' Revolt were influenced by his teaching is not known. But after his death his followers started their own movement, and become known as 'Lollards'.

'Lollard' is an old word meaning 'mumbler' or 'whisperer', a proper name for men who were hounded, persecuted and suppressed. Its members were at first 'poor priests', but as they expanded the doctrines of Wycliffe to embrace social matters they were joined by many laymen who preached without ordination, in open defiance of Church law. These men wandered the country, sheltered by supporters, living as best they could, preaching their new ideas at village greens, fairs and markets. They taught that the scriptures were the only true basis for all moral law, and that given the scriptures, every man and woman could arrive at the truth without the intervention of a priest. This destroyed the concept of the Church as the only mediator between God and man, and was an important statement on the freedom of the individual. Under conditions of continual harassment they secretly carried out the monumental work of translating the Bible into English. All copies were of course hand-written, and when found by the authorities were at once destroyed.

When Parliament met in 1395, it found a copy of the Lollard manifesto nailed on the door of Westminster Hall. After this, persecution intensified. Lollards were hunted down and charged with heresy and unlicenced preaching. Many were forced to recant before the clerical court, only to resume their activities afterwards. Others refused, and endured long imprisonment; and many, like the priests Will Sawtry and Will White, the tailor John Bradley, the currier John Claydon, were burnt alive. But their ideas spread among the people and attracted sympathy and support from many of their social superiors.

One man of importance who embraced the new ideas was the Herefordshire landowner, Sir John Oldcastle. He was a soldier of long service and a personal friend of King Henry V. In 1414 he was found in possession of Lollard tracts and accused of harbouring heretics. On being examined he was found guilty of heresy, and advised to recant and save himself. He refused, and was imprisoned in the Tower of London. With outside help he escaped from his dungeon, and, in hiding, planned a desperate revolt. He would abduct the royal family and lead the Lollards to occupy London; then he could halt the persecution, reform the Church, and expropriate its wealth for public uses. Messages were sent out to all sympathisers nation-wide, and large numbers of people, mostly artisans, craftsmen, labourers and peasants, began to move towards London. The weavers, always the most radical among the commons, made up the largest section. They assembled on St Giles' Fields, west of the city (an area now known as Soho), where they expected to have the help of their London supporters. But their plans were known to the king. The city gates were barred, and the suspected Londoners rounded up. Then, in a brief action, the rebel Lollards were attacked and dispersed. They left many dead on the field, while the king's men, in their heavy armour, had no casualties at all. Eighty rebels were taken alive. Oldcastle escaped.

Of the eighty, sixty-nine were condemned to death. On 13 January 1414, thirty-eight of them were dragged on hurdles from Newgate to St Giles, where they were hanged together on special mass gallows. A number of them were knights or small landowners. In the provinces local risings took place, but were easily defeated; the usual 'pacifications' followed. Oldcastle was outlawed, but remained at large for over three years, in spite of large rewards offered for his capture.

Lollardry was now treated as a capital offence, and many more were put to death for spreading its message. Finally Oldcastle himself was taken, badly wounded in his last fight, and hanged on St Giles' Fields. His body was then burnt as it hung from chains.

Lollardry had now lost all its leaders and intellectuals. The humble weavers, blacksmiths and carpenters continued to practise and propagate their faith as best they could, and many suffered for it. But the movement had ceased to be a threat to Church or state, and what remained of it after many years became merged with the general movement of the Protestant Reformation as the state itself saw fit to adopt many of its principles.

The poet Hoccleve advised the gentry to shun these dangerous theoretical and political activities, and to confine themselves to what was proper for their class. Paraphrased into modern English, this is what he says:

> Beware Oldcastle, and, for Christ's sake,
> Climb no more into Holy Writ so high.
> Read the stories of Lancelot of the Lake,
> Or Vegece on the arts of chivalry.*

SELECT BIBLIOGRAPHY

Cohn, N., *The Pursuit of the Millennium*, Paladin.
Dickens, A. G., *The English Reformation*, Batsford, 1964.
Jacob, E. F., *The Fifteenth Century*, Clarendon Press, 1961.
Loades, K. B., *John Wycliffe and English Non-Conformity*, Pelican Books.
Scattergood, V. J., *Politics and Poetry in the Fifteenth Century*, Blandford, 1971.

---

*Quoted in V. J. Scattergood, *Politics and Poetry in the Fifteenth Century*, Blandford 1971.

CHAPTER III

Jack Cade and the Kentish Rising; and the Cornish Rebellion

In the years following the Peasants' Revolt serfdom and villeinage died out in England, and by the middle of the fifteenth century most of the southern counties payed money rents for their land in lieu of dues and kind. The traditional manner of land usage continued, each village and the landlord holding a greater or lesser number of 'strips' scattered around the arable fields, and using the common land or 'waste' for the grazing of the cattle and horses, the feeding of pigs and geese, and for other essential purposes.

The state and society remained feudal. Every man was a 'vassal' of his overlord and subject to his control. At peasant level agriculture was carried on, to a great extent, socially. 'The custom of the manor' prevailed, and work was organised by agreements reached at village meetings and manor courts, where each man had his rights and his duties. The privileges of the chartered towns, the restrictions on trade and movement, continued to restrain the development of commerce. Yet in spite of this the formerly unimportant merchant class, who did not produce or cultivate goods but traded in them, became rich and powerful. They dominated and governed the towns, and became the holders of large sums of ready money. Some even began to trade in money itself. As part of the commons they frequently found themselves in conflict with the nobility, and could only improve their own status by improving the rights and privileges of the commons as a whole.

In 1429 Henry VI became king at eight years old. He grew into a man of remarkable piety and little wisdom. The great barons round the throne, who ruled their huge fiefs like little kings, competed fiercely for power. The house of York claimed the succession and were opposed by the king's party, the house of Lancaster. In 1455 began the twenty-year series of battles known, romantically, as the Wars of the Roses. This was in no way a civil war that concerned the public, but rather a number of glorified gang fights conducted by the barons with their private armies of retainers and foreign mercenaries. During the long conflict (many of the leaders changed sides at least once) the baronage performed one service to the people; they liquidated themselves, physically and financially. Thus, after the battle of Bosworth, the next king, Henry VII, was able to create a strong central state unthreatened by powerful rivals. He relied on the new aristocracy of capitalist landowners and the rising class of merchants and financiers.

The weak King Henry VI and the strong baronage did not make for good government. The throne was surrounded by plotting and corruption, and there was military defeat in France. The arrogant retainers of the barons robbed the public coffers without restraint. Moreover, a prelude to the barons' wars was the great Kentish Rebellion of 1450.

It was led by a man called Jack Cade, who claimed to be of the noble house of Mortimer, and signed himself by that name. His optimistic supporters dubbed him John Amend-All, or the Captain of Kent. His past is obscure, but he was an ex-soldier who made himself leader of a large movement in Kent that protested against oppression, injustice and misgovernment. Kent, as one of the most developed and wealthy counties, had much to lose by maladministration. And the government seemed unable to stop the frequent French raids on the coastal towns that left some of them looted and burning. Often depicted as a mountebank and ruffian, Cade must have been a very capable man. Lord Sackville said of him later, 'Whatever he was by birth, I warrant him a gentleman by his learning.' His claim to noble blood probably helped him win the support of many of the local knights and gentry who were in control of the county administration, as well as that of the common people. Thus when the unknown planners of the rising decided to act, the men of at least seven villages were officially ordered to assemble in arms by the lawful authorities; and a great armed crowd, estimated variously at from 20,000 to 45,000, set off for London to lay their grievances before the king and demand redress.

On May 31, they arrived at Blackheath. The rebels were well armed and at once began to fortify their camp, surrounding it with a ditch and palisades and putting up temporary structures for military use. This indicates that this was not a mere mob; rather a disciplined force carrying out a pre-arranged plan. They seemed well supplied with money, and paid for everything they required.

Cade's army lingered behind its defences for seven days. The reason for this halt is not known. Perhaps there were internal dissensions on policy; perhaps time was needed for drill and training. He may have been waiting for some sympathetic action in London. But any tactical surprise that had been achieved was wasted.

Whatever the reason, the king was given the chance to mobilise an army round London. Led by the archbishop, John Stafford, a delegation was sent to meet the rebels, discover what they wanted and negotiate for their dispersal; and they met not the disorderly rabble they had expected, but a disciplined army under able and courteous leaders. They were handed a document headed 'A Bill of Complaints and Requests of the Commons of Kent'.

Among the fifteen 'complaints' were: that the king was surrounded by corrupt favourites and that the crown's own income was taken by them, thus forcing excessive taxation of the commons; that justice could only be obtained by bribes and gifts; that debts to people for the maintenance of the king and court when travelling were not honoured; that 'true men' were unjustly accused of treason so that their land and goods could be sequestered by 'menials and others of the royal household'; that the poor and the commons were the victims of any of the king's servants who coveted their land; and that the system of tax collection was unjust and extortive.

It will be seen from these complaints that the rising was in no sense revolutionary, but a demand for a reform of the existing order. Among the 'requests' were that the king should continue to rule but with the aid of 'loyal and favourable lords', and that the Statute of Labourers be repealed or amended.

Two days later Cade had his reply from the king. Completely ignoring the carefully worded document, it commanded the gathering to disperse forthwith. It did not. On 18 June the king marched his army through London to give battle to the rebels; and on arriving at Blackheath found the camp abandoned and deserted. Cade had moved at last, and had retreated with his men back into Kent. Thinking the revolt now almost ended, the king stayed in London with much of his army and sent the rest in pursuit. This force caught up with the rebels at Solefields, near Sevenoaks, (now covered by the Park Grange Estate) where the road ran narrow between steep wooded slopes, an ideal site for an ambush. When the royal army had entered this bottleneck, it was suddenly assailed by flight after flight of arrows followed by a fierce rebel charge. Sir Humphrey Stafford and his brother, who led it, were both killed, along with most of their men. The rest fled in disorder, and a number actually joined up with Cade.

On hearing this news, the king panicked and left with his forces for Kenilworth, in the Midlands. The barons dispersed to their castles for safety, while the Lord Mayor pleaded for enough troops to be left to defend the city — but he was ignored.

Elated by victory, with no enemy at hand, Cade led his men back to Blackheath. Risings on a smaller scale began in the provinces, and recruits flocked to the camp. In Wiltshire the oppressive Bishop of Salisbury was dragged out of church and murdered, and a large contingent of Essex men set out for London.

The next step for Cade was obviously the occupation of the

8.   A panorama of London engraved by Nicholas Visscher in 1616. Southwark Cathedral is in the foreground, and 'traitors' ' heads on the gate-tower.

abandoned city, but he hesitated again. The Common Council and Aldermen of London debated their best course of action. They had little armed force except for the citizens' militia and the Tower garrison, which was not under their command. The great 'merchant princes' feared the destruction and loss that might follow a forcible entry. The ordinary citizens had much in common with the rebels, and could not be trusted to oppose them. Eventually the decision was taken to open the gates, and Cade marched his army across London Bridge into the city, cheered by the townsfolk. Passing over the drawbridge section, he ordered the ropes that operated it to be severed, so that he could not be cut off or isolated.

He rode in 'like a lordly captain', wearing the valuable armour taken from the body of Sir Humphrey Stafford. He declared to the citizens that he came as a loyal petitioner to the king, and that their goods and safety were assured. After conferring with the Lord Mayor on the problems of supply and order, he returned over the bridge to establish his headquarters at the White Hart Inn, one of the great 'transpontine inns' that then lined Borough High Street, the road commanding the approach to London Bridge and the city. The citizens of London and Southwark went about their work as usual.

There were some men, nobles and officials around the throne, who had made themselves notorious for their oppressions and misrule. Most had fled with the king, but there remained in London Crowmer the Sheriff of Kent, Malpas the merchant, Sir James Fiennes, and his brother, Lord Saye and Sele, Lord Treasurer of England. The rebels had sworn to deal with them. Malpas was not found, but his mansion was ransacked. Crowmer was taken, accused, tried and beheaded.

Lord Saye and Sele had taken refuge in the Tower but was surrendered by the governor, Lord Scales, on a promise by Cade not to attack the fortress. He was brought to the Guildhall to be tried formally by the justices who always sat there. He refused to plead, demanding his right to be tried by his peers. All day the dispute dragged on, until at last the crowd outside lost patience, rushed the courthouse and carried their victim to Smithfield, where he was decapitated.

The next day was a Sunday and Cade, with his leaders and his men, spent it quietly in Southwark. There is little doubt that the success of the rising was imperilled by these frequent periods of immobility and delay that characterised it. This probably reflects on the lack of a long-term policy. Of the plans, arguments and deliberations of the leadership we know nothing.

While the rebels kept the sabbath, their enemies were active. The great merchants, the rich aldermen, sought an audience with Lord Scales at the Tower. He had a considerable garrison under his command; there was a company of archers returned from France still in London, with other soldiers from the wars still under arms and orders. Also there were the armed servants and followers of the nobility of the city. Secretly they assembled, behind the Tower walls, an army of considerable strength. As the day drew to its close it set out, under the Tower officer Matthew Gough, to clear Cade's guards from London Bridge and isolate him in Southwark.

The attack was launched at dusk. The guards at the city or northern end were soon cut down, but the noise and shouting alerted the stronger unit by the fortified southern end. It was soon engaged, and a bloody battle began in the gathering darkness. Except for the open length of the drawbridge, the bridge had houses built along each side so that it was like a street, and in that narrow dark roadway, by the flickering light of torches and dim lanterns, men stabbed and hacked at each other. Reinforcements came running from the White Hart, and from the city. Neither side gave way. The dead and wounded obstructed the movements of the fighting men. Manoeuvre was impossible. Many, in the open section, grappled with one another until both fell into the river, where their armour dragged them at once to the bottom. The living stumbled over the dead, the wounded were trampled to death. The short summer night began to lighten, and the southern end of the bridge was still in rebel hands. Then Cade managed to set fire to the wooden houses beyond the drawbridge, and the flames swept across the 'street' and down upon the attackers. Screaming, the residents rushed out on to the contested bridge and added to the chaos and confusion. Some were burned to death. Many jumped into the river to escape the flames and were drowned.

Now a new element entered the battle. Lord Scales had in the

Tower some of the new-fangled weapons called 'cannons', and he decided to bombard the rebels. These guns were primitive iron tubes firing stone balls, very few of which found their mark. But the booming and flashing of the guns, never before known to the combatants, the hiss and splash of the balls as they fell into the river, added to the terror.

Eventually flames began to lick at the wooden drawbridge itself, and the Londoners had to break off combat and retreat towards the city. Among the numerous bodies that covered the bridge was that of the captain, Matthew Gough. The fighters on each side collapsed from exhaustion and were unable to resume the battle.

At nine in the morning both sides agreed under a flag of truce to stop fighting. The Londoners manned one end of the bridge, the rebels the other. It was stalemate. With the closure of the bridge, its essential lifeline, London came to a standstill.

The Londoners made the next move. There was no sign of aid from the king, whose cause they found themselves unwillingly upholding. Fearful of their ability to hold the city against further attack, they proposed negotiations. Cade and his officers agreed; they, too, felt they had done all they could. The king remained king, and they, his petitioners, remained rebels guilty of treason, each one of them subject to the death penalty. Cade consented to meet a delegation consisting of the archbishop, a cardinal and a bishop. These three high churchmen were all skilled and crafty politicians with a lifetime of experience.

They met in St Margaret's Church, Southwark, near the present St George-the-Martyr. The 'Bill of Complaints and Requests' was read out again and presented, and formally accepted for presentation to king and Parliament. The envoys then demanded that in return the host must be disbanded and sent home, while the government considered the document and the reforms urged. Cade replied that this would only be done if each man received a pardon written, signed and sealed in accordance with law, which would protect him against arrest for treason.

The clergymen then produced two 'Charters of Pardon', ready-made in advance, one covering Cade personally, the other all his men. These had no seal of royal approval, and could easily be repudiated by the king. They were rejected, and Cade demanded a separate pardon for each man, sanctioned by Parliament and endorsed by the royal seal. This, replied the priests, would take a long time — months were needed to assemble a Parliament. Meanwhile King Henry was raising an army that could destroy them with ease, and legally hang every survivor. Eventually Cade and his officers accepted a compromise. The 'Charters of Pardon' were handed over, and in return the delegates were given the rebels' muster-roll, so that a pardon could be made out for each individual man. Cade then signed an order for his force to disband and go home. He used as his signature the name he claimed was his by right — John Mortimer.

The next day most of his men left for their villages, confident that they had struck a great blow for justice and the commons, and that the reforms they demanded would now be put into effect. A small group, doubtful of the value of their mass pardon, remained near the White Hart with their leaders. Now news arrived that the authorities had decided that the pardon made out to John Mortimer did not apply to the leader of the revolt, who was not a true member of that family, but a commoner named Jack Cade. The government announced that it pardoned only those of the gentry and landowning class who followed Cade, ignoring the names on the muster-roll of the yeomen, peasants and artisans. It appears that the three great Christian prelates had lent themselves to a dishonourable deception.

Cade, knowing himself and his supporters duped, remained for a while at the White Hart then left with his remnant for Rochester. For a reason unknown to us they spent a day in an unsuccessful attempt to capture Queensborough Castle nearby. There is a theory that Cade had sent the movement's money-chest there for safe keeping, and its custodians refused to return it.

The king now announced a writ tantamount to outlawry against Cade, and put a price of 1,000 marks on his head and five marks on the heads of each of his followers who must have then split up and sought their own individual safety, as the next news of Cade is that of a lonely hunted fugitive, finally cornered and killed in a state of hunger and exhaustion. His slayer was a Sussex squire named Alexander Iden, who had been seeking him (and the reward) with a mounted band. His 'quarters' were displayed at Blackheath, Salisbury, Norwich and Gloucester as a warning to dissidents.

The rising was not followed by mass killings as the Peasants' Revolt had been. Probably the crown sat too insecurely on the head of Henry VI. Two of Cade's party, Nicholas Jakes and John Ramsay, were also quartered and their remains hung up at Chichester, Rochester, Portsmouth, Colchester, Stamford, Newbury, Coventry and Winchester. The wide distribution of the bodies certainly presumes that sympathy for Cade and his cause was nation-wide. A royal commission condemned another twenty-six to death, in a trial that became known as the 'harvest of heads'.

A few years later the Wars of the Roses began, during which King Henry was deposed, imprisoned, reinstated, deposed and imprisoned again, and finally murdered in the Tower — not by the commons, but by his own barons who had sworn him fealty.

In 1485 the Duke of Richmond won the last battle of the Wars of the Roses and made himself King Henry VII. He was the first of the Tudor dynasty.

In 1497 occurred the Cornish Rebellion, a protest against high taxation to pay for an invasion of Scotland. When the collectors arrived in Cornwall a blacksmith, Michael Joseph, roused his parish to resist. They were joined by the men of neighbouring parishes, armed with their traditional weapons of bills and bows. The Cornish peninsular was remote and backward and without a nobility. Its people considered themselves Cornish rather than English and spoke their own variant of Celtic. A war with faraway Scotland was no concern of theirs, and they refused to pay for it. In a short while an army of 15,000 gathered under the command of Michael Joseph and set off on the long march to London to protest to the king.

At Bodmin they were joined by the lawyer Thomas Flamanck, who told them that the king was breaking the law by taxing them for military purposes without first raising the old feudal dues to which he was still entitled. Passing through Somerset they were joined by a local nobleman, Lord Audley. There was no pillage on the journey of some 350 miles and how that great crowd was supplied with food is not known. Probably the surrounding people fed them as best they could.

They camped on Blackheath, hoping for the support of the Kentish men, but it never came. The king had a powerful army at hand, assembled for the Scottish war, and, without stopping to treat or parley, he attacked. There was a sharp short battle at Deptford, between London and Blackheath. The Cornishmen had little chance against the armoured cavalry and cannon of the king. They were soon routed, leaving two hundred of them dead on the field. Lord Audley was beheaded, Joseph and Flamanck were hanged. The rest were given a general pardon, as the king was eager to get on with his invasion of Scotland. The tax continued to be collected.

SELECT BIBLIOGRAPHY

Fagin, H., *The Commoners of England,* Lawrence and Wishart.
Simons, E., *Lord of London (Jack Cade),* Fr. Muller.

CHAPTER IV

The Pilgrimage of Grace, Kett's Rebellion and the Mousehold Community

As the fifteenth century drew towards its close, many wealthy landowners found that producing in bulk for the market had become very profitable, and that there was an insatiable demand for good English wool from Continental weavers. It was greatly in their interests to take over the many scattered strips of the manor fields, and turn them into large single units for cheap and easy working by landless labourers. The commons or wastes could be fenced off for sheep-walks, where one man and a dog could look after a large and profitable flock. So began the long process of the divorce of the English people from the land.

Overthrowing or ignoring manorial custom and the traditions of times immemorial, landowners started to enclose the wastes with fences, to merge the peasant-owned strips, to evict farmers in possession, to refuse the renewal of leases or inheritances. Where they could not evict, they forced their tenants out by fines or increased rents beyond their power to pay. They demolished farms and even villages in order to extend their grazing and unify the fields. Common land, essential to the peasants, was also enclosed to make deer-parks and hunting-grounds for the nobility.

The people did not accept this expropriation passively. For centuries they fought back with fence-breaking, hedge-pulling, riots and open rebellion.

In theory the state was opposed to the enclosures; they struck at the very roots of stability. It passed laws against them and decreed punishments for enclosers. But this was an activity of the rich and powerful and the new laws were not enforced. When villagers took their own measures, destroyed the hated hedges and reclaimed their land, that constituted a breach of the peace and was rigorously put down.

A poet of the time put it tersely:

> Houses where pleasures did abound,
> Nought but a shepherd and dog is found:
> Well-a-day!

Places where Christmas revels did keep
Is now become habitations for sheep.
Well-a-day!

The enclosures were rebuked by many people in high places. The scholar Robert Crowley warned the nobility and the landowners to remember their responsibilities to the common people. 'That you are lords and governors', he told them, 'cometh not by nature but by ordinance and appointment of God.' But the enclosures, and the riots and impoverishment that accompanied them, went on.

King Henry VIII came to the throne in 1509. Failing to obtain Papal agreement for his first divorce, he repudiated the authority of the Pope and set up a national reformed Church with himself at its head, which was to become the Protestant Church of England. In 1536, casting covetous eyes on the lands and wealth of the monasteries, he began to suppress them and disperse the monks, confiscating their possessions which he used to enrich himself and his subservient courtiers. The loot of the monasteries was the foundation of the fortunes of many of the aristocratic families of our own time.

Monastic life had long degenerated from the ideals of its founders, and the great abbeys and priories had to a great extent become, in the words of the king's indictment, centres of 'manifest sin, vicious carnal and abominable living'. Yet they continued to perform useful social functions; they offered overnight hospitality to travellers, distributed alms and relief essential to the very poor, and provided work on their estates for many laymen. Their closure brought great distress to the poor, the crippled and the helpless, who were often forced to become beggars, vagrants or thieves.

The dissolution of the monasteries and the religious changes stirred up revolt in many of the more distant backward parts of the country where feudalism was still strong. In 1536, in the north, occurred the so-called Pilgrimage of Grace and thirteen years later, in Devon and Cornwall, the Western Rebellion took place. Both of these began as religious movements but developed into protests against social and economic injustices.

The Pilgrimage of Grace, after local rioting all over the northern counties, began with a rising in Lincolnshire in October 1536, stirred by a rumour spread by monks that the suppression of the monasteries was to be followed by the closure of all local parish churches and the confiscation of their vestments, plate and valuables. Many of the gentry joined the common people and great crowds assembled.

The rebels were opposed to the closing of the monasteries and many of Henry's religious innovations. They demanded parliamentary and legal reforms, the restoration of the old Catholic holidays, with an end to enclosures, rack-renting and rising prices. On the

9. Interrogation techniques used to extract confessions from religious rebels in Tudor England.

whole they rejected Henry's new Church of England, and asked for the end of social practices regarded by the commons as unjust impositions.

A powerful nobleman, the Earl of Shrewsbury, called out his forces and forwarded the Pilgrims' grievances to the king. The king's answer was brief. He ignored their complaints, condemned the Pilgrims as false rebels and traitors, and ordered them to disperse at once and return to their homes. Such was the power and prestige of Henry VIII that they did so immediately.

A Yorkshire lawyer, Robert Aske, travelling to London, fell in with the Lincolnshire rebels. He seems to have been known as a champion of the people, for they insisted on his becoming their leader. He agreed to this reluctantly. After the collapse of the movement he returned to Yorkshire, where he found that county up in arms for the same reasons and was at once put in command. A group of dissident noblemen, headed by Lord Darcy, joined him. They entered York and occupied it, and assembled a force of 30,000 men at Doncaster. Aske made it clear that they were not opposing the king, but petitioning him to dismiss his 'evil councillors', Thomas Cromwell and Archbishop Cranmer, halt the dissolutions, end and restore the enclosures, and remedy other injustices. There were no long-term policies or plans in their programme.

The king was averse to an armed struggle that might develop into a civil war; so were the Pilgrims, although their aims were such that they could not be realised peacefully under Henry's autocracy. His army, led by the Duke of Norfolk, had only a quarter of the rebels' strength and was in no condition to fight. Norfolk arranged a truce with Aske, and again forwarded his demands to the king, who replied that the complaints were groundless, the words of presumptious men. But if the ringleaders were given up, said the king, the rest would be pardoned as an act of royal clemency.

This time there was no obedience as in Lincolnshire. The leaders drew up a plan for an agreement between the rebels and the crown. Aske himself carried it to the Duke of Norfolk, who received him politely. Norfolk could not promise that the king would grant it, but he did promise, on his own responsibility, a general pardon to all the rebels and the calling of a Parliament to consider their demands. Aske agreed. He seems to have been a reluctant leader, glad to be rid of the burden. He announced his satisfaction, repeated his loyalty to the king and returned to tell his followers that they could now return home to await events. Many did so gladly, but others were sceptical and stayed together under arms. Aske was then summoned to London for an audience with the king himself, an unusual honour and sign of favour, to explain directly to him the reasons for the rising. With some trepidation he set out on the many days' journey to the capital. Henry received him with all courtesy and grace, and they discussed the matter amicably. The king repeated the promise of a Parliament called to consider and remedy their grievances, and Aske returned to his men. All this took time, as Henry had hoped. The Duke of Norfolk's army was reinforced and plans were made to divide the rebels' leaders from their following.

In the Pilgrims' camp frustration increased and gave way to dissillusion. The days passed and there were no signs of a calling of Parliament; nothing was being done to fulfil the royal promise. In January 1536 the rebels lost patience and decided on action, against the advice of Aske; they attacked the important towns of Hull and Scarborough. The peasants of Cumberland and Westmorland besieged Carlisle. Probably the king anticipated this. His royal pardons were revoked, and, with the Pilgrimage divided between those towns, his forces easily routed them wherever they met. The leadership was captured, and Aske learned the value of the king's grace. He was executed in York, Lord Darcy was beheaded in London. Seventy peasants of the northwest were hanged on Henry's own order, in their villages or in their gardens. The monks of Sawley were hanged from their steeple; a female Pilgrim was burnt alive, a penalty reserved for women. In all, some two hundred people were killed for their part in the movement.

10. The fate of Robert Aske was execution on a gibbet similar to this one at Halifax.

The reign of the Tudors was a crucial period, representing the transition from medieval to modern times. The discovery of America altered the whole pattern of commerce. A new aristocracy filled the court and stood round the throne, a nobility based on the power of money rather than of birth. The landowners broke off the old feudal relationship with their peasant tenants based on mutual duties and obligations, and sought wealth by the pitiless exploitation of land and people. The peasant worked for the market, no longer for mere subsistence. He was not free, not bound to his piece of land; but his freedom, so long fought for, brought him little benefit. He lost the security of tenure he had as a serf, and the landlords were quick to take advantage of it. The cohesion of the manor was destroyed, and the process that was to turn England into a country of landless wage-earners was in operation.

Money now ruled. The merchant class became wealthier than the nobility, and sought to change everything that impeded its growing influence in the countryside, as in the towns which they ruled. Rules and customs thought to be eternal were breaking down, and there were as yet none with which to replace them.

The disappearance of the monasteries and the enclosures of land led to poverty and vagrancy on an unprecedented scale. It was

11.   Beggars being whipped through the streets, and sometimes hung as a punishment for being poor, 1577.

estimated that one-tenth of the population became homeless, wandering the roads and the counties in search of work that did not exist, supporting themselves by begging and stealing. Harsh laws were passed against them; penalties were flogging, branding, mutilation and hanging. But this was to no avail; the 'sturdy beggars' as the law termed the able-bodied unemployed, had no alternative means of surviving.

As wealth and power increased on the one hand, misery and discontent increased on the other. John Walker, of Griston in Norfolk, was hanged in 1540 merely for saying that the people of his county needed nothing but leadership for them to rise against the rule of the rich. Nine years later his words were proved true in what is called 'Kett's Rebellion'.

This, the last of the great medieval risings, was to hold its ground for some two months; during which time the rebels formed their own little 'commonwealth' and took over the third largest city in the country. By the end they had lost many in battle, on the gallows and on the block.

Their main grievances were the continuing enclosures of land and the evictions of tenants. Another boy king, Edward VI, was on the throne, and power was wielded by his Protector, the Duke of Somerset. Somerset and his peers had enriched themselves by monastic spoil, but he himself was a moderate, tolerant man who tried to halt the enclosures, the rack-renting, the 'monopolies' of the merchant princes and royal favourites. He issued a general pardon for fence- and hedge-breaking, but the rich objected and called for greater repression of the commons.

The country folk formed leagues to combat the landlords, raised funds for mutual aid and organised rent strikes. In 1549 there was widespread rioting through seven counties, with fence-breaking, ditch-filling and hedge-pulling to restore the land to the people. It took on the character of a class war. 'With clubs and clouted (patched) shoon', ran the saying, 'shall the deed be done'.

Open rebellion began outside the abbey at Wymondham, Norfolk, in July 1549, at the annual fair in honour of St Thomas à Becket. Among the crowds buying and selling, watching the entertainers and eating and drinking at the stalls, serious groups of men were forming, and speakers suddenly began to harangue the people. Obviously a plan was being carried out. Suddenly, with a cheer and a shout, a mass of men set off along the Norwich road to pull down the fences recently put up round common land by John Flowerdew, a grasping and unpopular small landowner. Flowerdew watched them in helpless rage, and asked them why they demolished his fences rather than those of Robert Kett, who had also fenced some waste nearby. Kett was a prosperous tanner who owned some land, and he had put up hedges and claimed the enclosure as his own. Unlike Flowerdew, he was liked and respected in the area, but a crowd visited him and told him that the people were reclaiming their own communal property, and his hedges too must come down. Kett at once agreed with them and said, 'Whatsoever lands I have enclosed shall again be made common unto ye and all men, and my own hands shall first perform it.' He then attacked the wealth and power of 'great men', and went on, 'Many horrible things of late years have ye endured, with many wrongs and miseries have ye been vexed and afflicted . . . Moreover, I promise that the hurts done to the public weal and the common pasture by the importunate lords thereof shall be righted.'* He then led the excited men and women to his hedges, and began uprooting them himself.

On the next morning, 9 July, a great meeting was held. Since time immemorial the popular assemblies of the commons had been held under a prominent oak-tree, and the tree chosen for this, known ever since as 'Kett's Oak' still stands, some three miles north-east of Wymondham by the A11 road. Here Kett was elected leader of the movement. He swore, 'I will never lay down the charge which the commonwealth has commanded me until your rights have been won.'

We know little about him, except that he was a man of mature age, from a respected family of tanners, a regular churchgoer and a member of the Guild of St Thomas à Becket. He must have possessed a strong personality and a ready tongue, and been self-confident, intelligent and able, to be selected as leader by his neighbours. All

---

*Alexander Nevylle, *Norfolk's Furies* (1607).

day the meeting went on, groups leaving to clear all enclosed land within a day's walk, and new supporters constantly arriving. Decisions were taken, plans made, messengers sent out to rouse the whole country; and a large band set out for Norwich, some nine miles away, where they began to clear new fences from Town Close, the citizens' communal pasture.

12. Kett's Oak at Wymondham during the 1940s.

Norwich was one of the largest and most important cities in England. The mayor, Thomas Codd, and his leading citizens had no doubts about the magnitude of the revolt. They knew that this was more than a local riot, and they sent off a messenger to inform the king, then at Windsor. Codd then went out and spoke to the rebels, advising them to go home. They refused. The next day Kett joined them with his main force, and camped at Bowthorpe, one mile to the west. To them came the High Sheriff of Norfolk and Suffolk, who in the name of the king ordered them to disperse. His attitude was contemptuous and insulting; he was not well received, but after some angry shouting he was allowed to gallop away in safety.

For two days Kett and his men debated their next move, and decided to set up a more permanent and defensible camp. The place chosen was Mousehold Heath, a large open space east of Norwich, the scene of the assembly of the serfs in 1381. The mayor refused them passage through the city and they made the long march round it. They were now 2,600 strong, with wagons, horses, and a baggage train. Within a week on the Heath they had grown to 20,000. Kett told them plainly that the die was cast; there could be no going back, and they must be prepared for desperate measures. 'Harmless counsels', he said, 'are fit for tame fools. For you who have already stirred there is no hope but in adventuring boldly.'

Mousehold Heath was then an area of high rough land with scattered coppices and woodland. It commanded a view of the city, with its strong wall and ten gates, beyond the River Wensum. On the heath stood the new palace of the Earl of Surrey and an old chapel. Kett occupied the palace and set up his headquarters in the chapel.

In Norwich the worried council sat for many hours. Some urged immediate battle against the rebels, others advised caution. There were too few troops at hand to make victory certain; many of the citizens and militiamen favoured Kett's cause and were well disposed to the rebels; defeat might mean the sack of the city. So the walls were manned, the city put in a state to resist if attacked, but the gates were kept open and there was no bar on persons moving in or out. There was much coming and going between the camp and the city, where the rebels were well received by the populace. Mayor Codd was neither for the rebels or the government; his interest was in preserving the great city of Norwich unharmed, and he maintained, for as long as he could, good relations with both sides. He and Kett were often together, and as chief citizen his signature often appears with Kett's on the rebels' messages.

The rebels worked hard to fortify their camp, digging deep ditches round it and erecting stockades. Huts were built for shelter, trees were felled for a clear view without cover for the enemy, and every day foraging parties left to collect food and arms. They raided the houses and estates of the rich and took away their oxen, sheep, poultry, deer, guns and powder. It is said that during this time the camp consumed 4,000 head of cattle and 20,000 sheep (these last were consumed with great relish, being one of the chief reasons for the enclosures). Their orders were that 'no violence or injury be done to any honest or poor man'. That there was little hatred in all this can be seen in a rhyming note left as a receipt by one party, which has survived:

> Mr Pratt, your sheep are very fat,
> And we thank you for that.
> We have left you the skins
> To pay for your wife's pins,
> And you must thank us for that.

Fear spread wide among the gentry. Many fled; others brought voluntary contributions to the camp, hoping to be spared the rest. Kett took a number of prisoners, men he thought might prove dangerous, whom he lodged in Surrey's palace and even in Norwich Castle itself. There was an absolute minimum of violence, and not one person was killed.

Church bells and beacons carried the news of the revolt far and wide through the county, and men left farms, shops and families, armed themselves and set out for Mousehold.

Meanwhile the camp was developing its own way of life. A large and ancient oak was selected as the meeting place; a roof was built under its spreading branches and a raised platform below. Here daily prayers were held (in the new form), and here the leaders of the revolt discussed policy and made their plans and reports in the full hearing of everybody. It soon became known as the 'Oak of Reformation'. The 'governors of the commonwealth' were Robert Kett and his brother William, who had soon joined him, Mayor Codd and ex-mayor Aldrich of Norwich, and their council was made up of two delegates from each of the thirty-three 'hundreds' of Norfolk. Their orders and messages were issued as from 'the king's camp', as Kett claimed that as the laws against enclosures had been passed by the parliament but not enforced, it was he and his men who were actually representing the crown and the laws by enforcing them. He described his following as 'the king's friends and delegates'.

A court of justice was set up to try breaches of peace and discipline in the camp, and that too sat in public under the great oak. There was no ban there even on those opposed to the rebellion, and many of these came to speak their minds to the insurgents, and were heard out, if sometimes heckled. Among them was Mayor Codd, a frequent speaker, and the Reverend Matthew Parker, later to be Archbishop of Canterbury, whose long sermon against the sin of rebellion aroused some resentment which was calmed by the singing of the *Te Deum* (in English, as the new style was), but Parker thought it best to leave in a hurry. The Oak of Reformation was the only spot in England where such freedom of speech existed.

Under the oak, too, the leadership drew up their manifesto, 'The Bill of Twenty-Nine Requests and Demands'. Among the demands, in addition to the end of enclosures and the restoration of communal land, were those for equitable rents, common rights for fishing and taking game, elections for local law officers to oversee the laws against enclosures, the establishment of a clergyman in every parish to teach the children (this was a forerunner of the later demand for working-class education), and added the clause 'That all bond-men may be made free, as God made all men free with his precious blood-shedding.' This last, the proposition that Christ's sacrifice on the cross freed all men of every social class, was to become a powerful argument in the great struggles for liberty in the next century.

The manifesto was forwarded to the king. The answer, from Protector Somerset, promised that when Parliament met in October it would discuss what redress could be offered to the people; meanwhile it ordered them to disperse, break up the illegal camp and return home.

This reply was rejected out of hand and the rebels strengthened their camp. Cannon were brought in from coastal forts, gunpowder from the port of Lynn. The local gentry seemed incapable of action, and many of them had fled from the district. News of the encamped rebels had spread round the country, and risings were taking place in other counties.

Kett and his men conferred under the oak. An army of 20,000 could not stay there for ever, behind their flimsy stockade. The next step was obvious. At their feet lay the great walled city; it had to be occupied. So far there had been no bloodshed. Nobody sought open war, and Mayor Codd had seemed to be a reasonable man. They decided to negotiate for the peaceful occupation of Norwich. Kett seemed to share the conviction of his men that they were really on the side of the king and would have his approval in the end.

They were forestalled. The great merchants and rich citizens had sent their own emissary to the king over the head of their mayor. One of them, Southerton, rode fast to London to press for immediate action to save the city from the rebels. He was received by the royal council, but it gave him little comfort. Because of the war against Scotland there was no force at hand that could face Kett's men. What troops were available, mostly Italian and German mercenaries, were on their way to Devon, where 10,000 rebels were besieging Exeter. Dangerous rioting had just been put down in five counties, and a strong garrison had to be kept in the Tower, as the mood was such that London had been placed under martial law. All that they could do for Norwich was to send one of the royal heralds, a most important official, to represent the king and offer pardon if the rebels disbanded.

Southerton and his companion, York Herald, with their escort, reached Norwich at noon on 21 July. York Herald put on his grand court armour, and over that his embroidered tabard bearing the arms of England, and rode into the camp. He took with him Mayor Codd and a small party of men-at-arms. On the rostrum under the oak he faced the rebels and offered them, if they would go home, the king's most gracious pardon. Some of those present were willing to accept; they had been too long from their farms and homes, and were anxious and frightened. But York Herald's words made no mention of the bitter injustices that had called them together, and contained threats of punishment for those who failed to beg the king's pardon and stayed united.

Kett made a brief and angry reply. He said, 'Kings are wont to pardon wicked persons, not innocent, just men. They for their part deserved no punishment and were guilty of no crime.' He added, 'I trust I have done nothing but what belongs to the duty of a true subject.'

York Herald, a brave man, immediately declared Kett a traitor, and ordered his men to arrest him. But this was not Smithfield at dusk, and Kett was not isolated as Wat Tyler had been. A great shout of anger arose and the rebels pushed forward. The arrest was not made. The herald and his company were allowed to leave in peace, followed by a number of peasants who had decided to accept his terms. The rest were left in no doubt as to how they were regarded by the government whose laws they were seeking to uphold.

This was the turning-point of the revolt. Mayor Codd ordered the city gates shut, the battlements manned, moved all his cannon to the eastern side of the city and opened fire on the camp. Kett's cannoniers replied, but the range was too great for either side to do any damage.

The next morning Kett led his men out to occupy the city. They encountered heavy fire from the guns and flights of arrows from the gate. The rebels shot back but ran out of arrows. Young boys risked death to gather up spent shafts from the field, and we are told that the wounded pulled the arrows from their flesh to give to their archers. At noon a great host swept down from the camp, crossed the River Wensum by wading and swimming, put the defenders to flight, rushed the gate and burst into Norwich. York Herald was still there and with the mayor rode into the market-place among the crowds. No weapons were raised against them, and again he appealed to them to lay down their arms and receive pardon. They shouted back at him, 'Be off! Plague take thee with thy idle promises!' He and his escort left for London, unharmed. Kett ordered the arrest of Mayor Codd and some others, posted guards to control the city and keep order, and left it to return to the camp with his army.

All next day they deliberated under the oak. They held public trials of captured noblemen, landowners and lawyers, but there is no evidence that any of them suffered more than brief imprisonment in the castle. Many were released if those who knew them in the crowd testified that he was a 'good man'. Mayor Codd was set free and resigned the mayoralty, his place being taken by Alderman Steward, 'a good and modest man, beloved of poor and rich'.

Meanwhile the state was at last reacting. A scratch force of volunteers, gentlemen, knights, squires, all with their followers and retainers, 1,600 soldiers and a body of Italian mercenaries, under the command of Lord Northampton, marched from London and reached Norwich on 31st July. The rebel guards, outnumbered, fled to the camp and Northampton passed through the gates into the Norwich unhindered.

Again the men of the Mousehold community attacked Norwich. There followed two days of bitter fighting in which the rebels lost more than four hundred men. Northampton and his men retreated, and now there was no repetition of their former error; the rebels stayed in the city, put out the burning buildings and kept it in their own hands. They took no revenge, put no man to death. For the next three weeks they were to be masters of the great city, while still occupying the camp on the hill.

The rebels were now at the peak of their power; but there were serious errors in their strategy. Instead of obtaining the support of the Protector, as they had expected, he and his government regarded them as traitors to be crushed. They had made no attempt to turn their local rebellion into a national movement, as had Wat Tyler in 1381. It remained a county affair, static, without development, and as such its destruction was certain when once the state marched against it. No attempt was made to link up with the rebellion under way in the west, and form a joint movement. There were a number of risings in the south inspired by Kett's example, but they remained small and separate, and were easily put down one by one. A body of troops and an executioner usually sufficed. Bad roads, vast distances and lack of communications made unification difficult. Kett had dispatched a force to capture the important port of Yarmouth, but it failed, with heavy casualties. The government was given time to divert a section of the army raised for the war against Scotland. There were 12,000 troops plus a large band of *Landsknechts,* 1,500 strong. These were German mercenaries, heavy armoured cavalry, with the reputation of being utterly without mercy or compassion. This force was placed under the command of the Earl of Warwick, known for his opposition to the Protector and a bitter enemy of the common people.

Arriving outside Norwich on the morning of Saturday 25 August, Warwick again offered the king's pardon for surrender, but also abused the rebels and told them that the alternative was fire, sword and death. Kett, he said, could not be included in any pardon. The offer was rejected as untrustworthy and the attack began. After two days of fighting with heavy casualties on both sides, Warwick entered the city by battering down the gates with cannon. He thrust towards the central market-place, and after many hours of street-fighting the rebels retreated and fled again to their camp. By Monday midday many of the houses were burning and isolated groups of rebels were still holding out in the narrow streets and alleys. These were shot down by the new 'hand-guns', and all taken alive were hanged at once. The market-place was filled with gallows, erected for the purpose despite the promise of pardon. Now the city and the camp faced each other across the River Wensum.

All next day Kett and his men sat in council under the oak. We know little of the discussion that ensued, or of the plans put forward. Their position was desperate: Warwick could blockade the camp and starve them out without making a direct assault. There could be no advantage in attempting another attack on Norwich. They could expect no additions to their strength or supplies, while Warwick could expect both. The course of the debate is not known, only the final decision. This was the strange determination to abandon the camp and face Warwick in the open, where he would have all the advantages of a strong cavalry force. Probably by now most of Kett's men expected nothing but death in battle or on the gallows; they apparently decided to uphold to the last the rights of the common people to their land and such liberty as the law allowed them, and to go down fighting for this cause.

There was in the camp an old prophesy often repeated. This ran:

> The country lads, Hob, Dick and Hick,
> With clubs and clouted shoon,
> Shall fill the vale
> Of Dussindale
> With slaughtered bodies soon.

It was decided to fight at Dussindale. The exact location known then by that name is uncertain, but it is thought to have been the low-lying ground about a mile north-east of Norwich, now reached through Gilman Road.

The camp was broken up and fired. A pall of black smoke hung over the place that, for some six weeks, had taken on some of the characteristics of a little communist community; where there were no class distinctions to alienate one man from another, where everybody was free to speak his mind, where each had his share in the common property and where their shared aims had created a sense of brotherhood. They gathered around the oak. Then, with their baggage-wagons and arms, Kett led his defiant followers to their final battlefield.

In Dussindale the ambiguous prophesy was fulfilled. Warwick's guns broke up the massed ranks of the rebels, the charges of his armoured cavalry smashed through them. The horsemen pursued the fugitives, cutting them down without mercy; they took no prisoners. A remnant made a ring of wagons lashed together and stood at bay inside it long after the field was cleared. On one of the wagons was a barrel of ale; this they opened, solemnly pledged each other and drank. Then they said a short prayer together and prepared to die. Warwick, seeing the battle won and unwilling to lose more of his men, sent to offer them mercy if they laid down their arms. The offer was rejected as untrustworthy. Warwick came in person and repeated it, with binding oaths; and the brave men threw down their weapons and were allowed to return home in safety.

By four o'clock in the afternoon, 'Kett's Rebellion' was over. Around the dale lay 5,300 dead rebels, with many more wounded and maimed. All those taken alive were killed on the spot, or hanged from nearby trees. Kett himself, well mounted, galloped away at the end of the battle when all was lost, to be captured later in a state of complete exhaustion.

Nine of the surviving leaders were part-hanged on the 'Oak of Reformation', then cut down and disembowelled alive and quartered. Thirty more suffered the same fate outside Magdalen Gate, Norwich, and three hundred were hanged around the city wall and left there until they decayed, poisoning the air. The dead of the battle were buried in one great pit. Warwick and his gentlemen, with the rich burghers of Norwich, held a special service of thanksgiving in St Peter Mancroft, the great civic church in the market-place. When he left for London he had with him Robert Kett and his brother William. They were imprisoned in the Tower, tried and sentenced for treason and brought back to Norfolk for execution. On 7 December Robert was dragged through the streets of Norwich on a hurdle to the castle, his body loaded with heavy chains, and was drawn by a rope round his neck to a gibbet projecting from the battlements; he was slowly strangled. William was killed in the same way at Wymondham, suspended from the abbey tower.

Protector Somerset paid dearly for renouncing his supporters among the common people. Warwick, grown in power and stature after his victory, eventually ousted him from his high position and he was beheaded on a trumped-up charge. And Warwick, who had aimed at a puppet monarchy with himself to pull the strings, was later executed for treason.

SELECT BIBLIOGRAPHY

Fagin, H., *The Commoners of England*, Lawrence and Wishart.
Groves, R., *Rebels' Oak*, Fellowship Books.
Scarisbrook, J. J., *Henry VIII*, Pelican Books.
Williamson, J. A., *The Tudor Age*, Longman.

CHAPTER V

The Civil War and the English Revolution

In the second quarter of the seventeenth century it became obvious that a crisis was approaching in the government of England. During the preceding period great changes had taken place in the social and economic relations of its people, their work and their lives. The land was now emerging rapidly out of the Middle Ages into modern times, out of a feudal past into a capitalistic society. Wealth was passing from the nobility into the hands of the merchants and men of business, but political power stayed in aristocratic hands. There was no need for surplus money to be kept locked up in chests or wasted on ostentation. The age of discovery, resulting in the opening up of the world markets, offered great opportunities for profitable investment, and rich traders needed ever larger sums for their expensive 'enterprises and adventures' which returned such large rewards.

The population had risen to almost five million, of which the majority still worked in agriculture; many of them as yeoman farmers, on small owned or rented estates. These had achieved a measure of prosperity and independence, and were militant in defence of their interests. There was also a class of peasants on rented fields and a much greater number of landless labourers, who eked out their earnings by engaging in cottage industry such as spinning, weaving or handicrafts. In fact, most of the industrial production of the country was based on the cottager and carried out by family units in their own homes. The goods men needed were now bought, not made at home, and a great impetus was thereby given to manufacture. Many of the landless villagers gave up working for the farmers and concentrated on their modest contributions to industrial production.

The increasing development of large-scale enterprises — mining, iron and metal-working, seafaring, commerce, as well as the trades and crafts of the towns — created a new and growing class of men who relied entirely on their employment by others, and the wages they received from them; the forbears of the modern working class.

The upper nobility, by and large, remained very rich. (It needed the efforts of 150 servants to bring Lord Berkeley to London to visit

King James I). They now ran their estates as large capitalist farms, working for the market and for export. If extravagance or misfortune reduced their standing they were ready to marry off their children into rich (though low-born) mercantile families, a thing that no Continental aristocrat would ever contemplate. Moreover, they would even send their younger sons to town to become traders themselves. Thus there was a merging of mercantile and aristocratic interests unique to England.

The strong central state, under the king, did not fully reflect these changes, although it had superseded many feudal institutions. Now it was the Crown that gave the orders that formerly came from the lord of the manor, the trade guilds, the clergy; that dictated to a certain extent prices, wages and taxes.

Religion, that all-important extension of politics and ethics into everyday life, was also decided by the Crown. The liturgy and ritual of the Church of England, 'as by law established', governed by its bishops, was ubiquitous. The one universal meeting-place of the people, high and low, was the church, and control of the pulpit meant control of the 'mass media'.

The outlook and activities of the merchant class had evolved its own version of Christianity, vaguely defined as Puritanism. It based itself firmly on the Bible, especially the Old Testament, and opposed the concept of a monolithic Anglican Church incorporating many relics of the old Catholic faith. The largest Puritan faction, the Presbyterian, was influenced mainly by the wealthy traders, sections of the gentry, and a number of peers whose grandfathers had grown rich on the loot of the monasteries, and who feared above all a return to Catholicism. With their belief in predestination, regarding acquired wealth as a sign of divine favour, they wanted a 'purified' church of partly self-governing congregations, with elected elders, based on Bible study, preaching, and with high moral standards and the right to punish infringements of them. This was to be the national church, controlled by Parliament; and the only permitted one. In the pursuit of worldly wealth the man who did best was the sober, thrifty, hardworking person, undistracted by the search for pleasure or entertainment, and these qualities of solemnity and abstinence became the great virtues of Presbyterianism. They were expert in finding and denouncing 'Popish practices' and 'idolatry' in the Anglican Church. The surplice, the organ, stained glass, altar rails, the rites of communion and baptism, statues, were abominations to them. These smacked too much of the old religion, with its ban on usury and its concept of ethical trading and the just price, to be permitted.

There were also a number of smaller sects, known as Independents, which stressed a direct, personal relationship between

God and man, and therefore the importance of the individual and his freedom. They declared that God took no heed of class or social divisions, which were not of His making, and that He would inspire with his 'inner light' and revelation peasant or workman as well as, or in preference to, gentleman, minister or bishop. They upheld the revolutionary concept of religious freedom, in which every one was at liberty to think and worship as they pleased, in accordance with their own divine promptings. (This freedom did not extend to Roman Catholics, for they were part of an international organisation pledged to restore the old order.) And they opposed any idea of a national church, clergy or ceremonial because it formed a barrier between God and man. Their following came mainly from the yeomen and artisans, the 'lower classes'.

In all this the controlling state remained largely feudal in form, with the monarch surrounded and advised by his chosen courtiers of the upper nobility and wielding all his ancient powers. The House of Commons, composed of the representatives of the business classes and the country gentry, was seen as a useful adjunct to the Crown; its principal function was to approve and make legal those taxes and levies that the king wished to impose, and to make him grants of money without interfering in the direction of affairs. The lower classes had no representation at all.

It was estimated at the time that the wealth at the disposal of the members of the House of Commons was three times greater than that of the peers assembled in the House of Lords. Yet the state clung to the idea that its power and future lay in the hereditary nobility, as indeed it once had.

The commercial class was demanding a larger voice in the government. There were obsolete practices that hindered the extension of trade. Sinecures given to favourites consumed a large portion of the king's revenues, some 40 per cent of which were spent on maintaining the court. He granted 'monopolies' that were an additional tax on goods in daily use. The king alone had the power to declare war. Wars were very expensive, and the House had to find the money to pay for them. Wars, if directed at the capture of bases for trade and the thwarting of rivals, could be very profitable. In matters like these the Commons demanded a say.

In 1625 King Charles I ascended the throne. He had inherited from his father James I, the idea of the 'Divine Right of Kings', a claim to absolutism in itself a relic of the feudal order. It seemed to him little short of blasphemy that Parliament should oppose his policies and wishes and put forward alternatives of its own. 'The business of a sovereign', he said, 'and the business of a subject, are clean different things.' He asked it for money, and it answered with 'remonstrances'. It sought to advise him in matters of religion; it was critical of his marriage to a French Catholic princess. Receiving little but opposition from his first three Parliaments, he dissolved each in turn, and for eleven years he ruled alone, an autocrat, in defiance of all English tradition. Thus he denied the merchants, the gentry and the religious dissidents their customary mouthpiece in the state. He imposed taxes which were by many considered to be illegal exactions, and men like John Hampden went to prison rather than pay them. Archbishop Laud rigorously enforced the rites of the Anglican church, and persecuted Puritans and sectaries. He tried his opponents in privileged courts like the Star Chamber, in which the rules of Common Law did not apply. He established a rigid censorship of the press.

In 1640 King Charles was forced to call a new Parliament. Archbishop Laud had tried to force his new prayer-book on the Calvinist Scots, and they had revolted against it. Money and an army was needed to put them down, and only Parliament could provide them. This was the 'Short Parliament', which sat for only three weeks. Instead of money, it presented Charles with a long list of complaints and criticisms. Charles therefore dissolved the Parliament.

Now the Scots raised an army and invaded England. Charles, with no power to oppose them, promised them a large daily payment (£850) to stay north of the River Tees. They agreed, subject to a treaty with an English Parliament, whose sympathies, they knew, would be with them rather than the king. Without a proper army and with no money, Charles announced with reluctance elections for a new House of Commons.

This was to become the famous 'Long Parliament' which, with changes and an interval, was to sit for twenty years and make itself the chief instrument through which the business classes and the merchants, in alliance at first with the working people, were to fight and defeat the king in open war, execute him for treason to the nation, establish a republic, destroy their own left-wing opposition, and restore a monarchy subject to parliamentary control. It was the 'revolutionary committee', through which wealthy commoners were to liquidate the remaining relics of feudalism in the state and in social relations, place power firmly in their own hands, and help England to become the world's first great capitalist nation.

When the Parliament assembled it found that, in the main, supporters of the king and his policies came from the remote, poor and backward parts of the kingdom — Wales, the west and the north, where people still lived and worked in the traditional ways, and many adhered to the proscribed Catholic faith. The majority group was Presbyterian, with a minority of Independents. A minority in the House of Lords supported the Presbyterians.

Under the leadership of John Pym, the Commons began two years of drastic reform. The king's chief adviser, Strafford, was impeached and beheaded. Laud and a number of his bishops were lodged in the Tower. It only just failed to abolish episcopy in the Church. An act was passed stating that the Commons could be dissolved only with its own consent, and that its dissolution must be immediately followed by elections for a new one. The king's prerogative courts were ended. To all this Charles had to give his royal assent.

The censorship of the press was lifted, and, in the political ferment of the time a flood of news-sheets, journals, and pamphlets poured from the freed press. New politico-religious sects appeared in public. In London and elsewhere there were great meetings and demonstrations of support for Parliament. Self-appointed preachers harangued the crowds without hindrance, and artisans and workers were eager to speak their minds on all subjects, sacred or profane. There was a great upsurge in the spirit and confidence of ordinary people, 'the base, common and popular', whose opinions had hitherto been of little account.

The final breach between the king and his Parliament came in January 1642. Rebellion in Ireland grew into a major armed revolt against English rule. A new army had to be raised to put it down. The king was the only legal authority with the right to lead an army and commission its officers. Pym and the Commons thought that, given this force, Charles would use it first to crush them and enforce his personal rule again; and they paused before giving the necessary approval and grants of money. But the Irish rebellion grew in strength, and the small English forces were unable to contain it. A Catholic-ruled Ireland would be a constant threat as a potential base for its co-religionists, France and Spain. An army was essential and Parliament agreed to provide it, in the Militia Bill, only if its officers were nominated and commissioned by itself. Charles refused to give the Bill the royal assent.

At this, the Commons passed and sent to the king a 'Grand Remonstrance', in 204 clauses, outlining all his acts it considered detrimental to the interests of the nation, and accusing him of working towards a royal despotism. It demanded that he should appoint as his ministers and advisers only those men approved by the Commons. It was also printed and distributed to the public as an appeal to the people against the Crown. The people backed it by tumults and demonstrations.

There was no republican faction in the Parliament. No member envisaged or desired a state without a king; what it sought was a compromise in which both sides could work out a system within which Crown and Parliament could co-operate harmoniously together for the progress of the kingdom, expressed as the recognition and expansion of the power of mercantile and financial interests.

King Charles' answer was to go in person, unannounced, into the precincts of the House of Commons, the one place in his kingdom which he had no right to enter, where no king has ever been before or since; a direct challenge to its privileges. He went to demand the surrender of Pym, Hampden and three other members whom he had accused of treason, a capital offence. On Charles's entry, accompanied only by his young nephew, the astonished members rose to their feet and doffed their hats. The king advanced through the House, seated himself in the vacated Speakers' Chair, and demanded the five members. He looked for them along the benches, but they were absent. (They had been forewarned.) He asked where they were, but there was no reply. He then spoke directly to the Speaker, William Lenthall. 'Mr Speaker,' he said, 'I must have these five gentlemen. Come, tell me where they are.'

Mr Speaker Lenthall hesitated a moment. Then he knelt before the king and answered, 'May it please Your Majesty, I have neither eyes to see nor tongue to speak in this place, save as its honourable members direct me, whose servant I am.'

The king controlled himself in the face of this defiance, answering briefly, 'Well, I see my birds have flown. I expect you to send them to me, or I must take my own way to find them.' And with this implied threat he strode out, with the cries of 'Privilege of the Commons!' in his ears.

The five members had taken refuge in London. There the alarm-bells rang out the tocsin, the gates were shut, the train-band put under arms, and the city prepared to defend them and itself. But Charles made no further move.

The king thought London, the stronghold of Parliament, with its citizens' militia, the train-band, and its violent crowds, a dangerous place to be. He left his palace at Whitehall for the safer north, took the decision for military action, and in August 1642 raised his standard at Nottingham, a feudal gesture calling all loyal subjects to rally to him in arms. The royalist minority in the Commons, and most of the peers, left to join him. The Civil War, which was to decide whether the supreme authority in England was the Crown or Parliament, had begun.

The principal support for Parliament came from the developed industrial parts of the country; London, the working cities, parts of the Midlands, East Anglia and the south-east. The king found his followers in Wales, Cornwall and the north, the cathedral cities, among the members of the Anglican communion, and the Roman Catholics who were still numerous in remote areas. The navy, and most of the sea-ports, opted for Parliament. This gave it the collection of customs and duties and the ability to import arms, as well as the taxes of the densely populated districts. King Charles had to rely mostly on gifts and offerings for his war-chest, and what he could raise from the country he held. His 'noble and gentle' supporters, used to living in the saddle, gave him a strong cavalry force and his nephew, Prince Rupert of the Rhine, came to command it. The rival forces became, in the slang of the time, 'Cavaliers and Roundheads'.

Parliament was backed by a number of separate armies raised by counties, mainly concerned with the defence of their own areas and each nominally independent. It named as its chief general the Earl of Essex, a moderate Presbyterian who sought no final military victory but a negotiated settlement, and showed no great eagerness to fight. There ensued minor skirmishes and small-scale battles all over the land as each side sought to strengthen its local position; then the king decided to advance on London, Parliament's main base.

Essex marched north to defend the city, and the first major battle took place at Edgehill, near Banbury, in October 1642, where the two armies met almost by accident. The king had 14,000 men, Essex 10,000. The royalist hopes lay in their dashing cavalry and Prince Rupert opened the conflict with a charge that swept away most of the parliamentary horse. But having scattered them, the Cavaliers found themselves unable (or unwilling), to re-form and turn about, and galloped on to raid the baggage train and the nearby town of Kineton. They came straggling back at dusk having left their infantry without support.

In their flight the Roundhead cavalry broke through and disorganised their own formations of foot, and the king's infantry, properly deployed, advanced to finish them off. It seemed the day was lost, and Essex seized a pike and went into the front rank to die with honour. But he still had two reserve regiments of cavalry left, now the only horse remaining on the scene, and they charged the royalist foot with such effect that but for the coming of night they might well have routed them. But they halted as it grew dark and Rupert's troopers returned; both sides drew off without a decision, leaving some 5,000 dead behind them.

Among the officers of Essex's cavalry reserve was a forty-three-year-old squire from the Isle of Ely, who was also MP for Cambridge. He watched the course of the battle carefully and led his men bravely into action. His name was Oliver Cromwell. He had noticed that the Cavalier horse was formidable in attack but that its lack of cohesion and discipline, and its inability to re-form after a wild charge, had almost lost the battle for the king.

Charles continued his march on London, and Essex strove to place his army between the Cavaliers and the city. He succeeded at

13.   Portrait of Oliver Cromwell.

Turnham Green, about six miles west of London, and, backed by the London train-bands, drew up across the road and the meadows. The two armies faced each other passively for a day. Then Charles gave up his plan and retreated to Oxford, which became his headquarters for the rest of the war.

Throughout the war, negotiations with the king were continued, and commissioners and delegations rode to and fro between London and Oxford. The king remained obdurate. Asked to assent to the Militia Bill for a short while, for appearances' sake, he replied, 'No. Not for an hour.' Nor would he budge on the matters of the bishops and Church government. He tried to raise foreign troops, even an army of Irish Catholics, to use against his own people. He made promises and broke them; he did not feel bound by agreements made with his subjects.

The war dragged on, with no sign of victory. Minor battles and sieges were draining strength from both sides. The public was growing tired of it, and a desire for peace at any cost was developing. Then Charles attempted another attack on London. Its men and women toiled to dig a ring of trenches and earthworks outside the city wall, and the train-bands marched out with Essex to give battle. In a forced march they broke up the royalist siege of Gloucester, and on the way back encountered their main force at Newbury, and in another great battle forced the king's retreat back to Oxford. But, on the whole, the war was going badly for Parliament, which was showing no great will for final victory.

'If we beat the king ninety and nine times,' said one of its leading generals, 'yet he is king still, and we are rebels.'

And Cromwell answered hotly, 'Then why did we take up arms at first? If so, let us make peace, be it never so base.'

In 1643 Parliament made an alliance with the Calvinist Scots. The Scots were to raise an army (at England's expense) and invade in the north, where support for the king was strong; and in return Parliament would set up the Presbyterian Church as the state religion, enforced by law, in defiance of its own Independent supporters. Freedom of conscience meant giving scope to the many sects of the common people who believed that Christianity really meant the equality of all people, and the Presbyterian merchants feared that more than they feared the king. In 1644 the Scots crossed the border and engaged the Cavaliers.

Meanwhile Cromwell was raising his own cavalry force, the 'Ironsides'. He chose Independents, men of his own mind: men who were convinced that in fighting the king and the bishops they were doing the work of God, as they could prove by many a biblical text. He found them among the yeoman farmers and artisans of East Anglia,

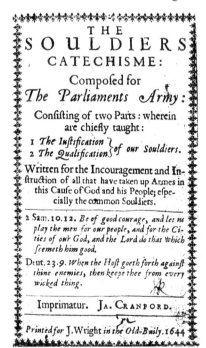

THE
SOULDIERS
CATECHISME:

Compofed for

The Parliaments Army:

Confifting of two Parts : wherein are chiefly taught :

1 The Iuftification } of our Souldiers.
2 The Qualification }

Written for the Incouragement and Inftruction of all that have taken up Armes in this Caufe of God and his People; efpecially the common Souldiers.

2 Sam. 10.12. Be of good courage, and let us play the men for our people, and for the Cities of our God, and the Lord do that which feemeth him good.

Deut. 23.9. When the Hoft goeth forth againft thine enemies, then keepe thee from every wicked thing.

Imprimatur. JA. CRANFORD.

Printed for J. Wright in the Old-Baily. 1644

14. The title page of *The Souldiers Catechisme*, 1644.

and, contrary to established practice, he chose his officers by merit, not by their social standing. 'I would rather', he said, 'have a plain russet-coated captain that knows what he fights for, and loves what he knows, than one that is a gentleman and nought else.'

By his analysis of the weaknesses of the enemy's horse, and the elimination of such faults in his own, his men were trained to charge in line, manoeuvre efficiently on the battlefield, and after a charge to re-form and charge again. He mounted them on slower, heavier horses, and relied on formation, weight and impact rather than speed and individual bravado. His discipline was strict, and morale high.

In July 1644, at Marston Moor in Yorkshire, Parliament won its first major victory. The army of the Eastern Association, joined by Scottish units, defeated a royalist force of 20,000; and the credit went to the Ironsides, who met and routed the formerly invincible cavalry of Rupert. The king lost 4,150 killed, Parliament, 300. However, the advantage gained was off-set by a great defeat in the west, the surrender of the entire army of Essex after much futile manoeuvring.

Cromwell saw that the war could not be won by separate armies and denounced the Presbyterians for lack of co-ordination and energy. With powerful backers, he demanded that Parliament raise its own fighting force, responsible to it alone, paid by it, and intent on complete victory. Parliament at length agreed, and in May 1645 its New Model Army took the field, under the command of Sir Thomas Fairfax, with Cromwell as Lieutenant-General in charge of the horse and second only to Fairfax.

This was truly a new kind of army, and its composition gave the Presbyterian leaders some misgivings. Under the Self-Denying Ordinance MPs had to give up their military commands (exception was made for Cromwell). This undermined the Presbyterian influence in the army. The businessmen in the House sought an accommodation with the king, once he was shorn of his powers; but what they really feared was too much power in the hands of the common people, the farmers and artisans. They sought no 'composition' with them! In the New Model Army there were large numbers of Independents and sectaries, who thought that as all men were equal before God, it was clearly his will that they should enjoy the same status in the world. As in the Ironsides, promotion was by merit, and many of its best officers were artisans, something formerly unheard of: Colonel Hewson was a cobbler; Colonel Pride, a drayman. Its soldiers were men of strong opinions, and enjoyed open discussion of them. Each man carried in his pack the portable 'Soldiers' Bible', with which to justify his views. The Old Testament prophets, denouncing injustice and oppression, were the ideal; the king, bishops and the Anglican clergy they regarded as Antichrist, and found traces of Popery even in Presbyterianism. They went into action singing psalms and marched to argument and discussion. Royalists dubbed them 'the Army of the Saints', and they were to prove a formidable revolutionary force.

In June 1645 the New Model Army met the king's main army at Naseby, and utterly destroyed it. Charles himself became a fugitive. The cabinet with his private papers was captured, with evidence of his plans to import 10,000 foreign mercenaries, to abolish the laws against the Catholics, to bring over an army of Irishmen, and, in place of his promised toleration of Presbyterianism, to set up an authoritarian Anglican Church.

Mopping up and the reduction of castles and strongpoints went on until the spring of 1646. The king surrendered himself to the Scots, hoping to effect a breach between them and England; the Scots sold him to Parliament for a large sum of money.

The last engagement took place at Stow-on-the-Wold in March 1646. The royalist commander, Astley, seated on a drum among his captors, said prophetically: 'Well, lads, you have done your work and now may go play — unless you fall out among yourselves!

SELECT BIBLIOGRAPHY

Brandon, L. G., *A Survey of British History*, Edward Arnold, 1951.
Buchan, J. *Oliver Cromwell*, The Reprint Society, 1941.
Cornforth, M., (ed), *Rebels and their Causes*, Lawrence and Wishart.
Hill, C., *God's Englishman (Oliver Cromwell)*, Weidenfeld and Nicolson.
Tawney, R. H., *Religion and the Rise of Capitalism*, John Murray, 1926.
Willey, B., *The Seventeenth-Century Background*, Chatto & Windus, 1934.
Woolwych, A., *Battles of the English Civil War*, Pan Books, 1966.

CHAPTER VI

The New Model Army and the Levellers

Though King Charles was nominally the prisoner of Parliament, he kept his royal state, held his court, was served on bended knee and allowed to carry on his negotiations with all sides, Presbyterians, Independents and Scots. Parliament continued to bargain with him for an agreed settlement. English legislation required the joint authority of King, Lords and Commons, and there could be no legal government without him. The Presbyterians wanted him to rule subject to their influence. Thus the revolution would be complete, with power wielded by the merchant class and the rich commoners, elected by a limited franchise based on property, and a national church enforced by law. The Independents now stood for a limited constitutional monarchy in a limited democracy, with religious freedom for all Protestants and radical changes in social relations. These demands were expressed largely through the many religious sects that dominated the thinking of the common people. A number of landed gentry supported them, the so-called 'Silken Independents'.

Now a secular movement developed to establish these aims as the law of the land through Acts of Parliament. Its supporters were called 'Levellers', and its leaders were John Lilburne, William Walwyn and Richard Overton. Lilburne had already suffered for his opinions. He had been imprisoned, kept in irons, flogged and pilloried by the Star Chamber and was to suffer under Parliament and under the Commonwealth. He was a rebel born — angry, aggressive, vituperative. Walwyn was the reverse — calm, compassionate, gentle, believing that the solution to all problems lay in the exercise of Christian love; and Overton was a cheerful man, a great wit and a high-spirited rationalist with a reputation for atheism. The writings, speeches and actions of these three were to influence considerably the progressive politics of their day, especially in the New Model Army. To the much debated question of the supreme power in the state, they replied that it lay not in the king nor in the Parliament, but in the 'sovereign people', a completely new concept.

The nation now had a Parliament dominated by the Presbyterian

15.   John Lilburne on the pillory after his trial at the Star Chamber in 1638.

'right wing', upheld by a 'left-wing' army under Leveller influence. with a king striving to exploit their differences in his own interests and still hoping for foreign intervention to restore him to his former power. The problem facing Parliament was to rid itself of the army which had become the chief threat to its policies. It decided to send part of it overseas to deal with the Irish rebellion and to disband the remainder, keeping only a small force of dragoons to maintain 'law and order'.

This was to prove difficult. Having paid off the Scots and sent them home, the state had economised at the expense of the army. The infantry had not been paid its basic eight pence a day for forty-three weeks, nor the cavalry its two shillings (for man and horse) for eighteen weeks; and it refused the army's requests for pensions for the disabled and the widows of the fallen.

In March 1646 the army was based on Saffron Walden, in Essex. General Fairfax was on sick-leave. In the great church there the Parliamentary Commissioners met the assembled officers, who demanded that the army be paid its arrears before discussing anything else. They sent in a petition asking for their money and care for the wounded and widows, and an indemnity for acts committed in the course of the war. Inside the church, to the astonishment of the Commissioners, were also seated a number of troopers and privates, rank-and-filers, who officially had no business there. Cromwell, in his seat in the House of Commons, heard the Presbyterians reject the petition and brand its signatories as 'enemies of the state and disturbers of the peace'.

Now something unprecedented occurred. The troopers, the rank and file of the cavalry, called their own mass meetings and each regiment elected two delegates (or 'Agitators', as they were called), to represent them and present their points of view. These Agitators composed a letter to Parliament stating their complaints, had it amended and approved by their regiments, and three of them, Allen, Sexby and Shephard, rode off to Westminster to present it.

It caused consternation in the Commons, who clearly saw in it the hand of the Levellers. The three troopers, questioned at the bar of the House, answered boldly that this was the agreed voice of the soldiers of Parliament, and that they were only its bearers.

The angry House ordered Cromwell to restore discipline and punish the mutineers. He arrived at Saffron Walden and at once sided with the army. He officially recognised the system of Agitators and saw that every regiment met and elected its own. With representatives of the officers they formed a Council of the Army. In the spirit of Christian brotherhood officers and men fraternised and the opinions of the privates were freely heard and discussed. In military matters discipline remained strict, but on all other matters the red-coated musketeers and the buff-coated troopers could speak their minds to the General and be answered fraternally. Suddenly the army had become an independent political force, the first ever

16.   The Sun Inn, Saffron Walden, used for meetings by the Parliamentarian army in 1647.

democratic army. Nothing like this was to happen again until the soldiers of the Tsar were to elect their soviets in 1917.

The Army Council demanded the arrears of pay. The order to disband was refused. The 'Irish Service' was refused. Some were even heard to say that the Irish were but fighting for what they themselves had fought for, their people and their freedom, papists though they were.

Soon the Agitators began independent action. A junior officer of horse, Cornet Joyce of the General's Lifeguards (he had been a tailor) 'kidnapped' the king. With five hundred men he rode to Charles at Holmby House and requested him to come away with him. 'Where is your commission for this?' asked Charles. 'Here!' answered Joyce, pointing to his troopers. The king went with him into custody, still treated with dignity and respect, pleased at the way his enemies were falling out. Cromwell and the 'Grandees', as the High Command was called, began negotiations with him.

Cromwell now became the army's spokesman in Parliament, and the voice of Parliament in the army. Fairfax returned to duty as a kind of neutral commander. The army, in its camps, billets, prayer meetings, preachings and Council, began to examine and discuss the concept of the state and its power, to find a new way of living based on social justice, equality and freedom of worship. The Bible, and mens' hearts and minds, were searched from end to end.

Most of the thinking soldiers adopted the basic philosophy of the Levellers — the 'Norman Yoke'. This held that all had gone well in England until William the Norman conquered it in 1066. He drove the native English from their lands and gave them out to his Norman backers, who then formed an aristocracy and imposed serfdom on the people; and their descendents held the land and made the laws still. Now it was for the native English, the common people, to cast off the alien Norman yoke and claim their land back from the heriditary usurpers. This combination of class-consciousness and nationalism was hard for the soldiers to resist. A republican sentiment manifested itself, regarding the king as superfluous and dangerous to a just society, and regarding the Grandees' meetings with Charles with suspicion.

The army moved to Newmarket, and called a rendezvous of the entire force, 21,000 foot and horse, to hear the Parliamentary Commissioners offer to pay off the arrears if the army agreed to disband. This was voted on by the men, one regiment at a time, and rejected. The call of home, farm or shop was strong in these citizen soldiers, but they declared that they were not mercenaries or professionals, but 'Englishmen with swords, which they would not put down until they accomplished their duty, for which they had fought and bled, to see a just and equitable settlement of the kingdom.' And for that purpose they would march on London, make a treaty with Parliament, and purge it of the 'rotten members' who stood in their way.

This caused panic in the city of London, where the ruling plutocracy called out the train-band for its defence. Parliament tried desperately to raise a new army to put down that which had won the war on its behalf. It bargained for a Scottish army to help it, and found that it had more in common with the Cavaliers than it thought. Its repression of public liberty increased; it imposed a new censorship of the press, stopped unlicensed preaching, persecuted the sectaries. The former revolutionaries were themselves launching the counter-revolution. Milton wrote sadly, 'New presbyter is but old priest writ large.'

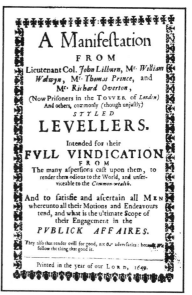

17.   The title pages of two Leveller tracts, 1649.

On its march to London the army received and protected Mr Speaker Lenthall and over one hundred 'left-wing' Members of Parliament, whose harassment inside and outside the House had been such as to inhibit and terrorise them. On its approach the city surrendered and opened its gates and the soldiers marched peacefully through, each with a sprig of laurel in his hat. The leaders of reaction in Parliament fled.

Now the New Model Army itself was showing signs of disunity. A split was growing within it over the principles on which the new England would be based. What were to be the rights of property?

Who was entitled to hold it? Whence did the state derive its power? What were the limits to its power? How were they to eliminate poverty? The Agitators did not see eye to eye on these matters with the Grandees and the 'Silken Independents'. The class issue was making itself felt.

To settle these problems a full meeting of the Council of the Army was held in Putney Church in October 1647, with Cromwell in the chair. The Agitators had brought with them a number of civilian Levellers as advisers. In the course of the debate they produced a programme they had drawn up with Leveller help, called 'An Agreement of the People',* which anticipated in many ways the Chartist programme of the nineteenth century. It was presented by a plain buff-coated trooper of the rank and file, Robert Everard. Its main points were religious freedom for all Christians (including Catholics), Parliaments of limited duration, universal adult male suffrage, and relief for the poor, sick and widowed.

It was on the question of the franchise that feelings grew high. Was a man without property, without 'a stake in the country', to have a voice in the election of its governing body? Yes, said the Agitators, in the voice of Colonel Rainsborough:

> Really I think that the poorest he that is in England
> hath a life to live, as the greatest he; and therefore . . .
> every man that is to live under a government ought first
> by his own consent to put himself under that
> government: and I do think that the poorest man in
> England is not bound in a strict sense to that govern-
> ment that he hath not a voice to put himself under.

The Grandees answered that the man without property could vote for the abolition of all property, that to hold property was a sacred and natural right, and it was for the defence of that property against interference that Parliament had fought the king. Rainsborough replied that if that were so, most of the soldiers had fought to enslave themselves, to give power over themselves to men of estates and riches.

The speeches grew more passionate; angry words were shouted. To maintain their essential unity Colonel Goffe called for a pause for prayer and God-seeking. The soldiers sought divine guidance in silence and meditation, and listened to the 'inner light' within them. A day of fasting and preaching followed, and the debate continued inconclusively. The unity of the army, the one hope for a just settlement of the kingdom, had received a severe blow. At the

---

*Its full title was 'An Agreement of the People for a firm and present Peace upon grounds of Common Right'.

proposal of Rainsborough a parade of the whole army was called at Ware, 'to settle these things'. At this parade one regiment of foot mutinied, and, marched in with the 'Agreement of the People' stuck in their hats, shouted for its implementation and marched past without orders crying, 'Justice! Soldiers Rights! Freedom!'. Cromwell himself rode up and quelled them, his sword drawn. Fourteen were arrested, a drum-head court-martial held, and one soldier, Richard Arnold, was executed by firing-squad on the spot. The rest of the army, Agitators and all, kept its ranks and looked on, knowing that its own survival depended on its unity. Fairfax, their greatly loved general, swore to resign if there were further disorders. But Cromwell then forfeited much of the trust in him.

A new situation of crisis arose. The king escaped from Hampton Court. He had been receiving the Grandees, the Presbyterians, the Scots, the Independents, and his old Cavaliers, and making contradictory promises to all. His principal hope lay in the Scots, who had agreed to invade England and restore him to the throne in return for a compulsory Calvinist Church enforced by the state (he had also promised Protestant freedom to the Independents, episcopy to the Anglicans, and Catholic emancipation to his Irish and foreign followers). He reappeared in the Isle of Wight, where he was lodged in Carisbrook Castle, and the Scots raised a large army to free him. There was little opposition from the Parliament to the royalist resurgence in the country.

Major royalist risings began in Wales, Essex, Kent and Surrey, and important castles and strongpoints captured. The New Model soldiers had once again to take the field against their own countrymen. In May 1648 the Scots crossed the border and drove south. For four bloody months this second civil war raged before the royalists were crushed. In a series of brilliant marches and campaigns Cromwell got himself between the two armies of the Scots, and, though greatly outnumbered, destroyed each in turn, at Preston and Warrington.

Parliament continued its endless negotiations with the king at Carisbrook. But the army was now thoroughly disillusioned and on the long march south had made up its mind. There was to be no more 'treating' with the perfidious king. It decided, in the words of Captain Allen, a former Agitator, that 'It was our duty . . . to call Charles Stuart, that man of blood, to an account for the blood he had shed and the mischief he had done against the Lord's cause and the people in these poor nations.'

On 2 December 1648 the army returned to London. On 5 December Parliament voted by a majority to work towards a settlement of the kingdom on the basis of the king's conditions. On 6 December, Colonel Pride, with a detachment of musketeers, stood at the entrance to the House of Commons with a list in his hands and detained all those members who had voted for it. The remaining House was nicknamed the 'Rump' (or sitting part) and ensured a Parliament of Independents. Moves were at once begun for a trial of the king for treason to the nation. There were no legal grounds for this, and the remnant of the House of Lords refused to consider it. A group in the Commons declared that the Acts of their House were the laws of the land, even without the approval of the Crown and peers. At Cromwell's insistence a commission was set up to try the king, although most people were opposed to it, including the Levellers, who thought it a political error. The court met in Westminster Hall, and the king refused to recognise its legality or even to plead guilty or not guilty; he demanded the right to trial by his peers. In law, he was correct, but this was a revolutionary tribunal that made its own law. After several days of argument (and many protests from outside) he was found guilty and sentenced to death, and on 30 January 1649 he was publicly beheaded in Whitehall proclaiming to the last that he stood for the laws of England. The army exulted, but many in the crowd wept. 'Church and state' had acquired an invaluable martyr and a wave of horror swept the royal courts of Europe.

The Rump declared the country a republic or 'Commonwealth' and set up a Council of State, with Cromwell as its President. The Levellers called for the acceptance of the clauses of the 'Agreement of the People'. Cromwell had their leaders imprisoned and ignored a petition for their release backed by 10,000 signatures. To break the influence of the Levellers in the army he ordered the most militant regiments to embark for Ireland. Some men of Colonel Whalley's regiment demonstrated in Bishopsgate, demanding their arrears. Cromwell acted with his usual speed, seized the leaders and condemned five of them to death. Four were reprieved, but Trooper Robert Lockyer, twenty-three years old and with seven years of service, was shot in St Paul's churchyard. He said, as the firing-squad was loading, 'I am troubled that so small a thing as contention for pay should allow my enemies to take away my life.' He then told his executioners that obedience to orders did not acquit them of murder. His body was followed to the grave by his comrades marching in step, with trumpets blowing, and many thousands of Londoners behind. All wore the sea-green ribbon of the Levellers.

There were simultaneous mutinies of Leveller army units at Banbury and Salisbury, demanding acceptance of the 'Agreement', and the two joined forces. Cromwell and his 'loyal' troops marched ninety miles in two days and surprised them asleep at Burford, in the Cotswolds. The Levellers were 1,500 strong, and expecting reinforcements, and after a brief resistance were defeated. Their leader, Captain Thompson, refused to surrender and fought until he was cut down. Three corporals who refused to resume duty were imprisoned

18.   The trial of King Charles I, 1649, from a contemporary engraving.

in the church and shot next day. Scratched into the lead lining of the font the visitor can today read the pathetic inscription: 'Anthony Sedley, Prisner, 1649'.

With this episode the army was 'tamed', and the apostasy of Cromwell established. He accepted the command of the Irish Service, and drove from the New Model men who refused to serve in it. The Leveller leaders, from their prison in the Tower, protested that the death sentence by court-martial in time of peace 'was both treason and murder'.

After crushing the Leveller mutiny Cromwell and Fairfax were awarded honorary degrees by Oxford University, the great stronghold of royalist sentiment; and the plutocrats of London accepted the rule of the Council of State and gave a great banquet in its honour. At the high table Cromwell and Fairfax were presented with gold plate of great value. The 'Agreement of the People' was conveniently forgotten.

The Good Old Cause, as the Levellers called their struggle for republicanism and democracy, was in eclipse. The history of the Commonwealth with Cromwell as Lord Protector, and the subsequent restoration of the monarchy after his death, lies outside the province of this book. But as the new king, Charles II, took his revenge on the regicides in 1660, and Major Harrison of the New Model was being drawn to his execution on a hurdle, a bystander sneered at him, 'Where is your Good Old Cause now?' And Harrison clapped his hands to his heart and answered, 'Here it is, and I go to seal with my blood . . . I go to suffer for the most glorious cause that ever was in the world.'

The old Agitator, Richard Rumbold, awaiting the executioner on the scaffold, cried to the watching crowd his testimony of faith. 'I am sure there was no man born marked of God above another; for no man comes into the world with a saddle on his back, neither any booted and spurred to ride him.'

The Good Old Cause did not die with its pioneers, nor did the 'Agreement of the People'. They lived on in the hearts of men and women who bequeathed their ideals to their children and in the nineteenth century the relevant clauses became the bases of our own democracy.

SELECT BIBLIOGRAPHY

Brailsford, H. N., *The Levellers and the English Revolution*, Cresset Press.
Hill, C., *Puritanism and Revolution*, Secker and Warburg, 1958.
Slater, M., *Englishmen With Swords*, Bodley Head.
Woodhouse, A. S. P. (ed), *Puritanism and Liberty*, Dent, 1951.

CHAPTER VII

Gerard Winstanley and the Diggers

There have been many visionaries and theorists of communism in England since John Ball preached his sermon on Blackheath. The first of them to put his ideas into practice was Gerard Winstanley.

In April 1649, two months after the execution of Charles I, the people of the parish of Walton-on-Thames in Surrey were surprised to see a group of about a dozen families of the labourer class encamped on the waste land of St George's Hill nearby. They had put up some rough huts and tents, tethered a few head of cattle around, and were employed in digging, manuring and planting the common — and this was on a Sunday morning! On being asked who they were, and what they were doing, their spokesman replied quietly that they were Diggers, or True Levellers, and that they were establishing 'the community of the people'; that they were throwing off the Norman yoke and taking back the land and its fruits as a common heritage that belonged to all, but had been stolen from them. They would not meddle with any man's property or break any fences, but only put into use land which was common and untilled; and this they would do without force or violence, but by the powers of love, reason and example. Any man could come and join them, and share their food and property.

Thus appeared the first recorded communist settlement in England. Its leader, spokesman and philosopher was Gerard Winstanley.

Little is known of his personal life. He was probably born in Wigan in 1609, where his father was a tradesman. He came to London to be apprenticed in the cloth trade, and set up his own shop. By 1643 his business had failed, and he supported himself by working as a cowherd in Surrey.

He seems to have come under Baptist influence in his youth, and agreed with their renunciation of the idea of an organised national church that one could be born into. (They rejected infant baptism, and only accepted mature members who came voluntarily to join them as a 'gathered church'.) He occupied himself with writing a series of religious pamphlets, in which he developed his ideas into a kind of rational humanism without a personal god or saviour, heaven or hell. Eventually he perceived God as 'reason' itself. He did not, however, reject the 'inner light' or 'voice' which spoke to every individual who would listen for it.

His rational outlook led him to examine human relationships and politics, and he must have read most of the radical literature of his time and found it wanting. For him, the essence of the matter was not the right of all to vote and to sit on councils, as the Levellers claimed. The rich would still own the land and its produce, the poor would still be in bondage to them. No matter what the law said, there could never be true equality between those who employed the labour of others for their own enrichment and those who had to provide that labour in order to live. This conflict of interest, based on property or the lack of it, was the principal obstacle to the rule of love. The land had been given to no man; it was the common heritage of all and had been taken from them, and kept from them, by force and fraud. 'The poorest man hath as true a title and just right to the land as the richest man.' Political freedom alone was of little use to the poor: 'True freedom lies where a man receives his nourishment . . . That is, in the use of the earth. A man had better have no body than no food for it.'

He claimed that there was enough unused land in England to ensure plenty for all, if it were well cultivated. Unlike many agrarian reformers, Winstanley was opposed to the expropriated land being redistributed as plots to the peasantry. This would only perpetuate the evils of 'property', which he saw as the major cause of oppression and conflict. He envisaged a classless society in which all men worked together on land they owned communally and shared the produce. There was to be no money, buying or selling, but an equitable system of exchange. There would be large communal store-houses to which people could bring their products and from which they could take whatever they needed. Magistrates would be elected, and punishments would be mild and corrective. 'What need have we of prisons, of whipping and hanging laws to bring one another into bondage?'

There would have to be a militia of the people for order and defence, and the national government would be through annual parliament elected by male suffrage. There was to be complete religious freedom, with marriage and burial becoming purely secular ceremonies.

Education was to be the right of all children male and female, followed by craft and trade training. Every incentive was to be given to the development and application of science, and 'inventors' would be the only people awarded honours. All of life, labour and mind would 'serve to add to the beauty of our commonwealth'.

Though he did not accept the Bible as literal truth, Winstanley could quote it widely in support of his views and he regarded the advent of the new 'commonwealth' as the fulfilment of the prophesied 'Second Coming of Christ', whom he hailed as the 'Chief Leveller'.

How was this great change in human affairs to be brought about? The state had its armed forces, the landowners their wealth and power, the churches their doctrines to prevent it: and pacifism and non-violence was part of the Diggers' creed. The only way was by the force of example. Let it begin with a small symbolic community, and soon thousands would see that this was a better way of living, renounce their property and possessions and join the movement. Even without them, there were enough landless and poor men to ensure its success.

Winstanley gave his ideas to the world in a series of small books, ranging from *The New Law of Righteousness,* which is a kind of manifesto in the simple language of the people, to *The Law of Freedom in a Platform* of 1652, in which he has fully worked out his policies on the basis of practical experience. They were not well received by most of the Levellers. Lilburne denounced the 'erroneous tenets of the poor Diggers at St George's Hill', and in a statement the movement stressed that 'it was the utmost of our aim that . . . every man, with as much security as may be, should enjoy his property'.

Winstanley, in his meditations, heard his 'inner voice' three times

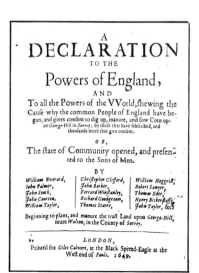
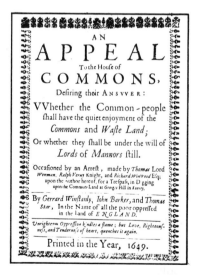

19. The title pages of two Digger tracts, 1649.

repeat: 'Work together; eat bread together; declare all this abroad. Israel shall neither take hire, nor give hire. Whoever labours the earth for any person or persons that are lifted up to rule over others, and doth not look upon themselves as equal to all others in the creation, the hand of the Lord shall be upon that labourer.'

Obedient to this call, Winstanley and his comrade John Everard gathered their small following and established their 'commonwealth' on St George's Hill. Most of them were poor labourers, but some were probably what we would today call 'drop-outs', people who had rejected their contemporary society.

The Diggers at once aroused suspicion and hostility among the local people, especially the freeholding farmers and clergy. They showed no desire to renounce their property. But there was sympathy as well; in the first weeks a number accepted the invitation to join them and 'make the earth a common treasury of livelihood to all mankind'. The strength of the community rose to about one hundred activists, of whom the names of seventy-three are known.

Prominent among the enemies of the colony was a local minister, Parson Platt. He and the lord of the manor, Mr Drake, were probably the organisers and financiers of the first attack upon it. About a hundred men rushed in, trampled the planted seed, burned some huts, carried away tools, and beat up and dragged away some of the Diggers. The Kingston JPs ordered their release and dispersed the mob, as there were no charges laid against the Diggers. True to their pacifist conviction, they had made no physical resistance, but sought to convince the attackers that they were acting wrongly.

News of this affair reached the Council of State. Preoccupied with the Levellers, the army and the royalists, they passed the matter on to General Fairfax, who sent a Captain Gladman, with two troops of horse, to investigate. Gladman met the Diggers, and reported that it was a trivial matter of a few homeless eccentrics and fanatics, and he brought Winstanley and Everard to explain themselves to the General. They stood before him 'covered' (that is, with their hats on) symbolising their rejection of rank. Fairfax, always a courteous gentleman, heard them out while they expounded their policy and stressed their doctrine of pacifism; and then dismissed them politely. He probably agreed with Captain Gladman.

This interview did much to publicise their activities, but a local mob attacked them so fiercely that they had to abandon their ground and leave. These reverses would have disheartened others, but the Diggers, confident that their way was right, returned after a few days and began to tend the land once more.

Their position seemed hopeless. Time and again their corn and vegetables were uprooted, their huts pulled down, their precious tools smashed or stolen, their cattle maltreated. Patiently they resumed their work, repairing and replanting. They cheered and encouraged one another with their songs. One begins:

> You noble Diggers all, stand up now, stand up now,
> You noble Diggers all, stand up now,
> The waste land to maintain, seeing cavaliers by name
> Your digging do disdain, and persons all defame,
> Stand up now!
>
> Your houses they pull down, stand up now, stand up now,
> Your houses they pull down, stand up now,
> Your houses they pull down, to fright poor men in town,
> But the gentry must come down, and the poor shall wear the crown,
> Stand up now, Diggers all!
>
> The club is all their law, stand up now, stand up now,
> The club is all their law, stand up now,
> The club is all their law, to keep poor men in awe,
> But they no vision saw, to maintain such a law,
> Stand up now, Diggers all!

In another song, the last verse includes the lines:

> But Freedom is not won
> Neither by sword nor gun . . .
> Then Clubs and Diamonds cast away
> For Spades and Hearts must win the day.

The great hosts of expected newcomers failed to materialise. In the face of continual persecution the Diggers continued their self-appointed task of reclaiming the land for the people. They sent speakers about the country to raise funds and start new 'commonwealths' on unused lands; and Digger colonies were founded at six provincial centres.

They were still working on St George's Hill in June, when a party of soldiers raided them, burned a hut and attacked a man and a boy at work there, causing them serious injury. Winstanley wrote protesting to Fairfax, but received no reply. Four Diggers were afterwards assaulted, one of whom was left for dead. Their cart, carrying wood to rebuild the simple shelters, was waylaid and destroyed, and their horse crippled. The local clergy ordered a boycott, forbidding their flocks to give or sell them food or shelter, or have anything to do with these obstinate heretics.

At last the law moved against them, and Mr Drake, lord of the manor, charged them with trespass before Kingston Court. They were not told the charge, they were not allowed to defend themselves or plead their case, their written defence was refused, and after hearing only Drake's case, the Diggers were fined £10 each, plus costs, which the court knew they could never pay. Bailiffs came and drove off their four remaining cows. (These were later rescued and returned by sympathetic strangers.)

The raids, attacks and assaults by local mobs at the instigation of parsons and landowners continued. Each time the Diggers returned and began again. A band of soldiers were sent under the orders of Mr Drake to burn their buildings and carry everything else away. Winstanley reported that they performed this duty with great reluctance and many apologies, one of them even leaving a small donation. Eventually, after eleven months of toil and struggle, the hungry Diggers, robbed of their harvest, abandoned the site and moved to Cobham Heath nearby, which they began to manure and dig. They were followed there by Parson Platt with a band of armed men, who destroyed everything they had brought with them. An armed watch was held on the heath by day and night, and an oath taken to kill every Digger who returned to it. And with that the brave attempt to throw off the Norman yoke and establish the community of the people seems to have reached an end.

The provincial 'commonwealths' fared no better. After a similar period of hardship they were destroyed by persecution, official or unofficial. No records remain of the fates of the Diggers. It seems that Winstanley and a small group were given employment for a while by a sympathetic and religious landowner, Lady Eleanor Davies of Pirton, Hertfordshire, who considered herself an inspired prophetess.

In 1652 Winstanley published his *Law of Freedom in a Platform*. After the chastening experiences of 1649 and 1650 he no longer seemed to think that 'community' could be achieved by mere example, but had to be imposed from above. Like so many other early reformers and philosophers he sought a 'prince' or powerful patron to put his system into practice. He dedicated his book to the great man of the day, Oliver Cromwell, with an appeal to him to win eternal fame by thus lifting the Norman yoke and ushering in the worldly millennium, or else to go down to history as a tyrant and despot for upholding it. 'Lose not your crown. Take it up and wear it . . . You have the power in your hand to act for Common Freedom. I have no power.' There was no response from Cromwell.

The Diggers and their ideals disappear for a while under the surface of history, to reappear, transformed, as part of the substance of the 'scientific socialism' of the nineteenth century.

SELECT BIBLIOGRAPHY

Petegorsky, D. W., *Left-Wing Democracy in the English Civil War*, Gollancz, 1940.

CHAPTER VIII

Monmouth's Rebellion

The Good Old Cause of political democracy, religious liberty and republicanism was to make a brief reappearance in the summer of 1685 — in the unlikely guise of the following of a Stuart pretender to the throne.

Charles II had many children, but unfortunately none of them was legitimate, and therefore at his death in 1685 the succession fell to his brother, the Duke of York, who became King James II. He was a Roman Catholic, and his ambition was to restore Catholicism and royal absolutism to England. He sought to achieve his aims by an oppressive state apparatus of spies, provocateurs, pressurised judges and rigged elections, with treason trials frequently leading to the execution block. Many of the opposition fled the country to find safety in the Netherlands.

Among these was James Scott, Duke of Monmouth. He was the eldest of Charles's sons, but unlike his half-brothers he claimed to be legitimate, the offspring of an early secret marriage between Charles and a woman called Lucy Waters; the proof of this was kept in a black box which was not obtainable. He was in his thirties, a soldier and an athlete, and a very personable and popular figure. He had one great virtue politically — he was a self-proclaimed Protestant; indeed he was known as 'the Protestant Duke'. Influenced by his exalted rank and military experience, the conspirators against James II made him their leader. These were a varied group, ranging from noblemen out of favour to old Cromwellian republicans. A plot was conceived among these exiles to invade England, put themselves at the head of a popular rising, remove James and his Catholic nominees and supporters, and propose Monmouth to Parliament as the new, rightful, Protestant king.

Money was gathered for this cause, but not enough. Arms were collected, but not enough. Soldiers, including foreign mercenaries and veterans of the New Model Army, were enrolled to lead the rebellion. The Duke of Argyll was to land in Scotland, Monmouth in the west country. The persecuted Scottish Covenanters would rise for Argyll; the oppressed dissenters and sectaries, with the

Anglicans, common and gentle of Dorset, Devon and Somerset would follow Monmouth. Both forces would advance on London, where a rising of militant Protestants would prepare for the surrender of the city. James would be dethroned, and, hopefully, Parliament would accept the legitimacy of Monmouth.

The Duke of Argyll left for Scotland. Monmouth, with three ships and 150 men, landed unopposed at the little port of Lyme (now Lyme Regis) in Dorset on 11 June 1685.

The western area selected for the landing was a prosperous part of the country, one of the most developed industrially, though manufacture was still in the 'cottage' stage. The basic product was cloth, and many of the townsfolk were self-employed artisans and their journeymen and apprentices, engaged in the various processes of cloth-making. It had been strongly parliamentarian in the Civil War and a fruitful recruiting ground for the New Model Army. The Good Old Cause was still secretly cherished by the veterans, and bequeathed to their sons. Firmly Protestant, with a large proportion of illegal dissenters and sectaries, it was expected to provide the Protestant Duke with a sufficient army; and large numbers of the Anglican gentry and nobility were thought to be waiting to join them.

The people of Lyme watched in surprise as the invaders disembarked, with their arms and four small cannon, and marched into the market-place. There a long proclamation was read out, accusing King James of poisoning his royal brother, of tyranny, of oppression, of perverting the laws of England, of seeking to destroy the Protestant faith and put England under the Pope and the Catholic powers of Europe. Therefore the Duke of Monmouth with his friends and supporters would make war on him and bring him to justice; Monmouth's own title and reward would be left to the decision of 'the Wisdom, Justice and Authority of a Parliament legally chosen and acting with Freedom'.

The duke then spread his banner to the wind — blue and gold, with the slogan 'Fear nothing but God' — and appealed for recruits.

Many young men came forward at once; 116 joined up, or one-third of the able-bodied male population; and the next day hundreds came in from surrounding farms and villages. Some were men of advanced age, old Cromwellians, New Model veterans, sectaries and their preachers. It seems that many of the volunteers looked somewhat sceptically on the duke and his few high-born leaders who seemed to embody not a little 'the world, the flesh and the devil'; but if they could get rid of King James, the first step would have been taken towards the revival of the Good Old Cause.

Here and there in Lyme ageing men came out on to the streets wearing the red or buff coats of the New Model Army that had not been seen for twenty-five years, and hastened to help in training the raw recruits. Many more sent their sons, or even enrolled with them. Every volunteer knew that there were bloody battles ahead, and, if defeated or captured, each of them had committed high treason and could be hanged, drawn and quartered.

For three days recruiting and training went on. The men were hastily taught the elaborate ritual for loading and firing muskets, handling the sixteen-foot pikes in unison, marching and manoeuvring in regiments and detachments. Horses were purchased or commandeered for a cavalry arm and a wagon train. But there was little response from the local gentry and nobility who had been expected to come in large numbers and make the army respectable. The Anglican clergy and their flocks and bishops stayed conspicuously away. Monmouth's following remained an army of workmen, shopkeepers, artisans and labourers inspired by radicalism, and therefore a threat to the whole social order. Once again the revolutionary outbursts of the Old Testament prophets provided the texts for the soldier-preachers, like the words from Ezekial; 'Remove the diadem, take off the crown . . . exalt him that is low, and abase him that is high . . . I will overturn, overturn, overturn it, and it shall be no more.'

Meanwhile reports from Scotland and London were eagerly awaited.

News of the rebellion soon travelled to the capital, and the startled king at once began to take counter-measures. The projected London rising was easily prevented by the arrest of hundreds of known radicals and sectaries, while strong army patrols guarded streets and buildings. The western county militias were called out. These were amateur part-time armies that paraded one day a month for training (much of which was reputedly done in taverns) and could be mobilised for local emergencies. Their function was to 'contain' the rebel army and prevent recruits and supplies reaching it until the regular forces arrived to destroy it. Meanwhile the royal regiments were being rapidly concentrated, armed and equipped. Lyme is 150 miles from London, some ten days' march for an infantry unit. The Protestant Duke had that time to train his raw levies, turn them into a disciplined fighting force and manoeuvre them so as to meet the royal troops with the maximum advantage. Marching against him were professionals of long standing with battle honours won on many fields in Europe and North Africa, under the command of the brilliant Lord John Churchill, later to win martial fame as the unbeatable Duke of Marlborough.

On 15 June Monmouth led his army north out of Lyme, now some 1,500 foot, with a scratch cavalry force mounted on carriage and farm horses unused to drill or to the noise of guns. Lord Grey was his General of Horse. He knew now that the London rising would not take place, that they had waited for a signal from him to act, while he waited for one from them that they had done so. He knew, too, that the Scottish rising was still-born, and Argyll captured. His one hope now was for a rapid increase in numbers, but the militia all round him made it difficult for his supporters to reach him. If he could take Bristol or Exeter, both large and important cities full of potential recruits, he would win a firm base from which to advance. He set his march therefore for Taunton, a Puritan stronghold, but first dispatched a force of musketeers and cavalry, under Lord Grey, to drive the militia out of Bridport, eight miles away. There a sharp fight took place in the village street, but, instead of charging the militia foot, Lord Grey and his cavalry turned tail at the first shots and galloped fast back to Lyme, leaving the musketeers to fight without support. In this first engagement the rebels lost thirty men, seven of them killed, but captured thirty invaluable horses. The soldiers drew their own conclusions on the merits of their cavalry and its noble commander. The main body marched on to find Axminster held by the militia, who were glad to abandon it after a spirited infantry attack, and a number who were captured enlisted under Monmouth. The next day Monmouth led his men into Taunton. Here there was little doubt where the townsfolk's sympathies lay. He was greeted by the whole population lining the streets to cheer him, all with sprigs of greenery in their hats. Doors and windows were garlanded and decorated, the church bells rang out a welcome, and the young ladies of a local academy for gentlewomen solemnly presented him with an embroidered silken banner they had made out of their petticoats. Enough men enlisted to add a new regiment to the army, now more than 5,000 strong. The stores of muskets and pikes had long been exhausted, and many of the recruits were armed with scythe-blades lashed on to six-foot poles; powerful slashing weapons, but not to be compared to pikes for resisting cavalry.

Monmouth spent three days in Taunton, revelling in his popularity, while the royal troops drew ever nearer. On the second day of his stay, under pressure from his leading captains and supporters, he summoned the justices, aldermen and civic dignitaries to the Market Cross and had his proclamation read out. Then, to the anger of many of his followers, he had himself solemnly declared King of England without waiting for victory or the approval of Parliament. The Taunton people at once began to hail 'King Monmouth', and did so on bended knee. He, in the manner royal, extended his had to be kissed, and began to 'touch' sufferers from scrofula, 'the king's evil', who could only be cured by the touch of a king. His republican soldiers accepted all this quietly. They would deal with this problem after their victory, which could only be won by maintaining their present unity. 'We submitted to it,' said Colonel

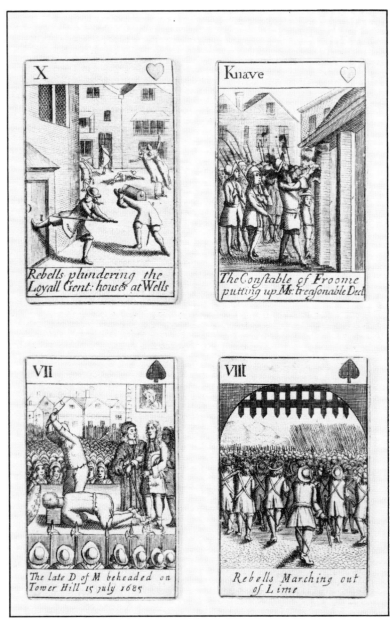

20.   Playing cards of 1685 illustrating Monmouth's Rebellion.

Nathaniel Wade. He was the son of a New Model major, commander of the Red Regiment and a sworn republican.

The new 'king' then declared that the Westminster Parliament was 'a rebellious and treasonable convention, to be pursued and prosecuted as rebels and traitors'. But still the respectable Anglican gentry stayed away, and their clergy and bishops repudiated him.

In the neighbouring towns the first units of King James's cavalry and dragoons were assembling. The foot regiments were approaching rapidly. In Monmouth's camp there was no clear strategic plan. He grew to be some 6,000 strong in foot, with about 1,000 horse. Lord Churchill (now replaced as King James's commander by Lord Faversham) expected him to attack and destroy the small royalist units as they arrived, one by one before they could concentrate, as he could easily have done. But, instead, Monmouth, after wasting precious days at Taunton, marched his whole army off towards Bristol, the great port and second city of the kingdom, intending to cross the River Avon by Keynsham Bridge. A night was spent at Bridgwater, and the army marched for two days through pouring rain. Royal troops were now all round them, and they were shadowed and followed by cavalry patrols. Keynsham Bridge had been breached by the militia, but Monmouth's men repaired it and the rebels marched across into the village, now only a few miles from Bristol. News came that the militia and regulars had fortified the city and put it in a state of defence.

As Monmouth's van rode into Keynsham it was furiously charged by 350 royal horse. There was a sharp fight, and the attackers were driven off. Monmouth decided that the whole of the royal army lay between him and fortified Bristol; he abandoned his plan, turned about, and marched to Bath, fifteen miles to the east. He found that city defended and sent his trumpeter, protected by military tradition, to demand that the Bath militia surrender their town to Monmouth, their rightful king. Despite the 'rules of war', their answer was to shoot him dead as a traitor.

The rebel army then turned south and camped for the night in the fields round Norton St Phillips (then known as Phillips Norton), soaked, weary and depressed.

There was no rest for them that evening. They were attacked by a strong body of regulars, foot and horse, and a battle ensued in which the half-trained rebels faced a cavalry charge and repulsed it, and fought the professional infantry along the fields and hedges until the enemy were forced to break off the engagement and run. Monmouth's four cannon had opened fire and acquitted themselves well, though out-gunned. Given a reliable regiment of horse, they could have counter-attacked and won an important victory. Cheered and inspired by this success, the outcome of sheer courage against superior arms, the rebels recovered their spirits and marched away next morning through Frome and back to Bridgwater; they reached that town in the evening of Saturday 4 July, and camped in the sodden meadows around it.

The weather was continually bad. It had rained for almost the whole fortnight of marching, and many of the men's boots were leaking and falling apart. For three days they remained encamped, resting under arms, and the royal enemy was content to rest too, worn out with their long forced march from London. Many of the rebels were local men and took the opportunity to visit their homes and families, and to take farewells that in so many cases were to be their last.

Monmouth's high command sought desperately to form a constructive strategy. They could try to evade the enemy and march direct on London, or make a second and more determined attack on Bristol. They could fortify a strongpoint and invite attack under the most favourable conditions. To add to their troubles King James now proclaimed a free pardon to all who would leave Monmouth's service and lay down their arms, and had he been included in it the 'Protestant Duke' would have availed himself of the offer and ended the campaign. But he was excluded and a price put on his head, dead or alive.

The council of war considered fortifying Bridgewater and standing a siege there, to the dismay of the citizens. But the royal artillery train was now in the vicinity, and the idea was abandoned.

More than two hundred of the rebels had already been killed and increasing numbers were taking the kings offer and deserting. The rebellion had passed its peak, and was beginning to decline. If there was to be any success it had to be won soon, or all hope would be gone. A decision was taken to march again on Bristol while it was yet defended mainly by the militia.

Suddenly the plan was dropped. Scouts came in with reports that the main body of the royalist forces, some 3,000-4,000 foot, with a strong cavalry arm and cannon, was camped for the night on the soft flat plain of Sedgemoor, cut by drainage ditches known locally as 'rhines'. They lay between the villages of Chedzoy and Western Zoyland, about three and a half miles away. They slept, thinking themselves safe till morning, having set up no defence works or entrenchments.

There and then Monmouth and his captains decided on that most difficult and risky of all military manoeuvres, a night attack. The troops were roused and stood-to, and the battle plans made. They would march along the Bristol road for some two miles, turn off down a narrow lane north of Chedzoy, make a detour across Sedgemoor and burst upon the enemy suddenly from their rear. Everything depended on surprise, and total silence was essential. At eleven o'clock on the night of 4 July, with the darkness intensified by a mist on the moors, the rebels marched out to battle. Orders were given that if any man spoke aloud or made any noise he was at once to be knocked on the head by his neighbours.

They reached the turn-off undetected. Five hundred horse under Lord Grey led the way down the lane and out on to the open moor. They were halted by a 'rhine' across their front that seemed too deep to wade and too wide to leap, and their guide went off in the dark to find the stone that marked the hard-bottomed crossing-place. He ran up and down, searching. So far all had gone well, but suddenly the protective silence was shattered by a pistol-shot. It may have been accidentally fired by a rebel, or deliberately by a sentry peering across the rhine. But over the water in the enemy's camp the drums began to beat and the soldiers turned out hurriedly and stood to their arms. In a few minutes, lines of musketeers faced Monmouth's men across the ditch. Grey's vanguard found their crossing, used it, and charged a body of royalist horse but were driven off and retreated to rejoin their main force. Only one troop of the rebel horse, under Captain John Jones, an old Cromwellian Ironside, stayed to hold the crossing. It was soon cut to pieces. Seeking another crossing-place, Lord Grey and his troopers were exposed to heavy musketry fire on their flank. Terrified by the noise and red flashes, the untrained horses turned tail, stampeded, and carried their riders out of the battle.

The following rebel infantry came up at a run and lined the ditches, and the two sides fought a point-blank musketry duel across the black water. On each flank the king's horse advanced across the rhines, wading them easily, and charged the pikemen and scythemen drawn up in defensive stands or squares. Soon some of these formations were broken and the horsemen pursued the fleeing rebels pitilessly, cutting them down as they ran.

As the light of the early sun broke through the mist and smoke, Monmouth looked about him. The king's cannons were now firing, cutting great gaps in his infantry lines, but his musketeers were still holding their ground, taking the royal shot and returning it as fast as they could load and fire. Squares were still withstanding and repelling charges of horse. This was the moment for decisive leadership, for a rally that could re-form the army and draw its remnants away with some safety and honour.

The Protestant Duke called Lord Grey and a few of his highest officers to him. There was a brief discussion; then they stripped off their metal breastplates, threw away their insignias of rank, dug in their spurs, and galloped away towards Bridgewater, deserting their posts and abandoning the men who were dying for them.

Long after this disgraceful flight the rebels fought on: but by mid-morning there were none left on the field but the dead and wounded. Here at Sedgemoor the last pitched battle on English soil had been fought, and the last great armed rebellion crushed.

The number of rebels who died at Sedgemoor has never been accurately ascertained. A militiaman who watched a mass burial in a common pit claimed to have counted 1,384, and another pile of 174 bodies. This would account for about a quarter of Monmouth's effectives. The royal army probably lost about fifty, with 200 wounded. For days after the battle the king's men scoured the surrounding country, hanging and butchering fugitives and wounded and any man they suspected of participation. King James gave his soldiers a free hand outside the law, and they took full advantage of it. All over the West Country men hung from gibbets by the score. Eventually the summary killing ceased, and six weeks of military repression succeeded it. About 1,500 men were rounded up and captured, and confined in appalling conditions to await trial. The charge was treason, and it embraced any person who gave food, shelter or aid to the fugitives, or even dressed their wounds.

Monmouth himself was found hiding in a muddy ditch dressed in peasant clothing, with no trace of his self-assumed regality left. He was sent to London and kept in the Tower, where he employed himself in writing abject and degrading letters pleading for mercy. He even offered to become a Catholic and act as informer. He secured an interview with King James, where he lay on the floor and grovelled, begging for his life. All this only moved the king to contempt, and on 15 July the Protestant Duke was beheaded on Tower Hill. The headsman botched the job, taking five strokes of the axe to decapitate him.

The Lord Chief Justice of England, Judge Jeffreys, was sent down to try the captives, and the travesty of law known as the 'Bloody Assizes' took place. He bullied, insulted and threatened prisoners and witnesses alike, and played the part of prosecutor as well as judge. His first victim was a seventy-year-old gentlewoman, Dame Alice Lisle, whose servants had given shelter to some fleeing rebels. She pleaded not guilty, claiming ignorance of the men's politics and activities. She was obviously weak-minded, senile and hard of hearing, but Jeffreys sentenced her to be burnt alive. As an act of clemency by the king, this was commuted to beheading.

Judge Jeffreys, with his four assistant judges, had to try many hundreds of prisoners during the short term of the assizes, and he did so by trying them in large groups. At Dorchester, on the first day, he tried ninety-eight of them, of whom thirty pleaded not guilty. All were sentenced to be hanged, drawn and quartered. In nine days he sentenced 1,336 rebels to death, apart from the normal business of the assizes. Executions were still being carried out a month later. So great was the pressure of work on the executioners (drawing and quartering was slow work, though butchers were employed to help out) that many men were reprieved to be sold off as indented labourers to work on the plantations in the West Indies. Great courtiers and noblemen competed for 'gifts' of chained gangs of those wretched slaves who could be sold so profitably to the English sugar-planters.

Few of the enthusiasts who volunteered so eagerly to fight under Monmouth's banner ever saw home and family again. Their deeds and struggles, and their terrible punishment, have become part of the tales and legends of the West Country.

King James had only another three years to reign. The powerful Whig nobility and plutocrats sought to be rid of him, but not through the medium of a radical army. In 1688 they treasonably invited the Dutch husband of his daughter Mary, Prince William of Orange, to invade England and assume the crown. William landed at Torbay with a large army of foreign mercenaries, and those statesmen, soldiers, justices who had opposed the treason of Monmouth so vigorously now deserted their lawful king for the pretender. James fled the country, the last of the ill-fated Stuart kings, and this act of treason by almost the whole of the Establishment has since been known as 'the Glorious Revolution of 1688'.

As Sir John Harrington wrote:

> Treason doth never prosper. What's the reason?
> Why, if it prosper, none dare call it treason.

SELECT BIBLIOGRAPHY

Chevenix-Trench, C., *The Western Rising*, Longmans.
Earle, P., *Monmouth's Rebels*, Weidenfeld and Nicolson.

CHAPTER IX

The Industrial Revolution

The 'Glorious Revolution' of 1688, and its Bill of Rights, laid the basis for a form of state suitable for the advancement of the industrial, mercantile and financial classes. A series of successful wars and the capture of new colonies and bases, east and west, added to the wealth of the traders and opened up great opportunities for money-making. English cloth, produced and processed in thousands of cottages and small workshops, continued to dominate the markets of Europe and, indeed, the world. What was known as the 'Golden Triangle' brought many a speculative city burgher into the ranks of the wealthy, and with the purchase of a country estate made 'gentlemen' out of him and his heirs. This consisted of sending a shipload of English textiles to an African port, disposing of it there, spending the money gained on the purchase of kidnapped Africans from slave traders, sailing them to the West Indies or America where they would fetch a good price, and returning home with a locally acquired cargo of sugar or tobacco.

The growing amounts of capital available for investment from the middle of the eighteenth century found its utilisation in carrying through the great changes in English life and work known as the Industrial Revolution. Within little more than the space of a century the country ceased to be a nation of self-employed villagers primarily engaged in agriculture and domestic crafts to become a population of largely town-dwelling propertyless wage-earners.

One of its earliest manifestations lay in the improvement of agriculture which called for increased enclosures of common lands and the old open fields. Scientific development of large-scale farming raised yield and productivity enormously, and the introduction of turnips, clover and other crops for cattle food ended the wasteful system of one-third of the arable land lying fallow for a year. Thus, with ample winter fodder, the huge autumnal slaughtering was abandoned. Herds increased, stock improved, and fresh meat became available all the year round. All this meant that far fewer people could produce much more food, and the need for a peasantry disappeared. Large numbers of small farmers, villagers, and those

The Industrial Revolution 113

who combined simple industry with a small holding found themselves completely cut off from the land, ruined, and made homeless. They had no option but to seek work as labourers on the new farms or the new industries, or to drag out a miserable existence on parish relief or in the workhouse.

An elderly stocking-maker, looking back on his childhood in the pre-industrial years, wrote:

> [The stockingers] lived at comparative ease and plenty, having right of common for pig and poultry, and sometimes for a cow. They each had a garden, a barrel of home-brewed ale, a weekday suit of clothes and one for Sundays, and plenty of leisure.

A jingle of the time expresses the situation forcefully:

> The laws imprisons man or woman
> Who steals the goose from off the common
> But lets the greater felon loose,
> Who steals the common from the goose.

The poet Goldsmith began his *Deserted Village* in 1770 with a topical lament:

> Ill fares the land, to hastening ills a prey,
> Where wealth accumulates and men decay.

Ingenious machines were invented that did the work of many men. Industrial production soared. The development of the steam engine from a pumping device to a locomotive capable of powerful and rapid traction and a source of power for other machines, marked the beginning of a new era. Enterprising businessmen were building novel structures called 'factories' (or mills) where they installed their own looms and other machines, worked at first by water and then by steam power. They owned the buildings, the machines and the raw materials, employed labour to process and work it, and claimed the finished product as their own. This was 'commodity production', now long taken for granted, but a revolutionary innovation in its time, the basic productive unit of the new capitalist system. They even broke the manufacturing process down into divisions of labour each carried out by different workers, thus putting an end to the pleasure of work and the pride of the craftsman.

The development of the railways, the demands for more and better machines, and those of the state for armaments and ships led to a vast growth of mining and the metal industries. Unimportant villages and small provincial towns situated in the coal and ore belts grew in a few years into huge conurbations — Birmingham, Leeds, Manchester, etc. England was entering that dramatic era that was to make it into the world's first great industrial nation, the 'workshop of the world' with the world's first great landless working class.

These early decades of the new capitalist system, unrestrained and uncontrolled by law or tradition, were, for the masses of the population, years of misery and suffering unique in our national history. The domestic producers were unable to compete with the new machines no matter how long or hard they worked. They went out of business in entire trades at a time. (The price paid for weaving a certain kind of cloth piece fell from thirty-nine shillings and nine pence in 1795 to five shillings in 1830.) The ruined craftsmen became paupers living in the punitive workhouses or rotting on the meagre poor-law relief, or sometimes they became the wage-slaves of the machines that had destroyed them, submitting to their iron discipline for fourteen or sixteen hours a day.

An anonymous 'Lamentation' sums this up:

> My trade and occupation
> Is ground for Lamentation
> Which makes me curse my station
> And wish I'd ne'er been born.
>
> I ne'er can save one shilling
> And must — which is more killing
> A pauper die when old . . .

The once prosperous, highly-skilled hand-loom weavers of East London are one example. Charles Greville, a courtier and man of letters, notes in his diary for 17 February 1832 —

> A man came yesterday from Bethnal Green with an account of that district. They are all weavers, forming a kind of separate community . . . They are for the most part out of employment and can get none; 1,100 are crammed into the poor-house, 5 or 6 in a bed. 6,000 receive parochial relief . . . The district is in a complete state of insolvency and hopeless poverty.

In the new factories and industrial installations the safety and health of the workforce received minimal attention. An article in the *Gentleman's Magazine* in 1782 decribed for its highly respectable readers the physical condition of the new proletariat.

> [They] are suffocated in mines and pits or gradually poisoned by the noxious effluvia of metals, oils, powders, spirits, etc. used in their work, and can exhibit as mournful a scene of blinded and lame, of enfeebled decrepid asthmatic consumptive wretches, panting for breath and crawling half alive upon the surface of the earth . . .

21. Hand-loom weaving in Spitalfields, 1747, as portrayed by William Hogarth.

22. A steam-driven, multi-spindle, spinning machine of the Industrial Revolution.

It was out of the pitiless exploitation of people such as these, and of children from the age of seven upwards, of hours of labour that made all life a matter of work and sleep, on wages based on bare subsistence level, that the early industrialists and their financial backers made their huge profits.

There was no direction in which the workers could look for redress, hope or improvement of their conditions. Their traditional

23.   Lowering children into a coal mine, from the *Westminster Review*, 1840s.

way of life, based on self-employment in a village community in which each man's opinion carried weight, had gone for ever and was replaced by the cruel spirit of pitiless competition.

That perceptive Tory and future prime minister, Disraeli, said of the workers in his novel, *Sybil:* 'They are not in a state of co-operation, but of isolation . . . Christianity teaches us to love our neighbour as ourself; modern society acknowledges no neighbour'.

It was useless to look to law and Parliament for protection and justice. None of the landless workers could vote or stand for election and the laws were made and enforced by those described by the poet Shelley:

> Those ungrateful drones who would
> Drain your sweat; nay, drink your blood.

'Combination', the forming of fraternal organisations such as trade unions for collective bargaining and the improvement of hours and conditions, was strictly illegal and carried heavy penalties.

The constant cry of the employers and capitalist to the government was a demand for complete independence from interference by the state. This concept was known as 'laissez faire' or 'leave us alone'. In pursuing his own interests, it was claimed, a man was also benefiting society. Freedom for the businessman, who must deal with booms and slumps and market forces, was essential in this new competitive society. Any attempt by the state to regulate hours and conditions of work and wages or to consider employees health and safety they rejected as an intolerable interference with their own personal and economic liberty, and that of their workers. Even the early efforts of philanthropists to restrict the age of employment of the factory children to nine and above, and limit their work to twelve hours daily were opposed as a tyrannical interference with the childrens' right to work. Not for the last time, the watchwords of 'freedom' and 'liberty' were cried as screens for the encouragement and protection of oppression and exploitation.

Across the English Channel, in France, however, a new conception of liberty was being developed, in which it was seen as a partner with equality and fraternity. In July 1789 the people of Paris stormed and destroyed the prison of the Bastille, symbol of their oppression, and England suddenly became aware of the French Revolution.

SELECT BIBLIOGRAPHY

Cole, G. D. H. and Postgate, R., *The Common People,* Methuen, 1938.
Derry, T. K. and Jarman, T. L., *Modern Britain,* Murray, 1979.

George, D, *England in Transition,* Pelican, 1931.
Hobsbawm, E. J., *The Age of Revolution, 1789-1848,* Mentor, 1962.
Scott, A. F. (ed), *Everyone a Witness (The Georgian Age),* Martins.
Thompson, E. P., *The Making of the English Working Class,* Pelican Books, 1968.

CHAPTER X

Tom Paine, 'Champion of the Common Man'

One of the major events in world history and in the development of civilisation, the French Revolution was interpreted, explained and defended to the English by one of her finest radical thinkers, a man who was to influence events over three countries and two continents. His life was full of travel and adventure. Better known and honoured in America than in his own country, he strove to the end for a fairer society, for genuine liberty and for the rights of the people.

Thomas Paine was born in the little Suffolk town of Thetford in 1737, the son of a staymaker and small farmer. His father's Quaker ideas no doubt left their impression on him. As the child of a tradesman he had but a rudimentary education at a local school, leaving at the age of thirteen to become an apprentice staymaker himself. The life did not appeal to him. Fired by ideas of glory he ran away to sea on board a privateer; it took three years for his father to find him, buy him out and bring him back.

His life for the next few years was not particularly happy or successful. He set up as a staymaker in Sandwich, but failed. He married, but his wife died young. He remarried, and it ended in a legal separation. He returned to Thetford where he found employment as an officer in the excise and revenue service at a wage of £50 per year, out of which he had to keep a horse. In 1772 his fellow clerks in the excise decided to press for an increase in pay, and it was Paine who wrote an appeal on their behalf which he sent to every Member of Parliament. He argued that only an increase in pay could keep the service free from the corruption that was a constant temptation to its underpaid officers. Shortly after, he was dismissed on a pretext.

Paine now went to London in search of employment, and there he met the American-born Benjamin Franklin, who was working as a printer while unofficially acting on behalf of the colonists. Franklin advised him to 'go west' and gave him a letter of introduction to some literary people in Pennsylvania. Paine took his advice. In 1774 he arrived and became first a writer for, and then editor of the *Pennsylvania Magazine*. His work showed from the first strong

24.   Portrait of Tom Paine by
A. Milliére after George Romney.

radical leanings, opposing the 'peculiar institution' of Negro slavery
and demanding higher status and greater freedom for women. His
articles were anonymous, but signed 'Justice and Humanity'.

Feeling was running high at the time in the New World. Settlers
and colonists felt themselves to be the victims of gross injustice,
being subject to heavy taxation without any voice or representation
in Parliament. In 1775 the first shots were fired at Lexington in the
conflict that was to become the War of Independence.

Paine at once flung himself into the struggle on behalf of his
adopted country. He joined the hard-pressed army of Washington in
1776, serving mainly as a liaison officer between the army and the
new Congress. It is thought that it was he that composed the clause in
the Declaration of Independence, soon suppressed, outlawing Negro
slavery. In his pamphlet *Common Sense* he was one of the first to
recognise that the war was not just a fight against economic
grievances, but a struggle for complete independence from England
and the establishment of a new nation. He developed this theme in a
series of booklets called *Crises*, which heartened the soldiers so much
that General Washington had them read out on parade. The first of
them began with a phrase that has since become famous: 'These are
the times that try mens' souls.' The pamphlets were a useful defence
of the theory and idea of a new nation-state to be formed out of the
'13 colonies and holdings of England', and to be called 'The United
States of America'.

His writings sold rapidly, running into many editions, and should have made him a rich man. But Paine insisted on the cheapest printing and lowest prices for his works to ensure their widest circulation; so he remained poor and in debt.

His reputation was not enough to keep him from personal troubles, and he left the army and took a humble position as a clerk. During this time he occupied himself with such inventions as a plan for an iron bridge, which in 1787 he brought to England in the hope of finding a backer for it.

He spent a short time in revolutionary Paris, then returned to London. Edmund Burke had just published his *Reflections on the Revolution in France,* which was an attack on the belief current in France that a state could be created by reason and will-power, and argued that a monarchy, an aristocracy and an established church were essential to the well-being of a nation, as the inheritors and communicators of its culture and morality.

Paine wrote in reply *The Rights of Man.* It began with an explanation and a defence of the French Revolution, and quickly became known as 'the Bible of the poor'. Previous social critics and reformers had been mostly intellectuals, like Godwin, and they had been too philosophical and learned for the semi-literate working man of the time. Paine used a simple style with words and phrases everybody could understand. It was the greatest work of the pre-socialist reformers, and became the handbook and manifesto of English radicalism for many years. In some ways it reverted to the Leveller ideas of the Norman yoke, in others it speculated daringly on the organisation of a rational state based on humanitarian principles. It urged a democratic republic founded on adult suffrage — 'The aristoracy are not the farmers who work the land . . . but are the mere consumers of the rent' — in which a graduated income tax paid for a basic 'welfare state' giving its citizens family allowances, free public education, retirement pensions at fifty, marriage and maternity benefits, and great public works to ensure full employment. The book went through eight editions in its first year of full publication, 1792, and many more in the United States of America, where it was reputed to have sold a million copies.

The government of England, headed by Pitt, were terrified of the French Revolution and its repercussions here. It banned *The Rights of Man* as a subversive work and imprisoned its publisher, a fate he predicted when he undertook its printing. A warrant was issued for the arrest of Paine on the capital charge of treason, but he was warned and fled to Dover, leaving for France only twenty minutes ahead of the constables. He was tried in his absence, declared a traitor, and outlawed.

Paine's works were well known in France and he received a hero's welcome. He was made a citizen and elected to the National

Convention, where he sat with the Girondists or 'moderates'. When the fate of the king was under discussion in September 1793, he supported the idea of a French Republic but opposed the execution of the king. With the fall of the Girondists and the rise of the Jacobins he was arrested and spent the next ten months in prison, and probably only the death of Robespierre in November 1794 saved him from the guillotine.

While in prison under threat of death he wrote most of his second major work, *The Age of Reason.* This was a powerful attack on organised religion, especially Christianity and other religions based on the Bible. It made a strict examination and analysis of the Old and New Testaments. Paine put forward as a replacement to religion his own vague deism — that the universe is the work of a supreme being who has made no revelations of himself or his wishes to mankind, but may be slightly comprehended through the rational examination of his works in the physical world.

This attack on Christianity, though it laid a foundation for the later, respectable, Higher Criticism, brought Paine a reputation as a propagator of atheism. He wished to return to England, but England was at war with France. He sailed to the USA in 1802, where he found his work for the Republic forgotten, and he himself denounced and ostracised as an atheist and infidel, an Antichrist and an agent of the devil for the damnation of souls. He died in poverty and isolation on a small farm that had been granted him formerly by New York State. After some years the English reformer, William Cobbett, author of *Rural Rides* and *The Political Register,* exhumed his bones and brought them to England where they could provide a shrine for radicals, humanists, and free-thinkers; but somehow they were mislaid at Liverpool, and never recovered.

The English people of the time were denied the right to vote or to sit in the legislature, or to disagree with the government; they were crushed by oppressive laws and the suspension of traditional legal safeguards like Habeas Corpus; plagued by hosts of spies and provocateurs, subject to some two hundred hanging crimes; divorced from the land and forced into wagework. To them the acts of the French Revolution seemed to point a way to their own emancipation. Under its influence and that of Tom Paine, societies and clubs were formed to study and popularise the idea of parliamentary reform and adult male suffrage as a beginning to political and economic reform. They had arrived, unwittingly, at the same conclusions as their Leveller forbears of 150 years before.

CHAPTER XI

The 'English Jacobins': the Reform Societies

The English radicals who admired the ideals of the French Revolution, so pithily expressed in the slogan 'Liberty, Equality, Fraternity', did not seek to import them literally into this country. A few did indeed favour an armed rising and an imposed democracy, but this was not practical politics and had no public support. The majority looked back on the long struggles for popular freedom at home and found their heroes in men like Sir John Eliot or John Hampden and others prominent in the Civil War, and to the supposed ideal of the Saxon popular government. They demanded not a revolution but the restoration of the people's ancient rights alleged to have been lost with the Norman Conquest; they quoted Magna Carta, Habeas Corpus and the Bill of Rights. The establishment had no difficulty in denouncing these ideas as myths and insisting that universal suffrage had never been part of the national tradition.

A glance at the structure of Parliament and the electorate at the time shows that radicals were correct in making the demand for their reform the primary aim. The legislature consisted, as today, of the Crown, the Lords and the Commons. The first two were hereditary, the Commons elective. But the whole system was so ramshackle and obsolete that it could not be called representative in any way, and in fact had hardly changed for many centuries. Property qualifications restricted the right to vote to a tiny proportion of the public. The great new conurbations of the Industrial Revolution, like Leeds and Manchester, returned no members at all to Parliament; while ancient towns, decayed or almost uninhabited, sent one or more. Sratton consisted of six houses and one elector, and was a constituency. New Romney housed eight voters, and returned two members. Old Sarum, in Wiltshire, the deserted and uninhabited site of a castle and a cathedral, sent as many members to the Commons as did the 10,000 electors of Westminster. Cornwall, a royal duchy, returned forty-four MPs (many of whom purchased their seats), while Rutland, the smallest county and completely rural, elected more members than Yorkshire, the largest and one of the most industrialised. Two hundred and three boroughs, most of them with less than 500 voters on the register, returned 405 MPs out of a total of 558. The reformer John Wilkes showed that the 254 seats needed for a majority in the House of Commons were elected by a mere 5,723 persons out of a population of almost nine million. Corruption was universally accepted. It was obvious that without a fundamental reform of the House of Commons and the electoral system, there was little hope of progressive and equitable legislation.

The later years of the reign of George III saw the formation of a number of clubs and societies demanding parliamentary reform. They were mostly local, opposed to violence, and occupied themselves in debate and discussion, propagating their policies by pamphlets and persuasion. Many of them were small and had to meet in taverns, where a hint to the landlord from the licensing magistrates would be sufficient for them to be refused accommodation, with the subsequent dispersal of the society for lack of a meeting-place.

In London the principal 'Jacobin' societies were: the Friends of the People, a very moderate middle-class body dominated by Whig interests; The Society for Constitutional Information, also largely middle class, notable for its Major John Cartwright, a keen democrat who had blighted his career by refusing to serve against the Americans. Neither of these two lasted very long, or had great influence. Next came the London Corresponding Society.

This was the largest and the most influential. Though its number fluctuated, it claimed at one time 10,000 members, each paying a subscription of one penny a week. Its aims were simple — universal adult male suffrage, a secret ballot, and annual parliaments. Moderate as these demands seem today, at the time they expressed a revolutionary programme; they rejected the contemporary system of government by a propertied or titled minority and upheld the concept of the sovereignty of the people as whole, and the rights of the individual in the state.

It has the distinction of being, in all probability, the first political organisation of the working class. It was founded in March 1792 at a meeting of nine men of the 'industrial classes' at the Bell Tavern off the Strand, who elected as their secretary and treasurer Thomas Hardy, a shoemaker. Their purpose was to hold debates and discussions on the politics of the day, especially as they affected the masses of the people, to work for the right to vote and the reform of Parliament, and to correspond with provincial societies sharing the same objectives. Here can be seen the emergence of a new type of person: the literate, intelligent, self-educated working man, who after a long wearying day at bench or workshop would seek to broaden his outlook and knowledge of the world and his place in it by reading and discussion. His aim was the improvement of his lot and that of his fellow-workers, and frequently he had learned the lessons of organisation and efficiency as a lay official in a nonconformist chapel; the type that was in time to create the English labour movement and the trade unions.

The LCS organised itself into 'divisions' each thirty strong; the members addressed each other, in true Jacobin style, as 'citizen'. Each division sent a delegate, subject to recall, to attend the weekly meeting of the General Committee. Delegates were also sent to meetings of provincial societies, to contribute and to report back, and to large 'national conventions'. Public meetings were held, petitions sent to Parliament, pamphlets and broadsheets written and distributed.

Its proceedings were not hurried. Every member was entitled to defend his viewpoint. It took five nights to debate the question of whether working men and artisans had the right to demand parliamentary reform. The 'ayes' had it.

Francis Place, a tailor and a well-known member (the LCS denied that it had any 'leaders'), recorded that at his division he had met with many upright, inquisitive intelligent men; and he describes the routine at the weekly meeting:

> The chairman (each man was chairman in rotation) read some book . . . and the persons present were invited to make remarks thereon, as many as chose did so, but without rising. Then another portion was read and a second invitation given. Then the remainder was read and a third invitation was given when they who had not before spoken were expected to say something. Then there was a general discussion.

The response of the government and its supporters was to denounce these men as Jacobins, an unpleasant smear that discouraged many from joining. Aided by many of the clergy, they organised 'Church and King' mobs that terrorised members and their families, assaulted them in the streets, raided their homes and destroyed their furniture and possessions. They sent innumerable spies and provocateurs into the movement, to report on the 'citizens' and excite them into acts of violence.

At length the government of Mr Pitt officially moved against the LCS. It announced the discovery of a great revolutionary conspiracy, and suspended Habeas Corpus, the Act which protects subjects against arbitrary imprisonment. A party of Bow Street Runners (or armed 'thief-takers') accompanied by high government dignitaries, raided the home of the secretary, Thomas Hardy, and arrested him on a charge of high treason, for which the penalty was death. They broke open his drawers and cupboards, took away his books and papers, and even rummaged through the clothing of Mrs Hardy, who was in an advanced state of pregnancy and remained in bed while the room was ransacked. Eleven other men prominent in the LCS were also arrested, and all were confined in the Tower of London, traditional prison of traitors, before being sent to Newgate Gaol. Hardy's house was attacked by a Church and King mob, and his wife died in childbirth as a result of the shock.

The prisoners were examined by no less a body than the Privy Council itself, and are reported to have treated that assembly with contempt and refused to answer questions. They were all committed to trial on a charge of treason.

Hardy was the first to appear before a Grand Jury. His trial lasted for nine days; the jury, bearing in mind the mandatory sentence of hanging, drawing and quartering, retired for three hours then returned a verdict of 'not guilty'. Emotions in the jury-room must have been intense, as their foreman fainted away after announcing it in a whisper. Hardy was carried in triumph through the streets. The next two to be tried, Thelwell and Horne Tooke, were similarly acquitted, and the other prosecutions were abandoned.

The French Revolution was entering its bloody phase under the leadership of Robespierre, and many English radicals lost sympathy and ceased to support it. In 1793 the government declared war on France, joining with autocratic governments like Prussia and Austria. The twenty years of the Napoleonic Wars began; as the poet G. K. Chesterton has pointed out, the English 'fought to keep themselves in chains'. In an emotional wave of false patriotism the public lost interest in the struggle for parliamentary reform. Any radical or critical sentiment was thought to express support for the French. The authorities became even more repressive. In 1795 and 1796 the 'Two Acts' were passed, which made mere writing and speech into treasonable acts, made 'incitement to hatred of the government' a criminal offence, and banned lectures, reading-rooms and public meetings except when licensed by magistrates. It also closed down taverns and public houses suspected of being centres of radical discussion or activity.

In this climate of danger and hostility the LCS and its contemporaries rapidly lost membership and support. It became torn with internal dissention, and in 1799 the government banned it officially, and membership became a crime. A section of activists went underground and continued to propagate the doctrines of liberty and democracy at great personal risk and with little success. Many went to prison, or were transported. Thomas Hardy returned to his trade and opened a boot shop.

The many Hampden Clubs, founded by John Cartwright to preach parliamentary reform in the industrial north of the country, continued an illegal existence, harried, persecuted, penetrated by informers. They developed a strong revolutionary wing which overshadowed the legalist element and began to accumulate stores of arms, mainly pikes and daggers and a few firearms.

In London, half a million signatures had been collected on a great petition for parliamentary reform; this was presented to the Commons and instantly rejected. On his way to open that parliamentary session in January 1816 the Prince Regent, deputising for his father, the mad George III, drove through a hissing, booing crowd and his carriage windows were smashed by stones. The reformers called a rally to be held in Spa Fields, Bermondsey, in March. The Hampden Clubs and other workers' organisations in Manchester planned a march to the capital to present petitions protesting against the suspension of Habeas Corpus and demanding relief for the poor; it was to arrive in London at the same time as the Spa Fields meeting and join forces with it.

Volunteers for the march were each to carry a rolled blanket over his shoulder in military style, as the marcher would spend five nights on the road. They were at once dubbed 'Blanketeers'. It was rumoured that arms would be carried and that they would be 100,000 strong. In the event, less than 1,000 men set off, cheered on their way from St Peter's Fields, Manchester, by a crowd of 12,000 supporters. A strong body of soldiers arrived and dispersed the crowd, arresting their leaders. The Blanketeers had already left for London, but they were subject to attack by the military and yeomanry (a Volunteer Regiment of the sons of well-to-do farmers and the middle class) until they were scattered or arrested. The march was over before it reached Derby. One stalwart, Abel Couldwell, actually finished the route and arriving in London alone, duly presented his petition. Many of the Blanketeers went home despondent and defeated; some were gaoled as 'vagrants', others were kept in prison without trial until released by the magistrates who could not decide what charges to bring against them.

The spies and informers sent in lurid accounts of sedition, insurrection and rebellion brewing all over the north of England. These they exaggerated wildly to earn their pay, and for a long time the government was in a state of fear and apprehension; the suppression of popular rights was intensified, and the suspension of Habeas Corpus allowed them to keep suspected persons in prison without charge or trial. The provocateurs were encouraged to organise small local risings that could be easily crushed and the leaders put away or executed. One such was the hated 'Oliver', who was later exposed and fled abroad for the rest of his life. He travelled round Derbyshire and posed as a member of Hampden Clubs and similar 'seditious' bodies. Working on the good faith of local radicals he managed to convince the men of a number of Pennine villages and towns that a mass rebellion was about to take place (he was helped by the isolation of these small communities and their lack of communications) and, on the night of 9 June 1817, a crowd of 400 men, armed with pikes and what guns they could seize or collect, left the little town of Pentrich to march to Nottingham, expecting to join there with a large rebel contingent from the north and march on London, gathering strength on the way. In London, they would form part of a great national people's army that would overthrow the government and set up a new, reformed state based on universal suffrage and social justice. 'Oliver' did not take part in the march himself, and its leader was Joseph Brandreth, a stockinger of Sutton-in-Ashfield in Nottinghamshire. Brandreth composed a verse for his men to chant upon the road:

> Every man his skill must try,
> He must turn out and not deny.
> No bloody soldier he must dread
> He must turn out and fight for bread.
> The time has come, you plainly see,
> The government opposed must be.

Chanting these crude lines the Pentrich men set off demanding, and getting, guns from the farms and country houses on their way. But there was no rebel army waiting to welcome them. They were the only contingent. A small body of armed men, under the same misapprehension, had been gathered by Oliver near Huddersfield to await them; but when they saw how few and weak they were, and that no reinforcements had arrived at the time given them, they wisely gave up the attempt and went home. Alone, the Pentrich men went on, seeking other companies in vain, expecting every hour to hear of the fall of Nottingham to the rebels. After some twelve hours of marching, they were confronted by a mounted body of the 15th Light Dragoons that was awaiting them and the rebellion was over. Realising now that they had been tricked, they flung away their arms and fled; and the dragoons began the easy task of rounding them up and taking them prisoner.

The outcome of the 'Pentrich Rebellion' was a serious one for Oliver's victims. Three men — Brandreth, Ludlam, a quarryman, and Turner, an old soldier and a stonemason — were found guilty of high treason and sentenced to be hanged, drawn and quartered. Eleven others were transported for life, three for fourteen years. Six suffered terms of imprisonment. Those condemned to death were spared the full rigours of the penalty, which even the government of that day considered too barbarous a spectacle. So, on 7 November 1817, before an enormous crowd in Derby, the three men were hanged wearing heavy iron fetters; and after hanging for an hour the bodies were taken down and publicly decapitated.

It seemed that the cause of reform in England was in eclipse. Yet the experience, knowledge and understanding gained by so many working men in the London Corresponding Societies, the Hampden Clubs, and similar organisations was to play an important part in the next great political movement of the common people — Chartism.

SELECT BIBLIOGRAPHY

Cole, G. D. H. and Postgate, R., *The Common People*, Methuen, 1938.
Barker, T. (ed), *The Long March of Everyman*, Andre Deutsch and B.B.C. Publications.
Gregg, P., *A Social and Economic History of Britain, 1760–1970*, Harraps, 1950.
Stevens, J., *England's Last Revolution (Pentrich, 1817)*, Moorland Publishing Co.
Stevenson, J., *Popular Disturbances in England, 1700–1870*, Longmans, 1979.
Thomas, M. I. and Holt, P., *Threats of Revolution in Britain, 1789–1848*, Macmillan, 1979.

CHAPTER XII

The Naval Mutinies of 1797

No account of the social struggles of the English people, however, brief, would be acceptable if it failed to notice the great naval mutinies of 1797, though these were largely non-political and more in the nature of strikes against conditions which had become intolerable than acts of rebellion.

The war against France was going badly. Britain had been driven out of the Mediterranean and Europe. The alliances had broken down, and Britain was left to fight alone. The brilliant young French general, Napoleon Bonaparte, was everywhere victorious. Now, with the enemy's fleet and army stationed across the North Sea and the English Channel, Britain feared invasion. Ireland was in a state of active rebellion, ready to welcome the French ashore. The Bank of England had suspended payments in gold, and paper money was replacing it. Following a bad harvest, the price of bread, the staple food of the masses, had soared, and consequently there was hardship and discontent throughout the land.

The one hope of the government lay in the Royal Navy; the war was now being carried on almost entirely by that service. In February the country had been cheered by the victory of St Vincent where Admiral Sir John Jervis had defeated a much stronger Spanish fleet. 'Jolly Jack Tar', with his rolling gait, tarred pigtail, high spirits and open shirt, was the great popular hero, welcome wherever he appeared. For landsmen the concept of the British sailor had been formed by the idealistic poems and songs then fashionable, like Dibdin's *Songs of the Fleet*, articles in the press and romantic pictures. Reality was very different.

Of all the oppressed, exploited and brutalised people of England then, the seaman in the Royal Navy probably fared the worst. He served, fought and suffered under conditions that would seem incredible to a modern rating. His pay had not been raised since the Commonwealth, 120 years before, and was a third of the pay in the merchant service. It was always in arrears, usually about two years behind, although some ships had not been paid off for much longer — it was thought that back-pay would encourage desertion. An Able

Seaman received twenty-four shillings a month, an Ordinary Seaman nineteen shillings, and out of this there were deductions for 'slops' — clothes, bedding, etc. — so that he usually got about ten shillings. Out of this he had to contribute to the upkeep of his family, who were often left to exist on parish relief.

Overcrowding was inevitable when small, wooden ships carried crews of hundreds. Nelson's flagship, *Victory*, of 2,164 tons, had a complement of 850 men. Each man off watch swung his hammock between the guns, his official allowance of space being fourteen inches in width. For victuals the men were divided into messes and each mess collected its rations from the purser. These were sufficient in quantity; but the quality was appalling. Salt beef and pork was sometimes years old, shrunken, hard and inedible (the sailors often used it to carve themselves little boxes for snuff and tobacco, and it lasted like wood and took a good polish). Biscuit was full of worms and weevils that had to be 'tapped out' before eating. Cheese was so hard that men used pieces to replace lost buttons on their coats. Full rations were very rarely issued. The pursers were notorious for giving short weight to the messmen, and the usual pound of issue was expected to be only fourteen ounces — pursers were paid an allowance for savings. Fruit and vegetables were rarely seen and scurvy was common. Ships' water rapidly became foul, and was replaced by 'swipes', a watery beer, or cheap vinegary wine.

The one bright spot was the daily half-pint of diluted rum, but this encouragement to drink was balanced by a flogging for any sign of drunkenness.

There were never enough seamen to man the expanding navy; volunteers were insufficient, in spite of generous enlistment bounties. The lowest types of criminals often opted for naval service instead of prison, and were willingly accepted. The ships could only be kept up to strength by the constant use of press-gangs, who roamed the streets kidnapping seamen or working men and carrying them off forcibly as captives without rights. Once taken aboard they might not return for years, if they survived at all, and friends and families were left to guess the reason for their absence. The docking of a merchantman or a naval craft was a boon to the press-gang, and many discharged seamen on their way home after a long voyage were knocked on the head and later found themselves on the deck of a ship possibly bound for the other side of the world. Landsmen of all trades, who had never been to sea, became unwilling sailors of the king and subject to his harsh 'Articles of War'. Even as humane and progressive an admiral as Nelson insisted that without the press-gang few of His Majesty's ships could put to sea.

When ships put into port after cruise or battle, there was no shore-leave for 'poor Jack'. Captains knew too well that many a

25. 'The Delegates in Council', by George Cruikshank, 1797.

sailor would readily take his chance of flogging or hanging by 'making a run for it'. So the seaman was really a prisoner on his ship, although perhaps only a mile or two from his home and loved ones, from whom he may have been forcibly snatched and might never see again. Though, when in port, visitors from ashore were allowed on board, this only benefited those who lived near ports — and the local whores of course.

The discipline aboard was brutal in the extreme. On many ships orders were enforced by blows and most offences, even quite minor ones, were punished by trussing on a grating and flogging with the cat-o'-nine-tails, a rope whip of nine thongs, a few blows of which were enough to strip skin and flesh and only a few more to expose the ribs. Sentences of 'a dozen', which seem to have been usual for ordinary breaches of discipline, were enough to incapacitate a strong man for many days. For more serious offences as many as 300 lashes could be imposed; this usually resulted in death. An offender could also be 'fllogged round the fleet', hauled from ship to ship to be flogged on each, and very few unfortunates survived it. French seamen who handled British naval prisoners of war, or bodies, called them 'the tigers'; not because of their ferocity, but because their backs were striped with scars of old floggings. (Corporal punishment in the French forces was abolished early in the Revolution.)

This regime brutalised and made callous the officers who ordered it and the crews who endured it. Their very lives depended on the nature of their captain, and his subordinates who took their examples from him. Many tales were told around the guns of savage martinets who ruled vessels that were hell-ships indeed; while those commanders who treated their men with justice and mercy, and addressed them civilly were rewarded with an extraordinary degree of respect, affection and devotion from their crews.

Such a man was Admiral Lord Howe, nominally in command of the Channel Fleet, which in April 1797 swung at its anchors in the waters of Spithead, off Portsmouth. Now aged seventy-one, he did not go to sea himself, and the acting commander was Admiral Lord Bridport. Howe himself was on sick-leave at Bath, with a bad attack of gout. It appeared an ordinary scene, the boats plying between the men-of-war, stores going aboard, an atmosphere of orderly activity as the fleet refitted. But things were going on, in crowded gun-decks and forecastles, in holds and 'tween-decks, that the Admiralty never thought possible. 'Jack' had taken all he could stomach and was clearing his decks for action. Everything was done in great secrecy and at great risk. Who the leaders were never became known, but they were obviously not the tough old sea-dogs of the crews; they must have been brought in by the press-gangs and the bounties — educated, literate men used to a better life. Crews met in secret conclave, sent messages and agents from ship to ship, elected delegates to a fleet committee which actually met on one of the ships; it drew up a list of grievances to be remedied and plans to enforce it.

On 16 April Lord Bridport embarked on his flagship *Queen Charlotte* and made a signal for the fleet to weigh anchor and put to sea. Instead of his seamen springing to their stations at the bosun's whistle, every man climbed into the rigging and joined in the roaring of three hearty cheers. The marines, there to enforce discipline on board, stood idly by; they leaned on their muskets and passively sided with the crews. From every ship in the squadron came the sound of cheering from men clustered on the shrouds and ratlins. An incredible catastrophe had occurred — the British sailor had refused orders.

The Admiralty should long have been aware that something was brewing on the lower decks. During the last years they had received petitions and letters from the crews of ships, unsigned by any individuals, posted on land, protesting against lack of pay, bad food and abuse of power; they had made no threats and stressed the loyalty of the petitioners. Therefore they were all ignored, and attributed to agitators in the pay of the French.

Now from each ship came a boat carrying its two delegates. They boarded *Queen Charlotte* without opposition, declared themselves the General Assembly of the Squadron, coolly took over the fleet, and established themselves in the admiral's great state-room. He and the officers, denied the use of the marines, decided to do nothing without instructions from the Admiralty.

The Assembly announced that it had, already sent letters to Lord Howe, 'the sailors' friend', stating their grievances and appealling to him to help them. Nothing had happened — Howe had forwarded their letters to the Admiralty, where, as usual, they had been ignored. A petition had also been sent to Parliament, observing all the formalities and ending: 'We, your petitioners, thereby humbly implore that you will take these matters into consideration and with your accustomed goodness and liberality comply with the prayers of your petitioners, and we are in duty bound ever to pray, &c.'

There was much fast galloping between Portsmouth and Whitehall. Meanwhile the Assembly sat in the state cabin, sending signals and instructions to the crews over the heads of the officers. The elected delegates of the sixteen ships were mostly of the promoted type of seamen, the pick of the crews — petty-officers, quartermasters' and gunners' mates, even midshipmen, not easily moved by mere agitators or 'Jacobins'. They rove a rope to the yard-arm, as is done when a seaman is about to be hanged, and left it there as a warning to both sailors and officers. It was never used. One of the main concerns of the Assembly was to prevent violence and disorder among the men, and preserve the astonishing solidarity of the whole fleet. Naval discipline was to be maintained, officers' orders carried out as usual, watches kept with customary strictness. 'However, no ship shall lift an anchor to proceed from this port until the desire of the Fleet is satisfied'. If all went well, each ship was to line the rails and give three cheers at 8 a.m. and again at sunset. Every man was to take an oath before his delegate 'that by his Maker the course we have undertaken be preserved until accomplished'. This oath was taken by the marines as well. In case of disturbance or counter-revolt on any ship, the red flag of battle was to be hoisted, or, at night, two lights, one above the other.

The fleet rocked peacefully at anchor. But it was now the sailors, not the Admiralty's fleet.

The Lords of the Admiralty responded with their usual lack of insight. A message was sent to Bridport ordering him to arrest the ringleaders and take the fleet to sea, and commanding the crews to resume full duty. Bridport replied that this was impossible, might lead to an even greater disaster, and begged that his order to put to sea be countermanded. The Assembly informed their Lordships that 'until there was full concessions of all their demands, the grievances of individual ships redressed, an Act passed and His Majesty's gracious pardon granted to all, the fleet will not lift an anchor; and this is the total and final answer'. They allowed one exception — if the French battle fleet came out they would at once resume full duties and fight.

The Assembly then signalled all ships that those officers regarded by the crews as tyrannical and unjust should be put ashore with their belongings; and this was carried out without violence or opposition. For example, the captain and six officers of the frigate *Hind* received an anonymous letter saying, 'Gentlemen, it is the request of the ship's company that you leave the ship precisely at eight o'clock . . . As it is unanimously agreed that you shall leave the ship we would wish you to leave it peaceable, or desperate measures will be taken.' They went, and the sailors rowed them ashore.

The Assembly also decreed, among many other rulings, that ships of war convoying merchantmen on trade routes should continue duty and not join the mutiny, thus avoiding antagonising the middle class of traders, whose support they saw as invaluable. The great fear of the Admiralty was that the sailors, in desperation, might sail the fleet off and give it up to the French, although all the messages of the Assembly stressed their loyalty to king and country.

Lord Spencer, First Lord of the Admiralty, came down quickly to Portsmouth to consult with Bridport. Concessions in pay and some minor matters were arranged, and Bridport went aboard *Queen Charlotte* to present them to the Assembly. He was piped aboard with full naval honours — as indeed were the delegates when they visited ships. Spencer's concessions were rejected as insufficient, and a full and official royal pardon for every man in the fleet was demanded. The delegates also decided to make no further demands 'in order to convince the nation at large that we know when to cease to ask, as we know when to begin, and we ask nothing but what is moderate and may be granted without detriment to the nation or injury to the service.'

This was not the tone or language of simple men misled by agitators. Spencer decided on further concessions to be approved by an Act of Parliament and a promise that no action would be taken against any man. This was read out to every ship's company by its captain, but its conciliatory spirit was undermined by Admiral Gardner, who addressed the Assembly, called them 'skulking cowards' and threatened to hang every fifth man in the fleet as an example to others. He was hustled off the ship to explain himself to Lord Spencer and the red flag, signal for emergency, was flown at the masthead.

The mutiny had now lasted for five days. The government had fortified Portsmouth, reinforced its garrison by 10,000 men, and trained its guns on the fleet. Mutineers on the Assembly's affairs went about the waterfront armed with cutlass and pistols. The townsfolk were confused, but support for the seamen was evident.

The squadron at Plymouth joined in and sent delegates. There had been bloodshed and scuffles on one ship, where the officers had resisted.

If anything happened, the French would soon know of it. Parliament met and passed a 'seaman's bill', voting an extra £370,000 for pay and agreeing to most of the demands. This was finally accepted by the Assembly and by the individual crews, and on 24 April the fleet at last weighed anchor and moved a few miles down the Solent, lying off St Helens to wait for a fair wind to the French coast. It did not come until 7 May, and when the signal to weigh anchor was made the crews did not obey. No royal pardon had arrived, and the men did not trust Admiralty promises.

Lord Spencer drove hard to Windsor and obtained the pardon, properly signed and sealed (much against the wishes of George III); he had a hundred copies made, and sent old Lord Howe, whom the sailors trusted, to distribute them on every ship and show the original to the Assembly. The mutiny was over, the common seamen had run the fleet efficiently for a month, had won many reforms, there were to be no floggings or hangings, and it was time for reconciliation. Portsmouth was in gala mood and the seamen had a grand triumphal march round the town; the ships' bands played 'Rule Britannia' and 'God Save the King', the military in the forts fired salutes. Lord Howe was carried shoulder high. Next morning the Channel Fleet put to sea to blockade Brest. The so-called 'Admirals of the Assembly' became seamen again, and the real Admirals set down to draw lessons from these astonishing events.

The mutiny of the North Sea Fleet stationed at the Nore off Sheerness, at the mouth of the Thames, was not so well conducted as that at Spithead, nor was the fleet so unanimous. It was a scratch squadron, with ships joining and leaving, and there was not the cohesion and fellowship to be found in a unified flotilla serving and fighting together over a long period. Here there could be no lengthy preparation and discussion before action.

It began like the Spithead affair, but not until that was almost over, with a refusal of duty on 12 May, when the Channel Fleet already lay off St Helens waiting for the royal pardon. The crew of *Venerable*, Admiral Duncan's flagship, gave three cheers as a signal, but Admiral Duncan, a popular commander, was able to keep control by a display of diplomacy, strength and courage. Together with the sister-ship *Adamant* they sailed off to watch the enemy in the mouth of the Texel. But the other craft, several ships of the line and nine frigates, gathered round the depot ship *Sandwich* (she was grossly overcrowded, carrying some 1,600 men instead of her usual complement of 400), elected their delegates and chose as their leader an unwilling seaman, Richard Parker. He may not have been very suitable but he had been a schoolmaster and could write a good document, and it was he who signed the proclamations and statements as 'Richard Parker, President'. Thus they lost the valuable anonymity that had been so useful at Spithead.

Things did not go smoothly. On some of the ships there was fighting with fatalities, and violence and humiliation against officers. The newly arrived frigate *San Fiorenzo* refused to participate, and was fired on by the crew of *Inflexible,* the cannon-ball causing some minor damage. This constituted 'making war on the king', a very serious matter indeed. But the rest of the fleet stayed solid under control of their delegates, maintained discipline, took an oath, and put bullying officers ashore. Delegates were sent to Spithead, to return after some days with the news that the mutiny there was over, and most demands granted by Act of Parliament. The Nore sailors then found themselves left in a state of war against the king, tantamount to high treason. There was little they could do but carry on the mutiny until they could force a pardon from king or government.

They also received a message from the Assembly of the Channel Fleet, expressing concern at their actions and violence, and begging them 'to make no unreasonable demands nor delay an amicable settlement by standing out for trifling objects'.

The Admiralty moved fast, in no conciliatory mood, sensing the divided emotions in the fleet. There was not much they could do by direct force, as the delegates were holding the officers as hostages. A battle between the fleet and 'loyal' ships would result in putting many craft out of action when all were so urgently needed. So instead they put a blockade on the Nore; no food, drink or stores could go aboard, and the fleet would soon be starved into submission.

In reply, the fleet blockaded the Thames estuary, allowing no ships in or out. Trade in London came to a stop, and the capital was faced with shortages. In a few days, over a hundred sail of merchantmen and fishing-craft were anchored round the Nore, running out of food and water. Some of them were looted for provisions, adding the crime of piracy to that of mutiny.

The desperate delegates now called for a settlement; this would include all that had been granted to the Channel Fleet, with arrears of pay made good to the last six months, shore-leave, and no abuse of the rights of corporal punishment. This, they said, could only be decided in face to face negotiations with the Lords of the Admiralty themselves, on board *Sandwich.*

The Lords of Admiralty declined the invitation, and on 6 June declared all the men to be rebels. After dark that night, with officials of Trinity House whose responsibility it was, boats left Sheerness and carefully sank all the buoys and markers indicating the safe channels through the dangerous sandbanks and mud-flats. The mutineers were trapped. They were unable to move out to sea — the idea had been broached of sailing across the North Sea and handing the fleet over to the Dutch — and unable to move inland or up-river because of the Sheerness and Thames forts.

A faction developed on ships demanding a return to duty, and relying on the mercy of the Admiralty. Fighting broke out on board, in which some died. Ships trained their guns on other vessels and threatened to sink them. Then two frigates were retaken by their officers, sailed through the fleet and sheltered under the guns of Sheerness fort. On 10 July several ships hauled down their red flags and opened the river to merchant shipping. Some of the delegates sailed away and gave themselves up to the French or the Dutch. The men offered to surrender their ships in return for a general pardon; and in the chaos the men of *Sandwich* released their officers, announced their return to duty, and as a token of sincerity handed over 'President' Richard Parker and their delegates. One by one the other ships surrendered.

The Admiralty, eager to get on with the war, announced a general pardon for all but the 'ringleaders'. Fifty-nine seamen were sentenced to death, of whom twenty-nine, including Parker, were hanged; twenty-nine were imprisoned, terms ranging from one to eight years; and nine were flogged, one of *Monmouth's* seamen being given 380 lashes. This time the Admiralty had won.

In a long statement before his execution Parker wrote:

> I stand subject to human passion the noblest of which is a tender sensibility at every species of human woe. Thus influenced, how could I stand by and behold some of the best of my fellow-creatures cruelly treated by some of the worst.

Standing in the shadow of the noose he said, 'I die a martyr in the cause of humanity'.

Of course, many naval officers were humane men caught up in a pernicious system. Admiral Nelson himself said of the Spithead men: 'I am entirely with the seamen in their first complaint. We are a neglected set and when peace comes, shamefully neglected.'

Captain Marryat, famous as the author of many fine tales of naval life, wrote in 1830:

> There is a point at which endurance of oppression ceases to be a virtue, and rebellion can no longer be considered a crime . . . The seamen, on the occasion of the first mutiny, had just grounds for complaint, and . . . they did not proceed to acts of violence until repeated and humble remonstrance had been made in vain.

Finally, here is an extract from a manifesto of the crew of HMS *Montague,* of the North Sea Fleet, which says much in a few dignified words:

> The Age of Reason has at length revolved. Long have we been endeavouring to find ourselves men. We now find ourselves so. We will be treated as such.

SELECT BIBLIOGRAPHY

Manwaring, G. E. and Dobree, B., *The Floating Republic*, Frank Cass, 1966.
Marcus, G. S., *The Age of Nelson,* Allen and Unwin, 1971.

CHAPTER XIII

The Reign of King Ludd

The Battle of Waterloo in 1815 ended the Napoleonic Wars, and left the Royal Navy the undisputed master of the world's oceans. The way was open for the extension and development of the Empire and of trade, and of the enrichment of financial, manufacturing and mercantile interests. But the victory brought no social peace to England. The first thirty years of the nineteenth century were probably the most turbulent and violent in our history. Denied representation, franchise or organisation, regarded with hostility by employers and contempt by their rulers, the only way in which the newly created working class could publicise their grievances and protest against injustice was by mass violence and the destruction of property. The riot, coupled with assault and arson, became the usual form of political and social protest and even of collective bargaining. There were serious riots throughout the land, provoked by desperate poverty, high food prices, new road-tolls and turnpike gates, taxation, enclosures, press-gangs and other 'social grievances'. There were riots, often leading to deaths, to rescue prisoners of the law and in support of strikers. The state replied with greater repression, spies, provocateurs and more savage sentences.

The first reactions of cottage and domestic workers threatened by machinery took place in the textile trades that were the first to be affected. No objections were made to the use of machines in mines and smelting works, which had never been domestic industries, but it was an elemental impulse to destroy the machines that could do the work of so many men and which drove families into destitution for the personal profits of their owners. It was often seen as an ethical, Christian issue.

There were widespread attacks on factories in the industrial areas towards the end of the eighteenth century. The Blackburn house of James Hargreaves, inventor of the spinning jenny, was attacked by an angry mob as early as 1768, and his machines destroyed. Richard Arkwright, who designed a wool-carding machine and installed it in his factory at Birkacre, Lancashire, was the victim of a mob that broke his doors down, smashed his machines and fired the building.

Two people were killed during this disturbance, and eight injured.

In Manchester in 1792 the first mill to install Cartwright's power-looms was burnt out by the hand-weavers, and it was a long time before they were installed anywhere else in the area.

The 'mob' was an ever-present and volatile element in the urban life of the time and would gather spontaneously when people were excited or incensed; once assembled, it was beyond the powers of the weak and timorous constabulary to control and could only be broken up by troops who had to be marched from barracks accompanied by a magistrate. He would read the Riot Act to the crowd, ordering them to disperse peacefully. If that was ignored, he could legally request the officer in charge to order his men to fire.

It was this wild crowd, easily led by demagogues, that formed the 'Church and King' mobs that had raided and terrorised radicals and 'Jacobins'. Now the privations of the people during and after the war made it reverse its objectives and incline to what it considered the interests of its own people.

At times the outbreaks reached the level of local insurrections, of revolutionary risings but without revolutionary aims, like the Gordon Riots in London in 1780 which terrorised the capital for twelve days, devastated whole areas, looted and burned houses, prisons and chapels. At one time thirty-six fires were raging in the city simultaneously. The riot was finally put down by the military with considerable loss of life just as the Bank of England was about to be attacked for the third time. The number of people killed in the streets was 210, and seventy-five died later from wounds; 450 were arrested, and sixty-two sentenced to death.

There was rioting for sixty-one successive nights inside and outside the Covent Garden Theatre, now the Royal Opera House, on account of an increase in the admission charges. Considerable damage was done to the newly rebuilt theatre in these 'Old Price Riots'.

In Bristol the rioters of 1831 controlled that city for several days, doing great damage to prisons, public buildings and private houses, many of which were ransacked. Casualties were twelve killed and ninety-four injured. One hundred and two prisoners were taken, of whom four were hanged. In Birmingham in 1838, the banning of reform meetings at the Bull Ring was followed by four days of fighting between the citizens and the police backed by troops. Lesser outbreaks were frequent throughout the country and posed a constant menace to the authorities.

There were now only two courses open to the people. One was direct action — rioting, the wrecking of the premises of oppressive employers, the destruction of the labour-saving machines. The other was to agitate and organise for the rights of legal trade unions for collective bargaining and negotiation, and for suffrage and representation in Parliament and local government. Both courses were illegal. The first appealed primarily to the instincts of the victims of the new system of 'free enterprise', the second to the more far-sighted and better educated. Many people participated in both spheres of activity seeing them as two aspects of the same struggle. In 1811 a cloth-workers' petition to Parliament, which requested a minimum wage only a little above poverty level was rejected, not for the first time. The petitioners then reported to the signatories, 'Had you possessed 70,000 votes . . . would your application have been treated with such indifference, not to say inattention? We believe not.' Thus the demand for the right to vote and to sit in the House of Commons began to loom large in the minds of the dispossessed people. But this was a long-term programme. Immediate relief for immediate problems seemed more likely to be achieved by violence. Often after serious disorders some concessions were made to quieten the situation.

An example of this is found in the Nottingham riots of 1799. The stocking-knitters sent in a petition to Parliament for a minimum rate, which, as usual, was rejected. Crowds gathered in the streets, smashed windows and attacked the houses of the principal masters. Mills were broken into and knitting-frames destroyed; 300 were smashed in one factory alone. The disorders continued for several days, during which time 300 special constables were sworn in and soldiers patrolled the streets. A stocking-frame was carried into Market Place and ceremoniously destroyed. The manufacturers unofficially contacted the workmen and the town council, and offered improved rates and conditions. The riots ended at once.

In 1811 the proprietors of factories in the stocking trade around Nottingham began to receive threatening letters, declarations and manifestos, bearing the signature 'King Ludd' or 'Ned Ludd' and an address given as 'Sherwood Forest' or 'Sherwood Castle'. Who this 'King Ludd' was, or if he ever existed, was never ascertained, but obviously a large secret organisation existed with a powerful individual or group controlling it. It may have been a name adopted from the legendary King Ludd who was said to have conquered London and built Ludgate long before the Romans came; it may have been taken from Ned Ludd, who, according to vague stories, was a half-witted boy in a stocking-mill who in a fit of fury at persecution smashed the stocking-frames. His address may have been a reference to Robin Hood. Many simple people believed that he actually existed and held court in the depths of the forest, sworn to redress the wrongs of the poor. Whoever they were, the 'Luddites' quickly became a force in Nottinghamshire, Lancashire and Yorkshire, able to summon on its missions large bodies of armed, disciplined and determined men, safeguarded and protected by the sympathies of most of the common people and even many within the professional classes.

The Luddites first appeared among the 'stockingers' of Nottinghamshire; their trade, relying largely on the European market, had been ruined by the long war and the blockades. They were skilled men who had served apprenticeships and knitted their wares on 'narrow' frames. Some mill-owners had developed a 'wide' frame on which unskilled workers could knit large pieces which were cut and sewn into form, instead of being made in one piece. These were cheap and soon fell apart, but sold well. These shoddy goods were ruining the market for the domestic producers. Following a reduction in the price paid to out-workers, parties of Luddites raided the mills and destroyed the wide frames and the goods they produced. A thousand frames and large stocks of stockings were destroyed in a few weeks.

Luddites met secretly by night in armed groups, some of which carried firearms. They advanced on the machines, smashed or burnt them, and dispersed quickly; a primitive and limited form of guerrilla war. The cut-up work dropped off sharply, and earnings rose by as much as two shilling a dozen pieces.

King Ludd claimed to be acting within the law. Under their charter the Framework Knitters Company had been empowered by Charles II to examine goods and destroy those below accepted standards. Their actions were selective — they sought only to destroy the shoddy stockings along with the machines upon which they were made. The JPs rejected this viewpoint and sent 2,000 troops into the area.

The punishment for machine-breaking was transportation to the convict settlements in Australia for up to fourteen years, and seven men were so sentenced at the March assizes. Parliament decided to raise the penalty to death. Very few members opposed this in the Commons, but the poet Lord Byron, in the House of Lords, made a memorable maiden speech in defence of the rioters:

> Are we aware of our obligations to the mob? It is the mob that labour in our fields, serve in our houses, that man your navy and recruit your army. They have enabled you to defy all the world and can also defy you when neglect and calamity have driven them to despair. . . . Suppose one of these men, as I have seen them, meagre with famine, sullen with despair, is dragged into court to be tried for this new offence under this new law; still there are two things wanting to convict and condemn him . . . twelve butchers for a jury and a Jeffreys for a judge.

Fear of the gallows did not stop the Luddites. Attacks on factories and mills spread into Yorkshire and Lancashire. The instrument used to smash machinery was a heavy sledge-hammer dubbed 'Great Enoch' after its maker, Enoch James, and King Ludd's subjects chanted as they swung it:

> Great Enoch still shall lead the van,
> Stop him who dare! Stop him who can!

Many masters turned their factories into little fortresses and manned them at night with their managers, foremen, partners, overseers and soldiers. Bloody battles ensued, in which firearms were freely used.

Mr Burton of Middleton, valiantly defending his power-looms, killed five Luddites. For this his house was burnt and his assassination attempted. Luddite attacks were accompanied by town riots against high food prices, and many shopkeepers were coerced into reducing the prices of bread and potatoes.

In Yorkshire the Luddites made war on the shearing-frames, which using unskilled labour did the work of the skilled 'cropper', who with great heavy shears trimmed and levelled the surface of the cloth. Mill owners received warning notes from King Ludd to dismantle the machines, like the letter sent to a Huddersfield manufacturer which read:

> You will take notice that if they are not taken down by
> the end of next week I will detach one of my Lieutenants
> with at least 300 men to destroy them . . . and if you have
> the Impudence to fire on any of my men they have orders
> to murder you.

At night the bands of Luddites, their faces smeared with blacking, met to drill and plan in the woods and on the lonely moors. They would march off to attack their objectives and pitched battles would often ensue. They cheered themselves by singing songs like these:

> And night by night when all is still
> And the moon is hid behind the hill
> We forward march to do our will
> With hatchet, pike and gun.
>
> Oh, the cropper lads for me,
> Who with lusty stroke
> The shear-frames broke
> The cropper lads for me!

Spies were sent to infiltrate the movement, to report the names and plans, to provoke attacks on prepared positions where they could be defeated and captured for the gallows. They had little success. Many small mill-owners succumbed and dismantled their machines, leaving the large and powerful factories to hold out. William Horsfall fortified his factory near Huddersfield, even mounting a cannon and cutting loop-holes in his walls. He was later murdered. William Cartwright of Rawfold's Mill in the Spen Valley filled his yard with armed supporters and soldiers, slept there himself every night, put spiked rollers on his stairs and mounted a cask of vitriol on top, to be overturned on to any invaders. He was attacked by a force of some 150 Luddites, and a sharp exchange of musketry-fire took place for about twenty minutes. Then the door was rushed by a party with hammers and axes; it was thrown back with many casualties, some fatal, and the attackers retired. Cartwright became the hero of the Tories and the military. It was said that he came out to two mortally wounded attackers and offered them drink and a surgeon if they would tell him who their leaders were. They preferred to die in silence. One of the soldiers defending the mill refused to fire and was sentenced to receive 300 lashes. Cartwright intervened on his behalf and the sentence was considerably reduced.

The Luddite movement, after a few successes, faded out. The raids grew less frequent, then stopped. The Nottingham stockingers formed a trade union, and the masters organised a committee to oppose it. Both of these 'combinations' were strictly illegal. The constables and the magistrates saw to it that the union was broken up. No move was made against the masters.

Long after the end of organised Luddism sporadic machine-breaking went on. As late as the eighteen-twenties a crowd of hand-weavers, armed with cudgels and pikes, were on their way to smash some power-looms in Lancashire when they saw a body of cavalry ride towards them with drawn swords. They cleared the road and the troopers rode up and halted. Their officer addressed the weavers and warned them of very serious consequences to themselves if they did not disperse. An old weaver cried out, 'What are we to do? We are starving. Must we starve to death?' The soldiers then took their day's rations from their haversacks, threw them to the weavers, and followed their officer away. After a long wait the crowd went on its way to attack the mill.

The 'reign of King Ludd' was shrouded in mystery. Nobody ever knew who was behind it, or why it ended when it did. Secrecy was a matter of life and death, and it was well kept. It was expensive in casualties and many of its activists ended on the gallows or in the convict settlements of Botany Bay. It was a backward-looking philosophy seeking to return to conditions which had already become obsolete. It was the last desperate struggle of a doomed class, the free domestic producers. The future belonged to the machines — and to their owners.

SELECT BIBLIOGRAPHY

Cole, G. D. H. and Postgate, R., *The Common People,* Methuen, 1938.

George, D., *England in Transition,* Pelican Books, 1931.

Hammond, J. L. and Hammond, B., *The Town Labourer (1760-1832),* Guild Books, 1949.

Walker, J., *British Economic and Social History, 1700-1977,* MacDonald and Evans, 1979.

CHAPTER XIV

Captain Swing: the Rural Rebellion

In the first half of the nineteenth century the foreign visitor to England would have noted that there were no peasants. In defeated France the great estates of the rich had been broken up by the revolution, and the bulk of its food production was carried on by free peasants working on their own land. In England the peasants had lost their land and the rights that went with it, and had become a class of propertyless agricultural labourers, working for farmers who owned or rented land. The losers were therefore better off than the victors. The landowners, squires, farmers, parsons and others of the rural gentry had greatly increased their wealth in the preceding years; the war had made agriculture very profitable. Immense sums were spent by noblemen and landowners on building or rebuilding their residences, making them into the much visited 'stately homes' of today, and on the landscaping of their parks in the best classical taste. Huge areas were devoted to their game preserves, where man-traps and spring-guns were set to maim or kill the humble poacher trying to take a rabbit or a pheasant.

The standards of the farm labourer, often a highly skilled man in his own sphere, had fallen drastically. The loss of commons and grazing rights (between 1770 and 1830 6,000,000 acres of common land had been enclosed, and lost to the people) had affected him to the extent that, even when in full employment, he was living in poverty and barely able to provide his family with enough of the cheapest food. In the industrial north there was now alternative and better paid, if unattractive, work available in the factories; but in the rural south the land-worker's position was hopeless. There were many reasons that made it impractical or even impossible to move, apart from the long and expensive journey of many days across England.

The farmers now looked upon themselves as businessmen rather than paternalistic employers with responsibilities for the welfare of their 'households', as had been the ideal in the past. Then the worker was usually engaged for a year at the annual hiring-fair, and 'lived in' with the master as a member of his household, with the option of continuing in this position if he proved satisfactory. His food was normally the same as that of the farmer and his family, and it was customary to share a common table (the farmer sometimes brewed a stronger ale which he reserved for himself). There was a mutuality of interest and a social relationship between employer and employed. The ethics and philosophy of the new captalism destroyed all this. It became more profitable for the farmer if his hands lived out and he employed them as he needed them, by the day or week, thus turning them into casual workers. He also saved on their food. He drove their wages down to the very minimum needed to support life: and later, as will be discussed, below it. They had no alternative but to submit.

The reasons given for this harshness were the post-war drop in food prices, the increased rents demanded by the landowners, and the tithes that had to be paid to the clergy — a flat 10 per cent of the annual product of field and stock, sometimes paid in kind but now mainly in money.

The farmer was enabled to pay wages below subsistence level by a system known as the 'Speenhamland Act', from the Berkshire village where it was first applied. In 1795 a group of magistrates met there to consider imposing a minimum wage that would reflect the fluctuating price of bread, basic food of the poor, so that however high it went, nobody would starve. Under pressure from the farming interests they drew up a scheme whereby there should be no minimum wage, but every worker whose wages were insufficient to live on would draw a weekly dole from the parish for himself and his family, according to the number of his children and the price level of the quartern loaf. This was the 'bread and children law'. Thus the employer was absolved from the payment of a living wage; he was subsidised by the rate-payers, and the worker was reduced to the level of a parish pauper even when fully employed. A 'means test' was rigorously applied, and any worker who possessed a trifle of property, or some small savings, was barred from the parish relief he now needed to live on.

This system spread rapidly throughout the south of England. The villages became the homes of poverty-stricken paupers, living on bread, cheese, oatmeal, and what they could grow in their little gardens. Parish relief, formerly only applied for by workers in order keep themselves alive when sick or unemployed, now became a necessity for many in order to maintain a basic subsistence level.

One aspect of the Speenhamland Act was the demoralising effect it had on the worker himself, and on his dependents. No matter how little he did, he could not fall below the relief scale. No matter how hard he worked (except in special tasks or periods) he could not rise above it. There seemed little point in working at all, except that traditional village self-respect demanded at least a show of it. This expressed itself in the heavy fall in the productivity of agricultural labour shown in the statistics of the time. Previously, patriotic writers had been proud to compare the sturdy, well-fed, independent English peasant with his downtrodden, famished French counterpart. Now this situation was reversed.

There is little written evidence of the attitudes of the victims of this system. The labourers had no Members of Parliament to speak for them, no trade unions to defend them. Scarcely literate, they wrote no books, kept no diaries, made no great speeches. Their actions, however, expressed their feelings quite clearly.

On every farmer's land was an area of high vulnerability, the stacks or ricks in which he stored his hay, straw, corn and peas. These were often thatched against the weather at considerable expense, and constituted an important part of the economy of the farm. They were, moreover, highly inflammable. On some Kentish farms, in the summer of 1830, a number of these in the region of Sevenoaks and Orpington unaccountably caught fire at night and burned out. Some were on the property of a farmer who had made himself disliked by evicting a family and destroying their cottage. These fires were followed by a mass outbreak of rick-burning, machine-breaking, intimidation and rioting that spread over many of the southern counties, and has been called 'the last labourers' revolt'.

An important part of the farm-workers' year was the threshing that followed the harvest, when the ears of corn were beaten out of the husks with flails. This gave employment to many men for some weeks

26. Rick-burning in Kent, 1830.

and, as the work was urgent, was better paid. Now a threshing machine had been devised, worked by the power of a horse, that could do the work in a shorter time with fewer hands; so even this scanty annual source of income was to be curtailed. On the night of 28 August 1830 such a machine, hired by a farmer at Lower Hardres in Kent, was attacked by a crowd of men from surrounding villages and destroyed. The following day another was smashed near Hythe. Elsewhere ricks of corn and hay blazed through the night. The village labourer, regarded by his social superiors as a passive simpleton, was protesting against his degradation in the only way open to him.

The next day a hundred rapidly sworn-in special constables and a body of troops under two magistrates proceeded to Lower Hardres, but all was quiet there. No arrests were made or charges laid. It was later said that a meeting of farmers had decided against the use of the machines, but the two which had been attacked continued to be operated. All round Kent, and soon spreading into other counties, rick-burning and machine-breaking reached an epidemic scale.

According to *The Times* of 3 January 1831, a Kentish farmer said of his labourers: 'I should be well pleased if a plague was to break out among them, and then I could have their carcasses for manure . . .' On the next night all his ricks were fired. The arsonists were well known locally, said the report, but no action could be taken for lack of information and evidence.

It soon became apparent that these were not sporadic acts of desperate individuals. *The Times* suspected 'an organised system of stack-burning and machine-breaking'. Arrests and sentences were followed by the firing of the ricks and barns of the magistrates. (They, and the JPs, were drawn from the country gentry, the squires and farmers from whom an objective judgement could hardly be expected.) Local councillors who served on poor law committees and the 'overseers of the poor' found their property set alight.

The first rural machine-breakers caught were tried before Sir Edward Knatchbull at Canterbury. His sentence was a very mild one, compounded, no doubt, of a mixture of conscience and appeasement. He sentenced them to three days' imprisonment and gave them a caution, hoping 'that the kindness and moderation evidenced this day . . . would be met by a corresponding feeling among the people'.

His goodwill had little effect. Arson and breaking increased in all the southern counties. Reports appeared in the press of bands of labourers, armed with clubs and staves, marching along the country roads in broad daylight, and attacks on property began in the full light of the sun. Now crowds amounting to hundreds of men from many villages began openly to surround the houses of gentry and farmers. They used no violence, made no threats. One of them was their spokesman; the rest remained silent. The speaker spoke of their grievances, described their poverty, and asked for money. A pound or two satisfied them, and they went away. Farmers told them that what kept them poor and prevented fair wages were land-rents and tithes, and promised support if they would agitate against these two evils.

Meanwhile, from Wiltshire to Kent, barns and ricks were burning and farmers dismantling their machines. Labourers assembled in large groups and demanded fair wages to replace parish relief. Two shillings and sixpence a day was the sum demanded (about twelve-and-a-half pence), and at Brede a party of farmers met a workers' deputation and a document was drawn up and signed by both sides in which the farmers promised to pay two shillings and threepence a day to an able-bodied workman with two children, and more for larger families; and to put the local overseer of the poor out of the parish. Then a crowd of about five hundred marched to the house of Mr Abel, the bullying and insulting official of parish relief, dragging with them the village dung-cart. They hammered at his door until he agreed to come out and to get into the cart; then he was drawn by women and children into the next parish, where he was deposited by the roadside. He went off to the nearest magistrate to lodge his complaint, and, as the crowd dispersed, each man was given half a pint of beer by the farmers, and a present of a large barrel of the same to roll home with them. In return, the villagers demonstrated against tithes at the vicarage requesting that the church set up a school for their children.

This was to be an example followed in many districts — an arrangement with the farmers for an agreed rate of wages and the expulsion of the local overseer of the poor if he had a reputation as a callous and uncivil official. Many farmers enlisted the support of their labourers in their own struggle against tithes.

Landowners and obstinate farmers now began to receive letters signed 'Swing', or sometimes 'Captain Swing', threatening fire and vengeance if the demands contained within them were not conceded. The letters varied from scarcely legible scrawls to fair examples of handwriting. They were received in places as far apart as Hampshire and Kent. Some of these epistles have survived. One, written in a good copy-book hand, reads:

> This is to inform you what you have to undergo Jentlemen if providing you Don't pull down your meshenes and rise the poor mens wages the married men give tow and sixpense a day the single tow shillings or we will burn down your barns and you in them this is the last notes.

this is to inform you what you have to underge Jentelmen if providing you Dont pull down your nes: chines and rise the poor mens wages the maried men give tow and six pence a day a day the singel tow shilings. or we will burn down your barns and you in them this is the last notis from W B

27. A 'Swing' letter.

Another, to a wealthy farmer in Oxfordshire, showed that across the land there was communication between the rebel labourers:

> Remember in Kent they have set [on fire] all that would
> not submit and you we will serve the same for we are
> determined to make you support the Poor better than
> they have been supported yet for they are all starving at
> present so pull down your Thrashing Maschine or else
> Bread or Fire without delay. For we are 5 thousand men
> and will not be stopt.

Much briefer:

> This is to acquaint you that if your thrashing Machines
> are not destroyed by you directly we shall commence our
> labours. Signed on behalf of the whole, Swing.

To the authorities it seemed that the entire south of England was in a state of open rebellion. Bodies of soldiers patrolled the road, hundreds of special constables were sworn in and placed on duty. Even light artillery was sent down. There was no resistance. Bands of men who met on the roads dispersed peacefully when ordered, obviously by a pre-arranged policy, and even allowed leaders to be taken into custody where they could be indentified. Many farmers showed sympathy with the plight of their labourers, paid the wages demanded and dismantled their machines. In some places, the hated workhouses (known as 'bastilles') were stormed and ransacked, and the burning of barns and ricks and machine-breaking continued until winter. Yet not one person was killed or injured by the followers of Captain Swing. Attacks were only made on property.

Thrown into a panic, the country gentry suddenly became aware of the deplorable conditions of the poor at their gates. The new pay scales were being widely accepted, or sums near them reached by agreement. The government, hard pressed for troops as so many were policing the industrial north, advised local magistrates to be firm in putting down rioters and arresting suspects, and hinted that they need not be too scrupulous in observing the strict letter of the law. Thus a man was committed to prison, after hearing a sermon on the virtues of 'quietness', merely for saying, 'We have been quiet too long.'

£50 REWARD.

The **TRUSTEES** of the **CHARITIES** in **DEDHAM**, having received Information, that a most scandalous and disgusting Letter has been sent to the Rev. W. M. Hurlock, Lecturer of that Parish, **THREATENING** him, and the Premises in his Occupation, with

DESTRUCTION,

DO HEREBY OFFER A REWARD OF

Fifty Pounds

TO ANY PERSON

who will give such Information as shall ensure the **CONVICTION** of the **WRITER** of the above-mentioned Letter.

Dec. 13th, 1830.

PRINTED BY SWINBORNE, WALTER, AND TAYLOR, COLCHESTER.

28.   Reward poster, 1830.

The Times, in its humane and reforming mood, looked for divine help for the labourers. In a leader on 6 December 1830 it wrote:

> Let the rich be taught that Providence will not suffer them to oppress their fellow creatures with impunity. Here are tens of thousands of Englishmen, industrious, kind-hearted but broken-hearted human beings exasperated by insufficient food and clothing, by utter want of necessaries for themselves and their unfortunate families.

By the end of the year there was a general willingness on the part of the magistrates to recognise the justice (and force) of the labourers' demands, and to legalise a minimum wage policy. This was stopped by a circular letter from the home secretary, Lord Melbourne, (not an old-fashioned Tory, but a 'progressive' Whig) condemning such a settlement. 'Reason and experience', he wrote, 'concur in proving that a compliance with demands so unreasonable in themselves, and urged in such a manner, can only lead, and probably in a very short period of time, to the most disastrous results.' Justices, he added, had no longer the legal authority to determine wages.

This circular was followed by energetic action by local authorities. Magistrates banned all further meetings of villagers; anyone proposing higher wages was arrested and imprisoned, and many were arrested without specific charges being made against them. Troops and constables were busy everywhere; soon justices were complaining that there was no room in the prisons for real criminals, so crammed were they with farm workers.

The burnings and coercions died away; and the trials of the arrested labourers began with the assizes. Few judges troubled to hide their political prejudices or anger against the accused. Said Mr Justice Park at Aylesbury, trying men accused of demonstrating for a reduction in tithes:

> It was highly insolent in such men to require of a gentleman, who had by an expensive education qualified himself to discharge the sacred duties of a minister of the gospel, to descend from that station and reduce himself to the situation of common labourers.

> Mr Justice Bosanquet dismissed the whole cause of the disorders with a wave of his hand: 'Though there might be some distress among the rural poor,' he said, 'It was much exaggerated.'

> Mr Justice Taunton:

> 'That man must know little of the gentry of England . . . who represents them as tyrants to the poor, as not sympathising with their distress and as not anxious to relieve their burdens and promote their welfare and happiness . . .'

The rebellious labourers killed or injured nobody. Yet when the trials ended, nine men were sentenced to death, 457 to transportation, and many hundreds to varying terms of imprisonment. Such travesties of justice must always occur when the influential and wealthy sit in judgement on those without power or money.

SELECT BIBLIOGRAPHY

Hammond, J. L. and Hammond, B., *The Village Labourer,* Longman, 1948.
Hobsbawm, E. and Rudé, G., *Captain Swing,* Lawrence & Wishart, 1969.

CHAPTER XV
The Rise of the Trade Unions

In the Middle Ages, when all production was on the small scale of the handicraftsman, the level of wages was determined by the trade guilds, independent societies which included both masters and their journeymen; they had all served a long apprenticeship and worked side by side at the bench. There was no need for separate organisations of wage-earners, as most journeymen expected to become masters themselves. The unskilled workman made his own separate terms. With the decay of the guilds, the growth of investment, new ways of working and a growing gulf between employer and employed, with less opportunity for an artisan to set up for himself, the state undertook the task of regulating wage rates. In 1563 this power was transferred to the magistrates, who enforced decrees in the areas under their control. Workers now began to form 'combinations' to protect their seperate interests, which eventually developed into trade unions.

The early history of these combinations (also known as trade clubs, lodges, or societies) is not very well known. Before the Reformation they usually began as quasi-religious cults to honour the patron saint of a craft, or a local saint, and grew into societies for mutual aid in a particular trade. They provided financial aid for members in need, for instance, insurance during sickness or unemployment; they ran burial clubs; they ceremoniously initiated time-expired apprentices into journeyman status; and drank together at their chosen tavern. At their meetings, naturally, wages and work came under discussion; in the traditional English manner Parliament was petitioned for redress of grievances. If unsuccessful, there was possibly a 'turn-out', or refusal to work. This later became known as a 'strike', probably from the maritime term 'to strike sail'.

The legality of these societies was doubtful. They could be prosecuted for acting in restraint of trade, and most justices would declare an action to raise wages illegal. But if an employer wanted a strike stopped, he had to bring the matter before a high court. This took time and during this period the strike would usually be settled, one way or another.

By the eighteenth century there were already many 'societies' or unions existing, all of men in skilled trades; some still masquerading as friendly societies, burial clubs, etc. Because of bad communications these remained local. The development of national movements was a by-product of the railway age.

As the century drew to its close and the industrial revolution proceeded, these primitive unions were beginning to worry the employers. The workers' concept of trade solidarity and discipline was the very opposite of the 'laissez-faire' philosophy of the capitalists, and they claimed that for a workman to have to observe maximum hours of work, a negotiated wages structure and safety and other regulations was an unbearable restriction on his individual liberty to work as he pleased. Unionism was denounced as tyranny, and yet again the defence of freedom became a catchword to perpetuate poverty and exploitation.

In 1799 the House of Commons received a petition from a group of master millwrights asking it to ban any combination of journeyman millwrights in the London area. This was a year of revolution in France, of internal repression, of war and mutiny; and the government of Pitt found treason and sedition everywhere. Largely at the instigation of William Wilberforce — who is better know for his campaign to free the slaves in the colonies — Parliament passed the Combination Acts of 1799 and 1800. These made it illegal for any worker to join with another to obtain an increase in wages or to decrease hours of labour, to refuse to work with any other man or to persuade any other man to stop working. It forced workers to give evidence against each other. Penalties were imprisonment and hard labour, while other clauses made it virtually impossible for an accused man to have an adequate defence or to appeal.

These Combination Acts, with their strict impartiality, also banned any organisation of employers. During the period in which the Acts were enforced against workers, no action was ever taken against any employer. Indeed, the radical bobbin-net-maker Gravener Henson tried every means to get the law enforced against an illegal combination of masters in Nottingham. The authorities steadfastly refused to act. The workers were now, officially, entirely at the mercy of the employers, who were openly backed by the whole power of the law.

A well-known example of the operation of the Acts was the case of the compositors of *The Times* in 1810. These men were prosecuted for 'combining' and suffered terms of imprisonment from nine months to two years. They were also harangued by the judge for taking part in a 'wicked conspiracy' and opposing 'the very employers who gave you bread'. To associate peacefully with one's fellow-workers in order to influence wages and conditions now became a

29.   A trade union membership card of the Order of
Friendly Boiler Makers, 1836.

criminal conspiracy, an act of rebellion against the laws of the land.

The Acts did not destroy the unions. They merely made them illegal and drove them underground; their existence was an absolute necessity for the workers. To protect themselves they functioned as secret societies, binding their members with terrifying ceremonies and solemn oaths. Anonymous intimidation, threats and coercion of employers took the place of rational collective bargaining. Even the government was loath to enforce its own laws, and preferred to await private prosecutions by employers — usually as an action of their own illegal combinations!

In 1824 the radical tailor, Francis Place, began a movement for the repeal of the Combination Acts and the legal recognition of the employees' right to organise peacefully for economic benefits. It was received sceptically by the workers themselves, who felt that the House of Commons as then constituted would never agree, and that legalisation must await the victory of the movement for parliamentary reform. Nevertheless, by clever tactics and with the help of some sympathetic MPs headed by Joseph Hume, Place secured from Parliament a Select Committee to inquire into 'matters affecting industry'. Among these 'matters' it quietly included the operation of the Combination Acts.

Evidence before it was given by carefully chosen working men, who testified that the Acts did not prevent what they were intended to prevent, but merely increased strife and enmity between masters and men, and drove honest people into criminal behaviour and into holding the law in contempt. Some employers were also found who objected to this legal interference in their business and gave evidence accordingly.

The Select Committee reported to the Commons with the recommendation that peaceful union organisation be permitted, with safeguards against 'violence and intimidation'. Most MPs were country gentlemen who had little interest in industrial matters; they regarded the new class of manufacturers with hostility as upstarts and the sitting was very scantily attended. The business was put through as quickly as possible, with the supporting members refraining from speaking. The recommendations of the Select Committee were accepted, among them those on trade unionism, and the Combination Acts were repealed. Trade unionism now became a legal activity and industrial relations entered a new phase.

Although recognised as an entity *within* the law, a trade union as an organisation had no status *before* the law. It was therefore unable to enforce agreements made with employers, or sue for restitution against dishonest officials who robbed it of funds or property. While the worker had a legal right to withhold his labour, he might still be prosecuted for acting in restraint of trade.The non-member or blackleg was protected under the clauses against 'intimidation'. The unskilled casual labourer remained without union protection or assistance. Employers were quick to act on these advantages, many of which were not remedied for a century, and some not at all.

CHAPTER XVI

The Tolpuddle Martyrs

A celebrated manifestation of the hostility, difficulties and dangers that still beset trade unionists occurred in 1834, involving six men who have become known as the Tolpuddle Martyrs. These were farm workers of the small village of Tolpuddle in rural Dorset.

The plight of the agricultural worker and the social results of enclosures have already been described. Tolpuddle was just one of thousands of villages to suffer. The peasant grand-parents of the villagers had lived in relative sufficiency, with common-land, grazing, fuel and gleaning rights and worked for wages only part of their time. However, the enclosures and other restrictions had reduced the villagers to the status of casual labourers, wholly dependent on their earnings. Petty crime and poaching were prevalent — although a boy of fourteen could be hanged for stealing a sheep, or transported for taking a rabbit or a pheasant from a game preserve.

In the industrial areas the workers were organising their unions and beginning to fight openly for improvement. They had the backing of local radicals, reformers and progressives, and the notice of the press. The countryman in his isolation had no champions, no prominent or eloquent spokesmen, no publicity. William Cobbett, in his *Rural Rides*, summed up his condition:

> Their dwellings are little better than pig-beds, and their looks indicate that their food is not nearly equal to that of a pig . . . In my whole life I never saw human wretchedness equal to this; no, not even amongst the free negroes in America.

Such was life in the picturesque villages of England under the rule of the squires.

Tolpuddle is one of many villages along the course of the little River Puddle, each sharing in an echo of its name. Straggling along the road from Bere Regis to Dorchester, it is set among pleasant water-meadows and gentle green hills. In 1834 it had a male population of 175, about half of them children. In most of the districts, the labourer's agitations had succeeded in winning a minimum wage of ten shillings, (fifty pence) a week. In remote Dorset it remained eight shillings (forty pence). On that wage even potatoes were a luxury and the labourers' usual diet was bread, oatmeal, beans, cheese and roots like swedes and turnips. Normal dress consisted of ragged second-hand clothes under a coarse smock.

A prominent and respected resident of Tolpuddle was George Loveless, a labourer of thirty-seven, with three children. Like many of the pioneers of the labour movement, he was a Methodist, a sect that stressed the importance of the individual and his personal character and behaviour. With great difficulty he had taught himself to read and write in the evenings after long days in the fields, and out of his tiny earnings had acquired a few religious books. His church accepted him as a lay preacher, and he had a local reputation as a fluent speaker. He was thus a worthy representative of the best type of working man of his time, who was able to maintain his human dignity and integrity even in the demoralising conditions in which he, his family and neighbours existed.

Such a man would not suffer tamely the oppression of poverty in the midst of a prosperous countryside. In 1832, with some other villagers, he met a group of the local farmers who promised that wages would be raised to the level of the surrounding districts. The labourers were doubtful of the value of this promise. They were reassured by their vicar, Dr Warren, who was present. 'If your masters should attempt to run from their word,' he told them, 'I will undertake to see you righted, so help me God.' The men returned to their work satisfied. But the promised rise was not forthcoming. The law-abiding Loveless then led his neighbours to call on their local magistrate, Warren Pitt, to ask his advice. Pitt offered to arrange a meeting of the farmers and their men at the County Hall, Dorchester, under the chairmanship of James Frampton, the presiding magistrate of the Division. A deputation from Tolpuddle trudged the seven miles to Dorchester on the appointed day, with George Loveless as their spokesman. There they found that Frampton did not act as an impartial chairman, but as the mouthpiece of the employers. He informed them that magistrates no longer had the power to impose wage rates and that there was no law that could compel masters to pay more than they chose to pay; and that workers must be content to work for that amount. Loveless replied that they were not now demanding increased wages, but the implementation of an agreement already made and promised. The masters denied making any such agreement. The Reverend Dr Warren was cited as witness, and his words quoted. He stoutly denied having said any such thing: and the men set out on the seven mile tramp home in a spirit of despondency and disillusion.

An unknown rural poet wrote at the time:

> The 'nobs' of Old England, of shameful renown,
> Are striving to crush the poor man to the ground,
> They'll beat down their wages and starve them complete
> And make them work hard for Eight Shillings a Week.
>
> A poor man to labour (believe me 'tis so)
> To maintain his family is willing to go
> Either hedging or ditching, to plough or to reap,
> But how does he live on Eight Shillings a Week?

Worse was to come. After this victory the farmers counter-attacked and reduced wages by one shilling, pleading hard times. Now the weekly income was seven shillings. George Loveless pointed out that it was impossible to live a lawful existence on this sum.

30.   The Tolpuddle Martyrs from part of the wall decoration of the old time Dorchester exhibition at Wimborne.

In the evenings after work the men of Tolpuddle took to meeting under the large sycamore tree on the village green. (This tree, known as the 'martyrs' tree', still lives though now it leans heavily on props.) It was here in 1833 that Loveless made a suggestion to the villagers. He had heard, he told them, of trade societies, or unions, which could be legally organised by workers to defend and improve their standard of living. He proposed that the Tolpuddle people form such a society and use it in common to bring pressure on their employers for an increase in wages.

Loveless had a cousin in London, and through him contacted by post the Grand National Consolidated Trade Union. This, the short-lived first attempt at a nation-wide organisation to embrace and represent both skilled and unskilled workers, was the brain-child of the visionary humanitarian Robert Owen. It still contained many of the earlier conspiratorial elements surviving from the years of illegality, including impressive ceremonials and the swearing-in of new members with binding oaths. The GNCTU offered to send down two delegates to help form the new union, and, in October 1833, these duly arrived in the village. They brought with them, as essential luggage, a large painting of Death, depicted as a skeleton with scythe and hour-glass to be used in the initation ceremony. They were received by a meeting of some forty men, held in the loft of the cottage of George Standfield.

The delegates explained the function and organisation of a union and read out the rules: lay officials, and a management committee of eight was to be democratically elected; every member was to pay one shilling entrance fee 'on his initiation' and one penny a week unless sick or unemployed; and so on. Plans were made for the withdrawal of labour if a man was discharged from work for union membership, or if there was a further reduction in wages. All acts of violence were banned, nothing illegal would be tolerated. No religious or political matters were to be discussed at lodge meetings, nor was there to be any obscene language.

On 9 December the Grand Lodge of Tolpuddle of the Agricultural Labourers Friendly Society was formed. In the circumstances, it was a dangerous step for the members to take. They were sure of the hostility of the farmers and squires, and these were the very Justices of the Peace who would have the power to arrest them and sit in judgement on them. They were also the employers who would not give work to a union member, and who owned the houses their workers lived in. Membership of the society could mean unemployment and homelessness, as well as prosecution for breach of some nebulous law. Therefore membership of the lodge was kept secret, not to be divulged to anyone outside the organisation, not even to wives and families. In spite of all this, everybody in the district soon knew of its existence and who were its members. Such things cannot remain unknown in a closed village society.

One person who heard of it was James Frampton, the Dorchester magistrate. A wealthy country gentleman, he was noted for the zeal with which he had combated the rural agitations of the period of

'Captain Swing'. He had read the Riot Act, called out the yeomanry, denounced the labourers, on many occasions when others found it hardly necessary, and his house was barricaded like a military stronghold (it had never been threatened or attacked).

As soon as he heard of the union lodge at Tolpuddle, though it in no way infringed the law, he began to correspond on the matter with the Home Secretary, Lord Melbourne. Melbourne advised the discreet use of 'trusty persons' — in other words, spies. Trade union legality was still very unclear; for instance, it may have been legal for the local men to found their lodge, but illegal for the delegates to visit them for that purpose. And as for an initiation — if an oath was administered it could be interpreted as a breach of the Act of 1797, passed with specific reference to the naval mutinies of that year, and strengthened in 1799, which made the taking or giving of secret oaths a criminal offence. (Freemasons were exempted — they were considered gentlemen.)

The 'trusty persons' were put to work; and it was not long before they had frightened the labourers Edward Legg and John Lock into turning informers. They were not spies, but timid and worried men whose fears had been aroused by skilful questioning and threats, and they admitted to taking an oath at their initiation in the upper room of the Standfields' cottage. The prosecution of the rural trade unionists now became possible.

On 22 February 1834, in public places in the village, official posters appeared headed in large letters 'Caution'. They warned the people that any person taking an oath not authorised by law, or administering it, and any person persuading or inducing another person to become a member of a society bound by such an oath, was guilty of a felony and liable to seven years transportation. Four days were allowed for any person affected to reveal his participation and throw himself on the mercy of the courts. This warning was signed by Frampton and eight other magistrates, two of them his relatives.

The notices must have caused some consternation in Tolpuddle. Because of their rural isolation, none of its men were aware that the taking of oaths was illegal. They had been instructed that the organisation of a union was within the law and had acted in that belief.

On Monday morning 24 February, one day before the expiry of the four days allowed, George Loveless left his cottage to go to work. He said good-bye to his wife and children, little dreaming that it would be more than three years before he came home again. In the street he was accosted by the local constable and arrested on a warrant. Thinking it a small matter, he went peacefully with him. The constable also arrested Loveless's brother, James, Thomas Standfield and his son John, James Brine and James Hammett, all

31. The martyrs' tree,
Tolpuddle.

Tolpuddle men who had rarely travelled beyond Dorchester, and all
members of the lodge.

The six men walked quietly with the constable the seven miles to
Dorchester, expecting to have to walk back when the problem had
been dealt with. They thought it would be connected with the
warning posters, and that an apology to the bench, a statement that
they acted in ignorance with no intent to break the law, would win
them a reprimand and a warning and their dismissal. However, they
were taken before Frampton and the Recorder, who produced the
shame-faced Edward Legg. Legg identified them as the six men who
had been present at Standfield's cottage and had administered an
oath to him.

To their astonishment and indignation they were henceforth
treated as common criminals. Taken to Dorchester Goal, they were
stripped, their clothes searched, their hair clipped short. Their homes
were searched, and in Loveless's cottage was found a box containing
the rules of the lodge, a subscription book and a letter from the
corresponding secretary. These were taken away to be produced as
evidence.

The six men were to remain in the cells of the gaol for more than a
month, faced with the realisation that they were considered
criminals, liable to a possible sentence of transportation to a convict
settlement in distant Australia, their families abandoned to fend for
themselves as best they could, perhaps never to be seen by them
again. Despair and bitterness did not destroy their honour. Loveless,
at least, was offered the temptation of gaining his freedom
by turning King's Evidence, but he indignantly refused. They were
visited by the prison chaplain, who tried to convince them that they

were idle rebellious men who sought to ruin employers who were sometimes almost as badly off as their workmen.

The Government, headed by Earl Grey, in its anxiety to combat rural unionism, took the case out of the hands of the Dorset magistrates and decided to prosecute in person. All the power and experience of the state was to be turned against six labouring men who had sought, in company with their neighbours, a legal way of supporting their families by hard work for a living wage.

The trial opened at the Dorchester Spring Assizes on 15 March 1834. The case had aroused great interest and the court was crowded with the public and the press. All the Dorset papers had been full of stories attacking and deriding trade unionism, linking it with the twin horrors of sedition and revolution and branding it as a menace to the freedom of the British working man. In an editorial the *Dorset County Chronicle* found one of its causes to be the growth of literacy among the people. It condemned 'a mania for diffusing among the lower orders an education altogether unsuited to their station in society'. It is not known if the wives and children of the accused were present at the trial. The walk of fourteen miles, and the anguish, may have been too much for them. But a number of Tolpuddle men were undoubtedly present.

With traditional pomp and ceremony the judge, Mr Baron Williams, was installed in the Crown Court. A Grand Jury was sworn in to decide whether the indictment was true and valid, so that the case could come to trial. This Grand Jury consisted of the nine magistrates who had signed the warrants for the arrests, plus a brother-in-law of the Home Secretary. To nobody's surprise it found the indictment to be a true bill, and a Petty Jury was then sworn to try the prisoners. This was obviously selected with great care — one man was rejected because he was a known Methodist. Juries had been known to return unexpected verdicts and to throw out cases — but not in rural Dorset.

The crime the prisoners were charged with was, in plain language, that of administering to Edward Legg an unlawful oath, contrary to the Unlawful Oaths Act of 1797, plus eleven other minor counts. The prosecution outlined the government's case, asserting that the accused were guilty under the Act of committing a felony. The two witnesses, Legg and Lock, were produced.

Legg frightened, embarrassed and reluctant to talk testified that he had attended a meeting at Standfield's cottage, where the six accused were present. He was taken upstairs, blindfolded, made to kneel, and heard some words being read which he did not understand. Something was said, as he was kneeling, about striking for wages, and it was to be kept secret, but he was not sure what it meant. His eyes being freed, he saw the two brothers, George and

James Loveless, standing beside the tall painting of Death. There was more reading aloud, 'but I don't know what it was'. He was then given a book to kiss, 'which looked like a Bible'.

This insubstantial nonsense, corroborated in terms equally tenuous by Lock, was almost the whole of the government's case. The precise wording of the oath, and how it had been sworn, was never stated in court.

The counsel for the Loveless brothers, Mr Derbishire, did his best. He urged the good characters of the accused, argued that similar ceremonies were long part of normal procedure in joining a union, and no legal exception to it had ever been taken before this. The Act of 1797 had only been passed in case of mutiny in the armed forces, and could not apply to civil life; and that the union had never tried to intimidate or threaten the employers or its members.

The prisoners were not allowed to give sworn evidence in their own defence, but George Loveless, as spokesman, was permitted to write a statement on behalf of all. He wrote:

> My Lord, if we have violated any law, it was not done intentionally. We have injured no man's reputation, character, person or property; we were uniting together to preserve ourselves, our wives and children from utter degradation and starvation. We challenge any man, or number of men, to prove that we acted, or intended to act, different from the above statement.

This was read to the jury ('mumbled', said Loveless) and was later to appear in the press. Volumes could not have said more, or with greater restraint and dignity.

The judge summed up. He directed the jury to find them all guilty if they were satisfied that an unlawful oath had been administered. Then he spoke of the cruelty of a union in exacting subscriptions out of the scanty pay of labouring, men, and stated that their major plan was the destruction of property.

The jury was out for a very short time, and their verdict was guilty. The Tolpuddle men were each given the maximum sentence possible — seven years' transportation: 'For the sake of offering an example and a warning,' in the words of the judge.

Having heard his sentence George Loveless wrote something on a piece of paper, which he afterwards threw to the watching crowd outside the court. It was a poem that has since become known as the 'Song of Freedom'. He was not its author, and never claimed to be, but it has often been wrongly credited to him. It read:

> God is our guide, from field, from wave,
> From plough, from anvil, and from loom;
> We come, our country's rights to save

We raise the watch-word, liberty,
We will, we will, we will be free.

God is our guide. No swords we draw.
We kindle not war's battle fires,
By union, reason, justice, law.
We claim the birthright of our sires;
We raise the watch-word, liberty,
We will, we will, we will be free!

A word must be said about James Hammett. It later transpired that he had not been present at the initiation, but his brother John had been, and the warrant had been wrongly made out for James. But John's wife was nearing the end of her first pregnancy and was about to give birth. In order to protect the young couple and the baby, Hammett deliberately took his brother's place under the charge, said nothing, and endured his brother's punishment. The other five knew, of course, but at Hammett's request remained silent. Such was the moral strength of these pioneers!

The six men were paraded in convict dress through the public streets, chained hand and foot and to each other. For two months they lay manacled in the hulks of the decaying battleships moored off Portsmouth as staging-posts for transportees. They had to endure the company of the most evil criminals, in unlit, stinking, overcrowded holds. They were even denied each other's company; George Loveless, as 'ringleader', was confined in a different hulk. The green valley of the River Puddle must have seemed very far away, and they were naturally full of anxiety for the welfare and safety of their families.

At length the convict ships arrived to take them away. On 11 April the five were packed into the *Surrey* and sailed off to New South Wales, arriving at Sydney after a voyage of sixteen weeks; four months of pitching and rocking, locked up in darkness with sea-sickness and vermin, permitted on deck for only four hours daily. For many convicts it was a sentence of death — they never survived to land. George Loveless went separately to Van Dieman's Land (now Tasmania), disembarking at Hobart. There he worked for a while in a chain-gang at road-making then was sent to a government farm, where he was freed from his fetters and became a stockman, looking after the cattle. His five comrades were widely separated over the country, many hundreds of miles from each other, assigned to different settlers' farms. The settlers 'bought' the convicts from the government for £1 each, and they were, to all intents and purposes, virtually slaves.

The sufferings and adventures of the six men during their life in Australasia cannot be described here. But at home in England the

32. A satirical cartoon entitled 'The Dorchester Unionists Imploring Mercy!!! of their King', *Political Drama*, No. 32, no date.

trial and its outcome raised a great storm of protest. It was quickly realised that although they were being punished for administering an oath, their actual offence was the legal act of organising a trade union. People asked why the Duke of Cumberland, Grand Master of the Orange Lodges, could continue to administer oaths without prosecution, as could Oddfellows, Masons, and members of similar societies. Petitions were signed, asking for the prisoners to be returned and pardoned, and forwarded to the king, William IV. He refused to take any action. Mass meetings were held on a scale never before witnessed, and petitions poured into the House of Commons. The case of the 'Dorchester Labourers' became a major topic throughout the country. Even many opponents of trade unionism had to admit that an obvious injustice had been done, that the law had been 'stretched' too far; while every organised worker saw it as an open threat to himself and his union. Sessions of Parliament were interrupted by MPs raising the issue, and it became an embarrassment to the government itself. The magistrate James Frampton, prime mover in the whole affair, added fuel to the flames when it became known that he had secured the refusal of parish relief to the dependents of the prisoners, saying to Mrs Standfield, 'you shall suffer want, you shall have no mercy.' He also refused them permission to visit the men in prison. The trade unions immediately launched a fund organised by the London Dorchester Committee which provided a regular income for all the dependents.

The authorities still insisted that justice had been done according to the law, but nevertheless ameliorated to some extent the conditions of the victims.

The demand for 'freedom and return' reached its height in April 1834 in a great demonstration to present a petition to the king through Parliament. Half a million signatures had been obtained, all mounted on one huge role of paper, and it was accompanied by 40,000 men marching in an orderly and peaceful manner. Home Secretary Lord Melbourne refused to see their deputation, but promised to pass the petition on to the king. There was a full-scale debate in the Commons, where a great speech for 'freedom and return' was made by Dr Wakly, member for Finsbury. Owing to the nature of the still-unreformed House, it was defeated by 308 votes to eight-two. He raised the matter again after almost a year, and was then casually informed by the Prime Minister, Lord Russell, that the royal pardon had at last been granted and the six men would be brought home and freed.

It took a further year before the first of them, George Loveless, arrived home on 13 June 1837. With the financial assistance of the Committee he was enabled to write his account of his experiences, published as a pamphlet under the title *The Victims of Whiggery*.

The other men followed, as they were located on their remote and distant stations (Hammett had to walk 400 miles to his) almost four years after their arrest. On 16 April 1838, they were the guests of honour at a banquet in London arranged by the Committee. Thousands gathered to cheer them as they drove past the Home Office with a band playing 'See the Conquering Hero Comes'.

The Committee raised enough money to buy and equip two farms in Essex, one of which was taken over by the Standfields, the other by the Lovelesses and James Brine. Hammett, the last to return, was always a quiet and secretive man. He was content to resume his old way of life as a labourer in Tolpuddle, and when he grew old and blind he refused to be a burden to his relatives and voluntarily entered Dorchester Workhouse, where he died in 1891.

On the hundreth anniversary of the arrests, in 1934, the Trades Union Congress organised a commemoration at Tolpuddle. Six cottages were erected, each bearing the name of one of the men, together with a community hall, for the occupation of retired farm-worker trade unionists, while George Lansbury unveiled a headstone over the grave of James Hammett.

In 1912, a Memorial Gateway was erected in front of the Methodist Chapel. It bears the inscription:

> Erected in honour of the faithful and brave men of this village who in 1834 so nobly suffered transportation in

the cause of liberty, justice and righteousness, and as a stimulus to our own and future generations.

SELECT BIBLIOGRAPHY

Frith, M. and Hopkinson, A., *The Tolpuddle Martyrs,* E. P. Publishing, 1974.
Marlow, J., *The Tolpuddle Martyrs,* Andre Deutsch, 1971.

CHAPTER XVII

The Reform Bill

The change from water power to steam power as the source of energy for industry changed the entire demographic map of England. Industry along with a mass of the population moved into the northern areas where coal was mined, and the transformation of the rural landscape into the 'black country' took place.

Under the eternal pall of smoke, in squalid streets in developing industrial areas, the new working class lived with few of the benefits of nineteenth century civilisation enjoyed by the middle and upper classes. They were overworked when employed, never very far from subsistence level, starved when they were unemployed, old or sick, denied any voice in government — the victims of an uncontrolled and avaricious free enterprise. Yet it was their labour and their skills that were turning Britain into the workshop of the world and the first industrial nation. Great wealth was acquired by capitalists, investors and employers; but little seeped down to the men and women on the factory floor, the miners, the shipbuilders, the iron smelters.

The reaction of the workers has already been described. It was mainly violent and localised. Riots, machine-breaking and arson had achieved little in the long run when compared with the sacrifices made. Thoughtful workers saw that the two great foreign revolutions, the American and the French, had resulted in the establishment of democratic republics with universal male suffrage. The idea grew that there could be little improvement here until the whole system of government had been changed and the working man without property had the right to vote, to sit in Parliament, to make the country's laws. Given the great numerical superiority of the poor, this, people felt, would result in the election of a radical government pledged to social reform and a revolutionary change in the lives of the common people. Shelley wrote:

> Let a great Assembly be
> Of the fearless and the free . . .
> All that must eternal be
> Witness the solemnity.

The demand for reform was bitterly opposed by the authorities, national and local. Their suppression of an orderly and peaceful public meeting in its support, in St Peter's Fields, Manchester, has become part of labour history, known as the 'Peterloo massacre."

A 'monster meeting' was announced for 16 August 1819, and the public was invited to this traditional meeting-place to hear the famous 'Orator Hunt' speak in support of reform. Every effort was made by the organisers to ensure that there would be no violence. Only the aged and the lame were allowed to carry walking-sticks. Knowing that the local magistrates were doubtful about the legality of the meeting, Hunt offered to surrender himself to them before it took place; this offer was rejected. As no ban was announced, more than 80,000 people, women and children included, gathered peacefully round the banners and the cart that served as a rostrum and listened in silence to Hunt's eloquent discourse. Around the perimeter the magistrates had assembled a large contingent of mounted yeomanry and several troops of regular cavalry. They suddenly decided that the meeting was illegal and ordered the yeomanry to arrest the speaker.

The horsemen, with sabres drawn, forced their way through the dense crowd and Hunt peacefully allowed himself to be taken into custody. Suddenly a trooper cried out, 'Have at their flags!' and the soldiers began to strike out in all directions with their weapons.

33.   The 'Peterloo Massacre' at Manchester in 1819, by George Cruikshank.

Women screamed as people tried to avoid the sharp sword-edges and get out of the way of the horses. The watching magistrates panicked and ordered the Hussars to disperse the crowd. The cavalry charged into the mass of unresistng people wielding their sabres. Confusion and chaos ensued as men, women and children tried to escape, and in a few minutes the Fields were empty except for articles of dress and torn banners — and eleven dead and many wounded. More than four hundred people were injured, mostly by sword-slashes; 113 of them were women.

No protest was made by the government to the perpetrators of this atrocity. Instead, the Home Secretary, Lord Sidmouth, sent a letter to the Manchester magistrates congratulating them on their handling of the affair.

The workers were not the only social class to demand reform. Their employers, the capitalists and the middle class in general, were almost equally deprived of any share in government. Despite the wealth, power and importance of the middle classes, the country was still ruled by the landowners, those relics of feudalism. They made the law in Parliament; enforced it as judges and magistrates; they officered the armed forces; they filled all the principal offices of administration. Out of a total adult male population (in 1830) of 6,000,000, there were only 839,000 entitled to vote, or roughly one in seven. The two great parties of the landowners, the Tories and the Whigs, contested the elections between themselves. The Whigs, with a reputation for liberalism, looked with favour on extending the vote to the middle class to whom they looked for support in their power-struggle against the Tories and the crown. The industrialists backed their own demands for representation by political organisation, calling on the workers for their help. The workers' movements, eager for reform, gave their backing in great public meetings and demonstrations, thinking that along with their employers they, too, would be enfranchised. Thus strengthened, the industrialists threatened a tax strike. 'No taxes paid until the Reform Bill is passed,' was the slogan. They exerted economic pressure, drawing out their money from the banks and insisting on payment in gold. They threatened to stop all business, to create a run on the banks, to buy up freeholds and so acquire voting power. The workers supported them with mass meetings and petitions.

The outcome of all this was the First Reform Bill of 1831, which proposed raising the voters to almost a million by extending the franchise to £10 freeholders and forming a number of new constituencies for the industrial areas while abolishing over-represented ones like Old Sarum. This was proposed as a practical safety-valve against revolution. 'We drive over to revolution those whom we shut out from power,' said Macaulay in the House of Lords,

'Reform, that you may preserve!' The Commons passed the Bill by one vote. However, King William IV dissolved Parliament to prevent it from becoming law.

The workers protested by rioting all over the country. At Bristol, for example, they broke into the prison, released the prisoners, and burned down the bishop's palace and the town hall. The military opened fire, and twelve people were killed.

In the new elections a Whig government was returned which passed the Bill, only to have it thrown out by the Lords; but eventually, under threat of cramming their chamber with new pro-reform peers, it was accepted and became the Reform Act of 1832.

Thus the employers and the middle classes won the right to vote and to sit in the Commons with the landowners. They were satisfied; they felt that reform had gone far enough. It had been won by their economic pressure; now the vote must be kept from their employees who would use it to make free enterprise less free and less profitable.

This desertion by their late allies shocked the common people. It was dubbed the 'Great Betrayal' and in a few years was to produce the first great national movement of the working class — Chartism.

SELECT BIBLIOGRAPHY

Lewellyn, A., *The Decade of Reform (the 1830s),* David and Charles, 1972.

CHAPTER XVIII

Chartism

It was not long before the workers saw the results of the 'reformed Parliament' of 1832, which they had helped to bring about. It was this government that persecuted the Tolpuddle Martyrs; and in 1834 it produced the Poor Law Amendment Act which completely changed the system of relief of the poor. It decided that the causes of poverty were mainly the 'fraud, indolence and improvidence' of the people, who looked on parish relief as a right to which they were entitled, despite the burden it laid on the ratepayers. The new Act took relief out of the hands of the local parishes and made it the responsibility of the national state. It put an end to external relief, decreeing that persons or families in want and unable to make a living must apply for admission to a 'Workhouse', also called a 'Parish Union', as there was one built for a number of parishes. There they would be fed and maintained. All the indigent, whether temporarily unemployed, sick, or aged, were alike classified as 'paupers', and the purpose of the workhouse was unashamedly punitive. The unfortunate inmates were treated much as felons, without civil rights. The food was deliberately 'coarse', meagre and unappetising. The sexes were segregated ('to prevent breeding') and old couples who had spent their lives together, as well as young couples henceforth saw each other only from a distance in the dining-room or chapel. Children were separated from parents and brought up in their own section, like orphans. Beer and tobacco, of course, were banned. No visitors were allowed, or visits made outside, without written permission from the master. All able-bodied inmates were put to work. The workhouse residents consisted of the fit, the mentally handicapped, the physically disabled, pregnant women, children, infants and the senile, all crammed together.

Due to the insecurity of work, recurring unemployment, the impossibility of most people to save for crises or old age, a large proportion of the working class expected to receive relief at some time, especially when past working age, and this was generally recognised. The prospect now offered them by the reformed Parliament was a pitiless, grudging, inhuman imprisonment, the break-up of families and the final indignity of a pauper's grave. Everybody knows the story of Oliver Twist and the astonished horror of the Chairman of the Board: 'What! Do I understand that he has asked for more, after he had eaten the supper provided by the dietary?' (The supper was a small bowl of thin gruel.)

There was mass resistance, especially in the north, to the new system, but eventually it was established everywhere. The workhouse became the constant dread of the people, as it was intended to be. Many workers endured hunger and even death rather than enter these 'bastilles'. 'If they want to die, let them die, and diminish the surplus population.' Mr. Scrooge's attitude was also that of the government.

More and more the working man became convinced that only a truly reformed Parliament, dominated by members of his own class, could help him. The idea grew into the naive belief that this would bring about the millennium and replace individual self-interest with a higher social motive. The demand for the vote and representation became the major political obsession of the people, predominating over all other issues. As a meeting of London workers resolved:

> In 1832 the working class, by their moral and physical organisation beat the Tories for the sake of the Whigs. By the same means . . . they can beat both Whigs and Tories for the sake of themselves.

In June 1836, a small group of men, headed by William Lovett, met to form the London Working Men's Association. This was to be a new type of society; membership was to be confined strictly to wage-earning proletarians. Its objects were a little vague but stressed social justice and political equality. It laid great emphasis on the need for popular education and the removal of the stamp duties which put newspapers beyond the reach of most people. Lovett was elected secretary, and he emerges as one of the great popular leaders of the nineteenth century. Born in 1800 in Cornwall, he was apprenticed to a rope-maker, but moved to London and taught himself cabinet-making, becoming the secretary of their trade society. He educated himself with the help of the London Mechanics' Institute and became a follower of the visionary socialist pioneer Robert Owen. He remained convinced that the education of the people would lead to their emancipation and that the major source of evil was the excessive ownership of property by individuals.

Under his influence, and with the help of Francis Place, the LWMA produced in 1837 a programme of demands containing six main clauses for reform:

1. Universal male suffrage;

2. Equal electoral districts;
3. Annual parliaments;
4. Payment for MPs;
5. Secret ballots (voting then was by open show of hands);
6. No property qualifications for MPs.

These six points summed up most of the demands of the reformers and radicals, that they hoped would usher in a new democratic and prosperous Britain and were adopted and supported by popular organisations throughout the country. At least three of them had been demanded by the Levellers in the seventeenth century, and were here resurrected. In a short while, all over the country, 150 different organisations declared their support or affiliation. These had been formed for different purposes — to work and agitate for a free press, for factory reform, for currency reform; to oppose the Corn Laws, the 'truck' system, and to support many different causes. All united round the 'six points', which were seen to herald the fulfilment of all their various objectives. Lovett and his modest LWMA found themselves caught up in a great national movement; and with the acceptance of the six points by the powerful radical middle-class Birmingham Political Union whose chief interest was currency reform, they formed a programme for which the whole of the unfranchised could unite. It was printed for the public in 1848, and was named by Lovett 'The People's Charter', and the movement in its support, 'Chartism'.

Only two major organisations of the people remained aloof — Robert Owen and his followers, and the trade unions; whatever the sympathies of their members, the unions themselves were absorbed in their local economic battles with the employers, and considered the Charter irrelevant. Their victories were to be won on the workshop floor. Many Owenites became Chartists and tried to convert the movement to a kind of early socialism but with little success.

It was decided that the campaign would begin with the six points drawn up in the traditional form of a petition to Parliament. This was to be put before the public at a series of great meetings and as many signatures as possible were to be obtained and presented to the House of Commons. Such was the enthusiasm that there was little doubt of its success if enough people signed. Meanwhile, a Convention of delegates elected at the mass meetings was to gather in London to arrange for the presentation of the Charter and decide on the action to be taken in case of its rejection.

The meetings were duly held, and the delegates elected. The numbers attending and approving the Charter were immense. In Glasgow, 150,000; Birmingham, 200,000, and Manchester claimed a quarter of a million. Never before had any cause gained such popular support. In the northern industrial areas, great torchlight processions were held with slogans like 'Universal suffrage or universal revenge', 'Fight to the knife for children and wife', 'More pigs and fewer priests'. Demands were made for arms, and stores of pikes, firearms and bullets were collected and concealed. Men met at night on the moors for training and drill. Already in the movement two distinct trends were appearing — in the ravaged north of England, 'Physical Force' Chartism, with demands for armed insurrection, and in Birmingham and London, 'Moral Force' Chartism, emphasising education and legal change. A number of radical MPs promised their support in the House of Commons.

In August 1838 the National Chartist Movement was officially anounced at a great meeting in Birmingham at which supporters of all opinions aired their views. Advocates of both physical and moral force were present. But the dominant feeling emerged that, in the words of John Stevens:

> Chartism is no political movement, where the question is getting the ballot . . . This question of universal suffrage is a knife and fork question . . . a bread and cheese question . . . If any man asks me what I mean by universal suffrage, I would answer: that every working man in the land has the right to a good coat on his back . . . a good dinner on his table.

The Chartist Convention met in London in February 1839, with

34.   A contemporary engraving of the Chartist attack on the Westgate Hotel, Newport, 1839.

fifty-four delegates, and sat until September. Its expenses were met by a national subscription of one penny a week from all Chartists. 'Missionaries' were sent all over the country to build the organisation, sell its considerable literature, collect signatures, and report back. They received the impression that large areas were under the influence of the physical force section and were preparing for armed rebellion. Under the leadership of a fiery Irish squire, Feargus O'Connor (he ran his own influential radical newspaper, *The Northern Star*) their slogan was 'Peaceably if we can, forcibly if we must'.

The great petition for the six points had now obtained 1,280,000 signatures; pasted together, the pages were over two miles in length and weighed six hundredweight. The Convention turned its attention to what it called 'Ulterior Measures' — what to do if the petition was rejected. There were divided opinions on this, as on most other matters. Eventually nine measures were approved, the most important of which was a call for a 'Sacred Month', a 'National Holiday', in other words, a general strike. How the striking workers were to exist was not made clear, nor how it could succeed while the unions showed little interest. There was to be a refusal to pay rents, rates and taxes, and a boycott of all non-Chartist tradesmen.

Meanwhile the government, anxious to preserve its image, and wary of a repetition of the Peterloo Massacre, took no dramatic repressive steps. It increased the numbers of its spies and secret agents and strictly enforced existing laws. It strengthened its garrisons in the strongly 'physical' areas, and put General Sir Charles Napier in command. Napier was a remarkable soldier and a Tory radical (there were such things then, and some of the 'physicals' were in that category) who sympathised with many of the Chartists' demands but was intent on preventing armed rebellion and civil war. He personally attended Chartist meetings and discussed policy with the leaders. When some of them expressed doubts about the value of his artillery, he held a special demonstration of gunnery for them, to prove his point.

The Home Secretary, Lord Russell, called on the middle classes to form volunteer corps, and offered them arms and training: an open invitation to class war.

In Birmingham the magistrates banned public meetings at the Bull Ring and called out the military to enforce it; this led to days of rioting and disorder in the streets. The Convention decided to move to that city, away from the more peaceful atmosphere of the capital. Lovett signed a placard of protest which was posted up in public places, and for this he was arrested. Birmingham was placed under martial law, and Lovett went to prison for a year. With the leader of the 'morals' behind bars the influence of O'Connor and the 'physicals' increased.

The great petition with its six points was presented to the Commons on 12 July 1839, by Thomas Attwood, MP, in a speech so conciliatory that it was little more than another statement of the poverty of the people rather than a demand for the Charter. Most of the Convention repudiated it. Lord Russell opposed it as an attack on property by the propertyless, and the House threw it out by 235 votes to forty-five.

Now was the time for the 'Ulterior Measures' and the 'Sacred Month', but the Convention suddenly realised its weaknesses in organisation and its lack of political preparation. The calls for a general strike went largely unheeded, and where it began soon died out. A bad harvest and an economic slump made it impossible to maintain. The other measures had little effect in the few places where they were attempted. Chartism was in eclipse, and the Convention dissolved itself.

The government now made large-scale arrests of Chartist leaders. General Napier explained at length how his forces could quickly defeat any rebellions. Feargus O'Connor's influence and his fiery orations and militant writings in the *Northern Star* did much to keep Chartism alive. If any plans were made for insurrection they were naturally kept very secret and little is known of them. There were sporadic outbreaks of violence which seemed to indicate that plans were made, but failed through lack of co-ordination and communication. At Newport, Monmouthshire, an attempted capture of the town might well have been intended as a signal for a national rising. O'Connor tried unsuccessfully to stop it, knowing that it could not be followed up.

The leader of the Newport Rising was a draper, John Frost, a popular radical who was that town's delegate to the Convention. He had been mayor and magistrate, but had been forced off the bench because of his democratic views. The occasion was the arrest of the Welsh Chartist, Henry Vincent, who was held in Monmouth Gaol and reputedly ill-treated. Frost, with others, decided to rescue him and gathered an armed crowd, mostly miners and some with firearms, in the hills on the night of 3 November 1839. The main rendezvous was the village of Risca, six miles away. The plan was to occupy Newport in the hours of darkness, stop the mails going through, and march on to Monmouth to free Vincent. The non-arrival of the mail coaches in other towns was to be the signal that Newport was taken, and they could begin the general rising. The night was wet and stormy, the untrained men straggled and lost themselves on the wild tracks, and it was broad daylight before the vanguard reached Newport and marched into the town. Troops and police had barricaded themselves in the Westgate Hotel overlooking the main street, and the rebels were met by a volley of musketry from the windows. For a short while they resisted, those with guns firing back, several times desperately trying to storm the hotel, even getting as far as the entrance passage. But their position was hopeless, and after a while they broke and fled, leaving behind them fourteen dead and fifty wounded, of whom ten died shortly after. Their defeat was followed by the arrest of 125 men, twenty-one of them charged with high treason. Frost and two others were sentenced to death, which was afterwards commuted to transportation for life.

Arrests were made of a number of leading Chartists, amid riots, violence and disorder in many areas; but the great national rising of the 'physicals' never took place.

Robbed of its leadership, with its organisation in tatters, Chartism continued to exist as an ideology but split into many factions. There were Christian Chartists, educational Chartists, even teetotal Chartists; but in July 1840 the National Charter Association, was formed. With Lovett still behind bars, O'Connor was its dominant figure; he seemed content to follow the constitutional line. Again the six points were drawn up as a petition; again the signatures were collected throughout the country; this time it was signed by no less than 3,317,702 persons out of a total population of 19 million. But, like its predecessor, it was rejected in May 1842 by a Commons vote of 287 to forty-nine.

The nation had entered the decade known as the 'Hungry Forties', when a series of bad harvests, coinciding with an economic slump and a tax on imported wheat, drastically raised the price of bread. The second rejection of the Charter coincided with great strikes in the industrial areas. In those factories that did not join in, the strikers simply pulled out the drainage-plugs from the steam boilers, thus stopping all the machines. This was known as the 'Plug Plot'.

The Chartists considered strikes a manifestation of support for their cause. They called for no resumption of work until the six points became law. For a while Chartism and trade unionism acted together. But the Chartists were unable to sustain a common policy and O'Connor even attacked the strikes in his *Northern Star*. The strikers returned to work. There were 1,500 arrests and seventy-nine men were transported to Botany Bay. Chartism had suffered its second defeat.

The movement was now at a low ebb. It seemed that the British worker could never win the vote or the political equality that would provide the basis for social justice. Moreover there was no chance of armed rebellion; the state was too strong and too quick-witted for that to be a possibility. Supporters and activists began to devote themselves to other reforms that seemed more attainable — the Ten-Hour Day, the Anti-Corn-Law Society, Owenist socialism, trade unionism. The National Charter Association itself became a

35.   Conflict with the military at Preston during the Plug riots, 1842.

36.   An attack on the workhouse at Stockport, 1842.

supporter and investor in O'Connor's Land Scheme, for taking workers out of industry and placing them on the land, each with three acres, a few head of cattle, and a cottage. This backward-looking plan for creating a new class of small peasants succeeded for a while, but then it lost money, was declared illegal, and wound up.

Generally, the strength of Chartism fluctuated as a reflection of the economic condition of the people. When there was a period of relative prosperity and work was plentiful it was neglected. During slumps and depressions, with mass unemployment which bore heavily on them, they recalled their political inequality and became militant. As Dr Finer wrote: 'Chartism became the gathering-ground of all too weak to fight a single-handed battle against poverty.'

All over Europe 1848 was a year of revolution and change. France became a republic again. Many of the despots of the Continent, especially in the German states, were forced to grant their people constitutions which included some of the six points still denied to the British. Under these democratic influences, together with an economic slump with high unemployment and numerous food riots, Chartism recovered something of its former strength.

A campaign was begun for a third petition, this time of five points only, and a new Convention elected to supervise it. (At O'Connor's insistence the demand for the secret ballot was dropped.) Two resolutions were put for action if the Charter were again rejected. One was that the Convention should then declare itself in permanent session, and proclaim the Charter as the law of the land. The other, that mass meetings should elect delegates to a National Assembly or People's Parliament, which would present a memorial to Queen Victoria over the head of Parliament and remain in session until the Charter was officially proclaimed. Neither of these seemed particularly promising. The second course was adopted, though there was a strong republican element in Chartism.

By March 1848 Chartists claimed that the signatures to the new petition numbered almost 6,000,000, and it was planned to present it to Parliament on 10 April through the medium of O'Connor, who was himself now a Member of the Commons. There was to be a great demonstration of support in the open space of Kennington Common (now Kennington Park) on the southern fringe of London. From there it would be escorted the two miles to Westminster by a great procession, with bands, banners and pomp, as an expression of the will of the people.

The government reacted as though faced with the prospect of a foreign invasion. Its lawyers discovered, they claimed, an old law of the seventeenth century which banned the presentation of a petition by more than ten persons. A new law was rapidly passed making it a felony to 'seek to overawe or intimidate both Houses of Parliament'.

37. The Great Chartist Meeting on Kennington Common, 10 April 1848, from the first Daguerrotype of a crowd scene.

The aged Duke of Wellington, now almost eighty and a bitter opponent of all popular causes, was put in military command of the London district. He collected large numbers of troops to be stationed at strategic points on the route and available to close all the Thames bridges; and he raised a volunteer force of 170,000 special constables, many of them armed with cutlasses.

On the day, a great crowd assembled on the common, estimated by the Chartists at 250,000 and by their opponents at 25,000. O'Connor arrived and was at once taken to see the chief of police. There he was informed that the march would not be permitted but that the meeting could be held. O'Connor agreed to comply. While the speakers addressed the quiet and orderly crowd, the petition was ignominiously delivered to Parliament in three cabs to be received by the honourable Members with jests and laughter.

A commons committee examined the petition and declared that some of the signatures were spurious, the work of stupid and ignorant practical jokers — it bore such names as Queen Victoria, Prince Albert, Punch, Pugnose, and so forth. And that the total was 'only' 2 million. O'Connor postponed his demand for a debate for three months, and when it took place the petition was once more rejected by 224 to fifteen.

This was the death-blow to the Chartist movement. The

Convention listlessly considered a call for insurrection but made no decision and gave no lead. There was some rioting in industrial towns which was easily put down. Great London demonstrations on the following Whit-Monday were dispersed by troops, police, and a heavy fall of rain. Half-hearted local attempts at rebellion led only to many men being imprisoned or transported. O'Connor, always an excitable man, lost his reason and was taken to a lunatic asylum, where he died some years later. Many leaders and members emigrated. In the convict settlements of Australia, and in gaols and hulks at home, the imprisoned democrats served out their sentences. Thus Chartism died.

Its last meeting of any size was, symbolically, at the burial of O'Connor in 1852. Yet many Chartists lived on to see some of their six points adopted and become the law of the land. In 1858 property qualifications for MPs were abolished, the secret ballot established in 1872; and the reforms of 1867 and 1885 gave the vote to every adult male householder. How far these extensions of democracy had been influenced by Chartism is disputable. But Friedrich Engels was to write of 'the glorious Chartist movement, when the English workman marched at the head of the European working class'.

SELECT BIBLIOGRAPHY

Hovell, M., *The Chartist Movement,* Manchester University Press, 1916.
Lovett, W., *Life and struggles of William Lovett,* G. Bell and Sons, 1920.
Ward, J. T., *Chartism,* Batsford, 1973

CHAPTER XIX
Votes for Women

The Reform Act of 1832 had considerably extended the franchise; but apart from working men another large section of the people was left without the right to vote or to sit in the House of Commons — that was the female half of the population, the women. In the struggle for the Act women had stood beside men in meetings and demonstrations, expecting that the franchise would be extended to them too. The legal position had not been clear. Lord Chief Justice Lee in a judgement of 1733 stated that, though women had no right to vote, they were not 'positively excluded', meaning that there was no law that definitely forbade it. It was the Act of 1932 that made 'positive exclusion' into a statute by restricting the new franchise to 'male persons'.

Life for working-class women in the nineteenth century was not easy. Factories, mills and workshops were filled with women workers, who were 'naturally' paid less than men. After a long day's labour they went home not to rest but to other tasks of housework, cooking and child-rearing. But at least employment gave them some nominal freedom; they were not entirely dependent on husbands or fathers and if necessary could earn their own livelihoods, even if it meant heavy physical labour in mines or metal works, or in domestic service. The view of the trade unions was that female labour constituted a threat to the wage of the male family breadwinner, who should be able to earn enough to keep his wife at home. Many women worked in small firms and sweatshops at depressed rates, and attempts by them to form their own unions were not successful. The Womens' Trade Union League was not formed until the 1870s. Yet in strikes they stood shoulder to shoulder with their male fellow-workers and were prominent in political struggles.

The status of women of the middle and upper classes was different. Until 1882 a married woman was incapable of holding wealth or property — everything she possessed became the property of her husband. She was a complete dependent, first on her father, then on her husband, a position believed to be ordained by nature and by God. All the domestic work was done by numerous low-paid servants, the children were brought up by 'nannies', and her life was idle and without responsibility. She could have no higher education and she was barred from the learned professions; in a crisis, like the loss of her supporter or his impoverishment, the only respectable way of earning a living open to her was to become governess to the children of a wealthy family, paid companion to a lonely single lady or untaught teacher in a private girls' school. These situations were regarded with contempt as 'domestic' and the literature of the period is full of descriptions of their unhappy conditions. She might also become a courtesan or a prostitute, in which case she was treated as a total outcast. (Bernard Shaw, in *Mrs Warren's Profession* (1894) made the point that this was probably preferable to the horrors of a nineteenth century factory or to servant life.)

The struggle for emancipation can be said to have begun with the publication of Mary Wollstonecraft's *Vindication of the Rights of Women* in 1792. It was a demand for equality and education; 'to be the friend, not the humble dependent, of her husband'. She described the conventional lady as 'a gentle domestic brute'. This attitude was generally condemned, not least by women. It was rebellion against the Bible and the sanctity of home and family.

To an active mind idleness is intolerable, and many women occupied themselves with charitable and social work. Florence Nightingale became famous for her organisation of the nursing service, but mainly for her work for the wounded and sick in the Crimean War. Some worked for political reforms, like the Marriage and Divorce Act of 1857, which protected the earnings of a deserted wife from her absentee husband, who had hitherto been entitled to them.

At the beginning of the Chartist movement the call for universal suffrage was regarded as applying to women as well as men, but by the 1840s it had been watered down to 'universal adult male suffrage'.

The first steps towards higher education for women were made under the leadership of Emily Davis. She opened Girton College for women in Cambridge in 1874. It was not part of the university and was received with scorn and hostility, but the students were entitled to sit for the university examinations and eventually to graduate with degrees. (The university maintained its ban on women students until after the Second World War.) Girton was followed by other colleges, to the consternation of many. The educated woman was looked on as a social misfit who had lost her femininity and charm in the process and become a terrifying blue-stocking whom no man would dare to marry.

Lord Byron had written in 'Don Juan':

> Oh all ye lords of ladies intellectual,
> Come tell me truly, have they not henpecked you all?

Tennyson mocked them as 'sweet girl graduates'. They became the butt of the wits of clubs and saloon bars. But this part of the battle was won. The progressive University of London opened its doors to women in 1878.

It was harder for graduates to break into the learned professions. In 1859 Elizabeth Blackwell, having taken a medical degree in America, had to be placed on the medical register here, which was at once amended to stop recognition of anyone with foreign qualifications only. Against enormous odds, barred from all English medical schools, Elizabeth Garrett qualified a few years later. All over the country, in every social class women were beginning to look upon themselves as victims of discrimination, were questioning their status and demanding equality.

The demand for political equality, in the form of the vote, found early expression in 1825 in a book by William Thomson with the unwieldy title which begins *An Appeal to One Half of the Human Race, Women, Against the Pretensions of the Other Half, Men . . .* Thomson was an early socialist thinker, and in his book he produced a valuable argument in favour of suffrage and equality for women. It had little effect. The matter became the subject of a debate in the Commons in August 1832, after the passing of the Reform Act. 'Orator' Hunt, the speaker at the Peterloo Massacre of 1819, now an MP, presented a petition asking that unmarried women with the necessary property qualifications should be given the vote. The petitioner was a spinster of great wealth who based her plea on the right of property which carried the right to vote. An important argument against female suffrage was that her vote was represented in her husband's, as it was he that owned the property, not she. But what if she had the property but not the husband? The debate was conducted by the honourable gentlemen with some mirth and a little genteel ribaldry and the petition was thrown out.

In 1865 a Liberal government was returned with a majority of seventy (the Liberals were the successors of the old Whigs). The workers, whose support had helped it to power, had been promised an extension of the franchise to include themselves, and a bill was put before the Commons reducing property qualifications to £14 in the counties and £7 in the boroughs, and any man who had £50 in the bank for two years would have the vote. This would enfranchise some 2 million workers and small tradesmen. At the second reading the majority was only five, and soon afterwards that the government fell and was succeeded by a Tory administration.

A great public meeting was called by the National Reform League in Hyde Park on 23 July 1866. It was banned by the police, who closed the park gates. The workers, in their tens of thousands, swept aside the 1,600 police and gained entrance by pulling down the park railings. The Guards were brought up from Wellington Barracks and advanced on speakers and audiences; the meeting broke up in a series of riots and skirmishes in the dusk. Later the Tory government passed the Reform Bill of 1867, which enfranchised ratepayers and most lodgers.

Thus the vote was won for the majority of the urban male working class. Only the agricultural labourers were now denied it; and four other categories: peers of the realm, convicts, the mentally handicapped and — women. In his speech on the Bill, Prime Minister Disraeli said that he saw no reason why women should not have the vote. But he went no further in the matter.

In the elections of 1865 the philosopher John Stuart Mill reluctantly agreed to stand for Westminster as a Liberal, with female suffrage as part of his platform. Some women who called themselves 'the suffrage leaders' drafted a petition and Mill presented it to the House in June 1866. He became known as 'the ladies' member', and he raised the whole subject of the women's vote as an amendment to the Second Reform Act that the word 'man' in the Act be replaced by 'person'. After a long debate it was defeated, but gained the support of seventy-four MPs. Women's suffrage was now established as a rational constitutional issue, not just a matter for male ridicule, and was to be raised many times in the future.

This encouraging result led to the organisation of a 'National Society for Women's Suffrage' through which women took the unprecedented action of addressing public meetings where they endured heckling and jeering. Queen Victoria wrote a letter condemning 'this mad, wicked folly of "Women's Rights" with its attendant horrors'; and of one of the speakers — 'Lady Amberley ought to get a good whipping.'

For the rest of the century the suffragists, as the constitutionalists came to be called, carried on a discreet political campaign, held meetings, wrote and sold literature, marched in 'respectable' processions, and had little to show for it. By 1900 the movement was almost dead. It was revived in 1903 by the formation of the Womens' Social and Political Union, pledged to militant action 'to secure for women the parliamentary vote as it is or may be granted to men'; this was more simply expressed in their slogan, 'Votes for Women'. Membership was restricted to women and it was independent of all political parties.

Its leading spirits were the widow Mrs. Emmeline Pankhurst and her daughters Christobel and Sylvia, and Mrs Emmeline Pethwick-Lawrence, a wealthy social worker and a fellow of Trinity College, Cambridge. The word 'Social' in their title was thought to be a euphorism for 'socialist', so as not to disturb the many middle-class ladies active for the vote. (The Pankhursts and a number of their supporters were members of the Independent Labour Party.) The WSPU had strong support among working women, who were able to influence some of the labour movement and its press in its favour. One of its prominent activists was Annie Kenny, an Oldham mill girl. Yet the new Labour Party would not support the women's vote as a priority, considering that, as the franchise stood, it would merely give it to the propertied class and strengthen Conservative and Liberal interests. They considered that it should wait for the coming of universal suffrage, in which it would be included.

In 1904 Keir Hardy, the first Labour MP, presented a Member's Bill calling for J. S. Mill's defeated amendment to the Act of 1867. Amid hoots and jeers it was 'talked out' by a debate on rear lights for vehicles. Suffragettes, as the militants were now called, had gathered round Parliament in great numbers, and at once held a protest meeting there in the face of police opposition and repression, the first direct unlawful action.

The policy of provocation, nuisance and publicity now became the line of the WSPU. In the lively political life of the time, usually conducted by great public meetings, they were continual disturbers of the peace, shouting, heckling, raising banners, drowning voices and ringing bells, and getting themselves manhandled by stewards and harassed by the police. The press soon called them 'the shrieking sisterhood'. At a Manchester meeting Mrs Pankhurst and Annie Kenny were arrested and sentenced to a fine or imprisonment for assaulting the police. They refused to pay the fine and became the first suffragettes to be imprisoned.

The House of Commons now contained a number of working-class members elected as Liberals, with some of the Independent Labour Party. In 1900 they met to form the Labour Representation Committee, forerunner of the Labour Party. Some of the group expressed their support of the principle of women's suffrage, but did not consider it an urgent matter. The WSPU set out to make it one.

On the one hand the WSPU kept its roots in the labour movement, sending speakers to trade union, socialist and labour meetings. On the other, it included 'ladies', often of high social standing, who had money and time to work for it and the leisure to go to prison if necessary. 'Votes for Women' became a national controversy that was opposed on all manner of social and religious grounds. Hilaire Belloc found the very idea immoral; others objected that election canvassers would have the right to approach other men's wives. Many of otherwise conservative opinions were found to favour it, while some people considered radical and progressive opposed it. The division cut across political and social borders. There was even a Conservative Women's Franchise Association. Some of the 'suffragists' thought they had most to gain from the Liberal Party

38.   Suffragette clinging to the railings of Buckingham Palace.

and worked for its candidates. The 'suffragettes' saw the Liberals as the party which had consistently accepted the principle of women's suffrage but refused it when in power. They pursued them relentlessly, turning their meetings into shouting contests and drowning the speakers' voices in chants of 'Votes for Women'.

At all public gatherings and occasions of state they provided noisy exciting disturbances, shouting, bell-ringing and giving away leaflets. They became the great bogey of all political organisers and a byword for disruption even within the sacred precincts of Parliament itself. If it was publicity they sought, they certainly achieved it. The press was full of their activities and they became a popular theme for music-hall comedians.

In the general election of 1906 the Liberals were returned with a majority of one hundred seats over the combined opposition; they were supported by fifty-two Labour members. The prime minister was Campbell-Bannerman, soon to be succeeded by Asquith. Most of the Liberal candidates had pledged themselves to support the women's vote, but there was no mention of it in the king's speech, which outlined the proposed legislation for the ensuing session. Mrs Pethwick-Lawrence called for 'a great revolt of the women against their subjection of body and mind to men'. Thus the suffragettes were going beyond their political demand for the vote and were anticipating the Women's Liberation Movement of the 1970s.

The struggle continued and more and more women found themselves in prison for acts of trespass, assault, violence or damage to property. Options of fines were refused. Some women made a disturbance in the gallery of the House of Commons, and when police went to arrest them it was found that they had chained themselves to the grill with keyless padlocks; they made good use of their time before they could be cut free. This tactic was used at Downing Street, at the homes of cabinet ministers, at Buckingham Palace itself, and resulted in imprisonment in Holloway Prison. They hired airships and balloons to drop leaflets on London, and even broke through police cordons on royal occasions to thrust petitions on the king and queen. Some of the actions, like pouring corrosive acid into ballot boxes or dropping ignited rags into letter-boxes became dangerously close to terrorism and involved themselves and others to some risk.

Mrs Despard, an elderly widow and a prominent member of the WSPU, quarrelled with the leadership and formed her own group, the Women's Freedom League. They described their policy as 'constitutional militancy' and refused to pay their taxes. Like the Americans in 1776, they demanded: 'No taxation without representation'. Mrs Despard's furniture, and those of her supporters, were frequently sold off by the bailiffs and as frequently bought back for them by friends. One even went to prison for refusing to buy a licence for her dog.

Fifty members of the WSPU were sent to prison for six weeks after a demonstration at Parliament in 1908. Among them was Mrs Pankhurst, who was still suffering from the effects of an assault by hooligans who were always zealous in helping the police disperse women.

Political protest was also carried on by great meetings and processions, often to welcome home those released from prison. On 21 June 1908, named by the WSPU 'Women's Sunday', they had called for a mass meeting in Hyde Park, in which seven demonstrations were to converge on the spot. At Victoria Embankment they carried beautiful embroidered or painted banners depicting great women — Boadicea, Joan of Arc, etc. There were many bands and contingents of women of all activities — writers, artists, actresses, nurses, factory workers and housewives. Special trains were run to bring supporters from the provinces. Hats, rosettes, ribbons, even dresses were worn in the WSPU colours: purple, white and green. There were twenty waggons as rostrums, eighty speakers, and 2,000 men as stewards to keep order and prevent the usual disturbances by rowdies or high-spirited youths out for a bit of fun. *The Times* estimated the attendance at more than

500,000. At the call of a bugle the resolution 'Votes for Women, without delay' was put and acclaimed by most listeners.

At the end of 1908, after two private member's bills for women's suffrage had won majorities in the House but were dropped by the government, the WSPU called for public support to 'Rush the House of Commons' as a protest.

There had been a demonstration by the unemployed that day and the approaches to Parliament were still filled with police. The attempt was easily thwarted, but a warrant was issued for the arrest of Mrs Pankhurst, Christobel Pankhurst and Mrs Drummond, known affectionately as 'the General', on a charge of conspiracy. They refused to be bound over and went to prison; three months for the older women, ten weeks for Christobel Pankhurst.

Imprisoned militants began to protest by the then novel idea of the hunger-strike, and the authorities responded by ordering forcible feeding. It was cruelly done by tying the victim to a chair, inducting a tube into the stomach through a nostril and pouring liquid nourishment down it. The response to this was to smash up the cell furniture. There were many outcries against this treatment of women, and the government reacted by releasing those whose health was deteriorating and re-arresting them when they were well again to finish their sentences. This was the infamous 'Cat and Mouse Act'. During 1913 and 1914 Mrs Pankhurst was released after hunger-strikes and re-arrested no fewer than ten times, her last arrest being from a stretcher on which she was being carried to a WSPU meeting.

The fight for the vote continued. Now the lay opposition was organising against the granting of it. Such societies as 'the Womans' Anti-Suffrage League' were formed; these advanced the theory that women were temperamentally unsuited for politics. This form of political activity, carried on by persons who proclaimed aloud their unfitness for it, provided an amusing Gilbertian paradox and was soon abandoned.

The elections of 1910 returned a Liberal government again, with the promise that it would make female suffrage an open question for the Commons to decide. An all-party group of MPs set out to draw up a bill which would be acceptable to most members, and became known as the Conciliation Committee. At this the suffragettes decided to suspend their activities and to await events. The committee eventually produced a bill which would give the vote to women of the middle class on a property qualification, even when that property was owned by the husband. This was accepted by the WSPU as establishing the principle. They supported it by a great procession to a meeting in the Royal Albert Hall. It was headed by a body of women marshals mounted on splendid horses (all riding astride!), followed by more than six hundred ex-prisoners dressed in white

39.   The 1910 parade of suffragettes in support of the bill giving women the vote.

each bearing aloft the broad arrow of prison garb; then professional and cultural contingents, and even a large section of men, many of them famous in various spheres. Bands, banners and tableaux made an impressive and colourful pageant.

The government gave the bill parliamentary time. Both Lloyd-George and Churchill opposed it, but after a long debate it was passed by a majority of 110. The government decided that the majority was too small for such an important measure, and it was shelved. A protest meeting outside Parliament was brutally dispersed, but on government instructions no prosecutions were made.

This was regarded as betrayal. Militant activity was resumed, and in a short while more than two hundred women were in prison again.

At a given signal on 1 March 1912 almost every window in London's main shopping streets, Oxford Street and Regent Street, was smashed simultaneously by female window-gazers with hammers, and at the same time the windows in Downing Street were broken. The stone-throwing era had begun. This time the police raided the WSPU offices in Clement's Inn and arrested Mr and Mrs Pethwick-Lawrence and Mrs Tuke. Mrs Pankhurst was already in detention for a former offence, and Christobel Pankhurst, warned, fled to Paris. Among the evidence given in court by the police was the revelation that on the office shelves were found a number of books in

French! The arrested were all sent to prison for nine months, and were ordered to pay the prosecution's costs. Mr Pethwick-Lawrence refused, was declared bankrupt and his home sold up. For this, he was expelled from the Reform Club.

However widespread their attacks on property, the suffragettes were always careful to avoid injury to any person, although they claimed that some of their militants had died later as a result of hunger-strikes and forcible feeding. There was to be one fatality in their struggle, which can however be regarded as self-inflicted. On Derby Day, 4 June 1913, as the runners in the big race had passed Tattenham Corner, Miss Emily Wilding Davison, with the WSPU colours in her coat, ran out from the rails in front of the kings' horse in an attempt to halt it. She, horse and jockey were flung into a heap. The horse and rider were injured, Miss Davison died soon after in hospital. She had been a prominent activist for many years and had attempted a protest suicide while in prison. Her comrades gave her a most impressive funeral.

After this, militancy reached a new peak. Famous works of art in public exhibitions were slashed or damaged, like the Rokeby Venus in the National Gallery. Small and inefficient bombs were placed, like the one that damaged the medieval stone screen in the sanctuary of Westminster Abbey. Arson was attempted, especially at homes of Cabinet ministers, and was frequently successful. The movement was developing towards outright terrorism. Services in churches and cathedrals were interrupted, the king was openly insulted when he appeared in public. Arrests and convictions rose, and a large part of the public was alienated from the cause. The campaign was referred to in the Commons as 'a phenomenon absolutely without precedent in our history'.

The struggle for female suffrage and political equality seemed to be building up to a dramatic climax when it suddenly ended. The country found itself at war. The rival groups of European governments organised calamity for their subjects, and the war of 1914-18 began. Hailed in some quarters as 'the war to end wars', but known now as the First World War, it was to cost the British and Imperial forces 947,000 dead, and a total estimated death-roll to both sides of 8,412,000. Beside this colossal crime against humanity the misdemeanours of the suffragettes seem petty indeed.

On the declaration of hostilities, the British government ordered the unconditional release of all imprisoned suffragettes. The WSPU suspended its activities and most of its members devoted themselves to the war effort. They joined the women's services, worked in factories and in transport, and Mrs Pankhurst became one of the government's experts on the recruitment of women into industry, where they were tolerated by the unions as 'diluted labour'.

Quietly, almost as an anti-climax, in January 1918 Lloyd-George's government gave the vote to all women on reaching the age of thirty, only twenty-three MPs opposing it. In November women were enabled to stand for election to the House of Commons. Sixteen female candidates contested the first post-war elections in December 1918, but the only one elected was the Countess Markievicz, in Ireland. She was a Sinn Fein candidate, and, in accordance with that party's policy, never occupied her seat. The first woman to sit in the House of Commons was Lady Nancy Astor, elected by Plymouth in 1919 — a Conservative. Subsequent Acts of Parliament extended the franchise so that today, in Britain, all citizens of the age of eighteen — with the exception of peers and people confined in prisons and mental hospitals — have the right to vote.

SELECT BIBLIOGRAPHY

Fulford, R., *Votes for Women*, White Lion, 1976
Raeburn, A., *The Militant Suffragettes*, Harrap, 1950.
Rooke, P., *Womens' Rights*, Wayland, 1972.

Epilogue

It took three hundred years of strife and struggle, from the first manifestos of the Levellers in the 17th century, for Britain to win its present parliamentary democracy with universal suffrage for all its citizens, regardless of sex or colour. It has been said that all the great political battles have been won and that it is typical of our time there is nothing left to fight for.

Yet the promised millennium of the pioneers, the reign of harmony, social stability and universal justice has failed to come about. There still remain extremes of wealth and poverty, gross inequalities in education, housing and health care. The poor remain too poor, the rich too rich. Many valuable reforms have been won by the people since the end of the Second World War, but many are yet unrealised. Prominent among these is the right to work, to practise one's skill or profession, to support oneself and one's dependents by one's labour and thereby make a contribution to the national well-being. To a wage-earner, all other rights may seem of secondary importance. Workers are still often forced to strike to win from their employers the elementary freedom to belong to a trade union which can negotiate on their behalf; a right which the law recognises. Few people can look forward with confidence to a calm and secure retirement. The statesmen of all nations still rely ultimately on war and violence to solve their problems, both internationally and internally.

Throughout the long struggle of the common people for a voice in public affairs, for the redress of injustice, there has appeared consistently the ideal of a new and revolutionary form of state, the basis of which was to be not the power and profit of individuals, but what the Bible calls 'love', the trade unionist 'solidarity', the socialist 'fraternity'.

This desired society has been known by many names over many centuries: the Kingdom of Heaven on Earth, the New Jerusalem, the Rule of the Saints, the Digger Republic, the Co-operative Commonwealth, and so on. These early concepts, often associated with religious movements, remained unattainable ideals. It is no longer so. We are rapidly advancing our understanding of nature and the universe, and of our own minds and bodies. We have the knowledge and the means to make the desert yield an annual harvest, to compensate with the aid of technology for most natural shortages, to produce almost without limit, to reduce necessary human labour to a few hours weekly and provide leisure and prosperity for all. The potential exists at last for the establishment of an ideal society here on earth. But this can only be achieved after a radical reorganisation of our present economic and social relations.

The alternative is not the peaceful continuance of things as they are. It is the decline of Britain into a nation torn by civil strife, class war and poverty, into a continual struggle for a basic livelihood, and its possible transformation in a nuclear war into a scarcely inhabited radioactive wilderness.

This is the great challenge of our generation, the culmination of the long battles for political freedom. There are still great causes to be fought for, and won.

A Select Chronology

1348   The Black Death devastates England.
1351   'Statute of Labourers', freezing wages to pre-plague levels.
1369   War with France renewed.
1377   First Poll Tax levied. Riots in London after trial of Wycliffe.
       Death of Edward III. Richard II becomes king.
1379   Second Poll Tax.
1380   Third Poll Tax. Archbishop Sudbury becomes Chancellor.
       Walworth becomes Mayor of London.
1381

30 May	Poll Tax collectors attacked at Brentwood, Essex. **Peasants' Revolt** begins.
2 June	Armed attack on new Poll Tax collectors.
3 June	Abel Ker and party cross Thames into Kent.
5 June	Ker in Dartford. First council of rebels issue policy statement.
6 June	John Legge and his forces defeated *en route* to Canterbury. Rebels enter Rochester, take royal castle.
7 June	Rebels enter Maidstone, free John Ball from prison. Wat Tyler emerges as leader.
10 June	Tyler and rebels enter Canterbury with popular support. Hales' manor sacked in Essex. Riots in Cambridgeshire.
11 June	Kentish rebels advance on London.
12 June	Rebels camp on Blackheath. King Richard and court move from Westminster to Tower of London.
13 June	Corpus Christi Day. John Ball preaches after Mass. King rows down Thames for abortive meeting with rebels at Rotherhithe. Rebels enter London. John Wrawe and his rebels enter Bury, Suffolk.
14 June	Sudbury and Hales killed by rebels in Tower of London. King meets rebels at Mile End. Most demands granted, charters of freedom promised. Rebel activity in Suffolk and elsewhere.

15 June	Charters of manumission written and distributed to rebels. King meets rebels at Smithfield. Murder of Tyler, collapse of rebellion in London. Rebels attack Bury Abbey. Revolt and riot in Ely and St. Albans.
16 June	Abbot of St. Albans capitulates to rebels. Cambridge townsmen burn University records. Rebels leave London to return home.
22 June	King at Havering-atte-Bower, Essex, to direct 'pacification'. He receives and rejects delegation of Essex rebels, and annuls charters of manumission.
28 June	Last stand of Essex rebels crushed at Billericay, Essex.
2 July	King formally and officially revokes all charters of manumission.
15 July	Execution of John Ball at St. Albans.
3 November	King opens Parliament and declares general pardon for all rebels, except for 287 named men. Official end of rebellion.

1384   Death of Wycliffe.
1399   Deposition and death of Richard II.
1450

31 May	**Cade's Rebellion.** Rebels assemble on Blackheath.
18 June	Cade retreats from Blackheath.
20 June	Cade ambushes royal forces near Sevenoaks.
27 June	Cade enters London. Sets up headquarters in Southwark.
27–28 June	**Battle** on London Bridge.
30 June	**Cade negotiates** with high-ranking clergy. 'Bill of Pardons' accepted. Most rebels return to their homes.
11 July	Cade killed and 'quartered'.

1455–1485   'Wars of the Roses'.
1492   Columbus discovers America.
1497   Enclosure of common lands and wastes begin.
1509   Henry VIII crowned.
1536   King Henry begins the dissolution of monastic institutions.
        'Pilgrimage of Grace' against dissolutions and land enclosures.
1549

9 July	**Kett's Rebellion** against enclosures, rack-renting and trade monopolies.
July	'Commonwealth' formed on Mousehold Heath, Norwich.
21 July	Kett and rebels negotiate with York Herald.
22 July	Kett attacks Norwich and eventually occupies it.
25 August	Earl of Warwick attacks Norwich, rebels driven out.

Kett and followers break up Mousehold Camp, fight last battle at Dussindale. Mass executions follow defeat.

7 December   Kett hanged at Norwich.

1549   **'Western Rebellion'** in Devon and Cornwall.

1625   King Charles I crowned. Calls, and dissolves, his first Parliament.

1626   Charles calls second Parliament, which produces 'Petition of Rights'.

1629   Parliament protests against Charles's policies, and is dissolved.

1629–1640   King rules without Parliament. Period of autocracy.

1639   First 'Bishops' War' against Scotland.

1640   Charles calls 'Short Parliament' and demands money. Parliament refuses, and is dissolved. Second 'Bishops' War'. Scots invade England, defeat Charles at Newburn. Charles calls 'Long Parliament'. Struggle between king and Parliament intensifies.

1641   Parliament passes 'Grand Remonstrance'. Irish rebellion begins.

1642

January   King Charles breaches privilege by entering House of Commons to arrest five members. He fails, and goes north to raise an army.

August   King raises his standard at Nottingham. Start of **Civil War**.

October   First major battle at Edgehill. Both sides claim victory. King advances on London; checked at Turnham Green, he retires to Oxford.

1643   Parliament concludes 'Solemn League and Covenant' with Scots. Cromwell forms his cavalry, the 'Ironsides'.

1644   Battle of Marston Moor. Parliament and Scots defeat royal army. Parliamentary army under Earl of Essex surrenders in Cornwall.

1645   Parliament establishes New Model Army of Puritan Independents, under Fairfax and Cromwell. Battle of Naseby. New Model Army destroys main army of king.

1646   Last engagement of Civil War at Stow-on-the-Wold. Victory of Parliament. Charles surrenders himself to Scots at Newark. Scots 'sell' him to England. King kept at Holmby House; negotiations for settlement of kingdom continue. **'Levellers'** appear as a political movement. Parliament (Presbyterian) moves to disband New Model Army (Independent). Army mutinies at Saffron Walden, refuses to disband or move to Ireland. Soldiers elect 'Agitators' as delegates of rank and file. Cornet Joyce and Ironsides 'kidnap' and hold King Charles.

Army negotiates directly with him, without success. New Model Army marches on London.

1647 King escapes from Hampton Court to Isle of Wight, makes 'Engagement' with Scots. New Model Army holds 'Putney Debates' to determine future social order in England.

1648 Second Civil War and Scottish invasion. Fairfax crushes royalists, Cromwell defeats Scots. Colonel Pride 'purges' House of Commons. Trial of King Charles.

1649 King Charles executed in Whitehall; England declared a republic. Cromwell crushes Leveller mutinies in Army and leaves with forces to put down Irish Rebellion. Winstanley sets up short-lived **Digger community** near Walton-on-Thames.

1658 Death of Cromwell, Lord Protector of the Commonwealth. New Model Army disbanded.

1660 Restoration of Monarchy. Charles II crowned at Westminster.

1685 Death of Charles II; succession of James II. **Monmouth's Rebellion**, and 'Bloody Assizes'.

1688 'The Glorious Revolution'. King James flees after landing of William of Orange.

1698 Savery invents the steam engine (pump).

1706 Union of Scotland and England as one kingdom.

1709 First smelting of iron with coke.

1712 Newcomen builds steam engine (pump and power).

1748 Huntsman's crucible steel process.

1758 Lord Bridgewater begins canal system.

1785 Cartwright's power-loom at work.

1789 French Revolution begins. Fall of Bastille. *Declaration of Rights of Man.*

1791 **Tom Paine** publishes *Rights of Man*.

1793 Britain at war with France.

1794 *Habeas Corpus* suspended.

1795 Berkshire justices adopt 'Speenhamland Scales'. Seditious Meetings and Treason Acts passed.

1797 **Naval mutinies** at Spithead and the Nore.

1799 First Combination Act against trade unionism passed. Corresponding Societies suppressed.

1803 First steam-powered ship.

1807 Slave trade abolished.

1811 **Luddites** begin destruction of machines.

1813 Stevenson builds steam locomotive.

1817 March of **'Blanketeers'**.

1824 Combination Acts repealed. **Trade unionism** legal.

1832 First Reform Act extends franchise.

1834 **'Tolpuddle Martyrs'** convicted and sentenced.

1836 London Working Men's Association formed.

1838   **People's Charter** published and campaign opened.
1839   First Charter Convention held. Peoples' Charter thrown out by House of Commons. **Newport Rising.**
1840   National Charter Association formed. Second Charter Petition rejected by Parliament.
1848   'The Year of Revolutions' in Europe. Third Charter Petition rejected by Commons.
1858   Property qualifications for MPs abolished.
1864   **International Working Men's Association** (First International) founded.
1865   Extension of franchise.
1867   Marx's *Capital* published. Second Reform Act further extends franchise.
1872   Secret ballot in parliamentary elections.
1876   Compulsory adult education.
1878   London University admits women.
1888   'Bloody Sunday' in Trafalgar Square.
1903   Formation of **Women's Social and Political Union**.
1911   Payment of MPs.
1914   First World War begins.

Index of Names